YELLOW FEVER
The Dark Heart of the Tour de France

YELLOW FEVER

The Dark Heart of the Tour de France

Jeremy Whittle

HEADLINE

First published in 1999
by HEADLINE BOOK PUBLISHING

10 9 8 7 6 5 4 3 2 1

British Library Cataloguing in Publication Data

Whittle, Jeremy
Yellow fever
1.Tour de France
I.Title
823.9'14

ISBN 0 7472 2207 X

Typeset by
Letterpart Limited, Reigate, Surrey

Printed and bound in Great Britain by
Mackays of Chatham PLC, Chatham, Kent

HEADLINE BOOK PUBLISHING
A division of Hodder Headline PLC
338 Euston Road
London NW1 3BH

www.headline.co.uk
www.hodderheadline.com

For Deb, Murf and my parents – and for all the riders
who've paid the price

Contents

Acknowledgements

My profound thanks to all at Headline, particularly to my editor Lorraine Jerram, for her unwavering support, encouragement and guidance and for sharing the belief that the Tour de France is the world's most remarkable annual sports event.

The opportunity to write this book owes much to the love and support of Debbie Lewis and my family – and to Peter Waxman's obsession with his Roberts bicycle. I'd like to thank Jan Quinlan, Ruth Jarvis, James Poole, Peter Cossins, David Chappell and Andrew Warshaw for their help along the way.

Thanks also to the assortment of characters in the Tour's press room, far too numerous to list but including Mike Price, Andy Hood, Phil O'Connor, Steve Wood, Stephen Farrand, Simon Brotherton, Susanne Horsdal, Graham Jones, François Leuillot, Samuel Abt, Andrew Longmore, Pierre Ballester, Michael Enggard, Philippe Van Holle, Ulrik Sass, Jill Jemison, Gilles Comte, Graham Watson, Anna Powley and particularly to Andrew Hodge for all his help and enthusiasm during the 1998 Tour.

Most of all, thanks and respect to the Société du Tour de France for steering their ship into harbour, even when many would rather have seen it sink – and to all the professional cyclists whose courage and resilience never fails to amaze me.

1998 Tour de France

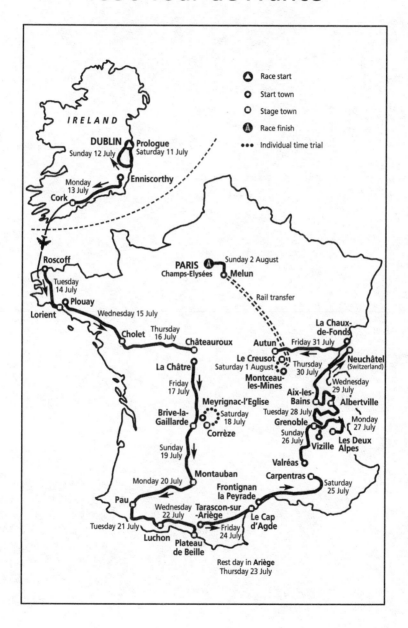

Preface

The broken and cracked race has disappeared into the swirling Alpine mists, far from the everyday world, clinging to its withered traditions on a dark summer's day. The 1998 Tour de France, exhausted by scandal and controversy, brought to its knees by days of rancour and paranoia, is close to breakdown. In a shroud of drizzle, the riders pedal towards the summit of the massive Col de Galibier, site of the monument to race founder Henri Desgranges. Hidden in official cars on the *route du Tour* is the race organisation of the modern commercialised Tour, which has found itself overwhelmed by the biggest doping scandal in the history of the sport. The Tour appears mortally wounded. It has taken on the air of an anachronistic curiosity, an emblem of outdated tradition; stung by a loss of credibility and rejected by modern French society.

But then, after all the bad news, after Chris Boardman's horrific crash and Richard Virenque's dramatic tears, after the midnight arrests and the dawn raids, after the lies and the half-truths, something good is about to happen. Italy's Marco Pantani, the irrepressible 'Pantanino', 'Pantagiallo', the mercurial climbing genius, sets about rescuing the shattered Tour de France dream. As he and defending champion Jan Ullrich waft in and out of view in the chill mist engulfing the giant Alpine pass of the Col du Galibier, Pantani, known to his devoted Italian fans as '*Il Pirata*', suddenly darts ahead of the field. The little man's attack, five kilometres from the summit of the Galibier, brings cheers of excitement and relief from a packed press room, weary of reporting the tidal wave of

1

doping revelations unveiled by the persistent French police. In the split second it takes the red-haired Ullrich to wonder whether to chase Pantani's violent acceleration or to look for help from the other riders around him, the Tour is lost and won. By the time the young German makes up his mind, Pantani has vanished ahead into the gloom.

Fifty kilometres across the Alpine peaks, at the ski resort finish of Les Deux Alpes, we watch transfixed, as on the TV screens above our heads Pantani bounds clear of the struggling Ullrich and crosses the bleak 2,645 metre summit of the Galibier pass with a growing advantage. After pausing to don a rain cape in the shadow of the Desgranges monument, the Italian launches himself into the steep descent with the skill and aplomb of a downhill skier. In the appalling visibility and freezing rain, his speed touches sixty miles per hour on the long plunge towards the Romanche valley, as TV motorbikes battle to keep pace with him.

Behind Pantani, a frozen Ullrich, now isolated from his Telekom team-mates, is in a state of panic, chasing both the Italian and his other close rival, America's Bobby Julich. In the swirling chaos at the summit, Julich, struggling to put on a flimsy rain cape as he drops away from the pass, slews into a parked camper van; but after a brief pause, he joins the race once more. Forced to chase alone, Ullrich's strength wanes with every kilometre to the foot of the final climb, while Pantani's lead keeps growing as he approaches the steep haul to the finish. With his Tour hopes ebbing away, Ullrich suffers another blow – a puncture at the foot of the final haul up to Les Deux Alpes. But at least his shivering wait for a new wheel from his Telekom team car gives his two team-mates Bjarne Riis and Udo Bolts the chance to catch up. Very soon, Ullrich is going to need them. Les Deux Alpes is certainly not the steepest or the longest of the Alpine climbs and is far from the torture rack that is its more renowned near-neighbour Alpe d'Huez, but for the exhausted and frozen Ullrich it's simply a hill too far. Further up the hairpins, Pantani is still in full flight as the German, with Riis and Bolts close behind, leadenly pedals up the seven per cent grades. By now, his face is stretched into a rictus of suffering and his eyes are puffy and watering. Even Riis, his mentor and friend, can do little to help him as he draws alongside.

Behind Pantani, the Tour's race director, Jean-Marie Leblanc, takes his traditional place watching the dramatic closing stages from the sun-roof of his red Fiat. In spite of the rain pouring on his head, Leblanc has lost his troubled frown for the first time since the Tour began and looks calm, almost as if he's enjoying himself.

Up at the ski resort Pantani, soaked to the skin but with a relieved smile on his face, crosses the finish line to a roar of approval from the thousands of 'tifosi' who have flooded over the nearby Italian border. Behind him, the distraught Ullrich is being overtaken by riders he passed earlier in the day. The final kilometres devastate him as he battles to cling on to the slipstream provided by team-mate Riis's back wheel. When he finally crosses the line to a chorus of heartless booing and crude insults from soaked French fans, he is almost nine minutes behind Pantani and has lost all hope of Tour victory. Barely able to pedal through the finish, the German seems on the verge of collapse as tears well up in his eyes. Gingerly, almost tenderly, Riis and Bolts support him through the usual unceremonious scrum of journalists, race officials, police and photographers crowding into the chaotic finish area. As the trio disappear towards their hotel, the worldly-wise Bolts puts an arm around Ullrich's sagging shoulders, while Riis, who has known enough dark moments of his own, grasps the broken champion's left wrist in consolation.

In the press room, there's a moment's pause as the day's dramatic events sink in. Quickly though, the stillness is filled by a chorus of ringing mobile phones and the steady, rhythmic drumming of a thousand laptop keyboards.

Introduction

'This is the war of cyclists – that's what we call it . . .'

1988 Champion, Pedro Delgado, describing the
Tour de France

Shortly before midday on 5 November 1998, Jean-Claude Killy, President of the Société du Tour de France, strode on stage at the Palais des Congrès in Paris and said the dramatic words that the world of professional cycling needed to hear.

'We all touched rock bottom on 17 July this year,' asserted Killy. 'If the 1998 Tour de France was chosen by history to live through this Calvary, it is because the Tour is so great. Because the Tour is so great, it lives on. And because it lives on, it will never again be the symbol of doping, but a symbol of the war against doping.'

The former Olympic ski champion's words finally acknowledged the horrors of the 1998 Tour de France, the eighty-fifth edition of the world's most famous endurance event which had finished only three months earlier, just a stone's throw away in the shadow of the Arc de Triomphe. A Tour which had started with high ambitions had fallen apart in a whirlwind of shame. French sport and culture had been shamed just days after the country tasted World Cup euphoria, as the most dramatic doping scandal in modern professional sport engulfed the race.

Before the 1998 Tour began in Dublin, riders like Richard Virenque, a French household name; Alex Zulle, the highest-paid professional in the sport; and world number one, Laurent

Jalabert, had entertained high hopes of final victory. For Zulle and Virenque, leaders of the discredited Festina team, their Tour ended in ignominy when they were thrown off the race and then strip-searched in police cells by the French drugs squad. French champion Jalabert, clad in the colours of his national flag, walked out on the Tour in disgust vowing never to return, even as the police descended on his team's hotel.

The drug abuse that we all privately knew had been prevalent in professional cycling, yet that the sport had publicly refused to acknowledge, was unflinchingly laid bare by the French judiciary. The old denials and the years of cosy complicity were mercilessly exposed as professional cycling's cocooned world came under scrutiny. The 1998 Tour became an explosion of truth in a world accustomed to deceit and white lies. It left us all – riders, sponsors, promoters and journalists – scorched and dazed and, to some extent, guilty. In the absence of any concrete evidence to dispel the tidal wave of scandal and gossip, every race, every rider and, sadly for those with nothing to fear, every victory was thrown into doubt. The suspicion of doping, let alone the proof of doping, devalued the Tour dream. The cornerstone of the Tour's appeal, the myth of unrelenting sacrifice and suffering that was at the heart of the modern race and of the Tour's timeless fascination, was kicked away.

But it would be wrong to believe that all professional cyclists use performance-enhancing drugs as a matter of routine. There are some riders, although it is impossible to know how many, perhaps more aware of life after cycling than others, who do not buckle under the strain of peer or sponsor pressure and carve out respectable careers within the sport without resorting to doping.

Originally, this book was to be the personalised story of one year in the long life of the Tour de France, but the events of July 1998 overtook that intention. This is the story of the collapse of 'Planet Tour'; the surreal, introspective world of professional cycling; a sport in which broken collar-bones are as common as broken dreams.

On Planet Tour, European bike racing's unreal world, just about anything goes. Professional riders pedal elegantly out of hotel lifts without raising an eyebrow; race vehicles ignore all normal driving conventions and throw caution to the wind; and the Euro-roving pack of journalists saunters unshaven into town halls to breakfast on wine and canapés at the local mayor's expense.

On Planet Tour, women are usually one of two things: podium publicity girls or brow-beaten PR people; but most of all, in this man's world they're unavailable, out of bounds. In this chauvinistic environment women are only painful distractions, reminders of that other world beyond the crowd barriers and press passes, the finish lines and security men; the normal world of children and schools, of home and friends. No – professional cycling's monastic tradition finds it hard to welcome women to Planet Tour. Talk to the fiercely protective managers, masseurs and officials behind each cosseted, shaven-legged star and you'd believe that the mere sight of a woman was enough to reduce a rider's competitive will to jelly.

This is also my story. I was down on my luck, uninspired and unemployed, until a series of coincidences plunged me into a journalistic roller-coaster ride, playing a bit-part in sport's greatest road movie. An insomniac's obsession with breaking away, with escape, found its home in a nomadic foreign sport, on the endless ribbon of tarmac that is European bike racing. Out on the roads of France, Italy, Belgium and Spain there are no stadiums or terraces, no grandstands for a masterly view; just a crackling race radio, the sun-roof of a press car and the endless road stretching ahead.

At the eye of Planet Tour's whirlwind are the professional riders themselves: the tanned, gaunt characters, cared for as if they were thoroughbred racehorses, whose triumphs and disasters are the lifeblood of the sport. They've been memorably labelled 'toasted whippets' but in truth they will always be the 'convicts of the road', prisoners of their own profession. This is the story of these convicts of the road; of moments snatched with athletes who may be champions but can often seem exploited and lonely men, living in a ruthless world of few comforts; a world without women or tenderness, without children and friends. They are Planet Tour's prisoners of pain, battling physically and spiritually with their own limitations.

Over the ruptured cobbles of Belgium, the smooth tarmac of the French Riviera and the brutal gradients of the Alps, Dolomites and Pyrénées, flock each year's new crop of young professionals; starry-eyed after glittering amateur careers in Italy, France and Spain. Each season they come and go. Many – too many – fall by the wayside, burnt out from racing too much, too soon, suffering from injury or fatigue, poor form or lost morale. Only the very best cling on to their contracts and eke out a fruitful career.

Until the 1998 Tour's scandals shook the foundations of the sport, the top professionals were idolised by fans from Colombia to Catalunya, fans who saw only their daring and sacrifice, their athletic elegance and grace in the heat of the afternoon. Under the summer sun, the riders hurtle past with the 'festival', the fête of the Tour, dreaming of bids for glory, of do-or-die heroics, of the chance of a career-making moment of success and even, for fewer than a handful, of final Tour victory. Most dread the loneliness of the Tour's time trials, or the 'race of truth' as the French call the *'contre la montre'*, and the cruel Russian roulette of the mountain stages, where hidden dangers and sudden unexpected failures make survival the overriding objective. Only a few see such stages, part of the very essence of the Tour's mythology that make the old race such compulsive watching, as opportunities and springboards. Most see them as days of pain and anguish, to be squared up to, survived and ticked off. They are prepared to fight tooth and nail for the honour of finishing the great race, for the distinction of entering a pantheon filled with tales of heroism and suffering.

Through the camera lens the Tour field sweeps anonymously past as a blur of lean, brown legs turning effortlessly as the miles recede under their sparkling wheels. That seductive image hides the brutality of the sport. Other than when they win, the riders can seem faceless automatons, athletic caricatures; Euro-rovers without homes or nationality. They exist only to shore up TV ratings, to support sagging sponsors, to reaffirm French cultural traditions of the man and the soil, of the boy and the earth. While we live our normal daily lives, they are out there somewhere on the Novotel-Sofitel-Fimotel treadmill, floating in their monastic nether world, racing and training their way through time as the seasons and the years slip behind them.

Shockingly, its skin taut as a drum, that complicated and cocooned world ruptured during the 1998 Tour. Everyone involved came face to face with the awful reality of its darker side. Because this was the July when the world caught an unwelcome glimpse backstage, when the blinkers dropped from its eyes and instead of athletic grace, sacrifice and camaraderie, it saw only deception and fraud.

'Doping is the biggest enemy that sport has ever had to

face,' said Jean-Claude Killy, that crisp and sunny November morning.

'We will never give up the fight against doping,' he pledged, 'because we believe that the ethics of sport are unique.

'We will never give up,' he concluded, 'because we believe in the strength and dignity of man.'

PART ONE

Day 1

My own story has a less than ideal beginning.

On a cold April morning in 1994, I stood anxiously in the foyer of the Hôtel de France in Compiègne, watching sleet sweep horizontally across the Oise river. One by one, riders from the Motorola cycling team, also billeted in the hotel, filed past, grunting tense greetings. Outside, they clambered into their waiting team cars before making their way to the start of the Paris–Roubaix in Compiègne's Place du Palace.

Paris–Roubaix, the toughest and most traditional French one-day race, has the same grip on the French imagination as the Grand National exerts on the British. The race falls each April and is organised by the Société du Tour de France, the most powerful race promoters in professional cycling. It may not have been *Le Tour* – after all, no other event is; but it was everything to me: it was my First Big Race. It was my initiating brush with the spring race known universally as

'*L'Enfer du Nord*' – the 'Hell of the North' – and it marked the beginning of my journey into the surreal world of the European circuit, the Disneyland of professional cycling.

The hotel foyer was empty and silent. For those quiet moments, I stood poised on the edge of reality, as nervous as the greenest new professional waiting for the start gun. The magazine that had hired me had barely any budget to pay my hotel bill let alone hire a car, so I was hitching a ride with the editorial team from a French magazine. The clock above the reception desk ticked on. There was still no sign of the battered press car, containing Jacques and Pascal. I grew more tense as the sleet outside darkened the sky. Surely, after our friendly, drunken dinner the night before, they wouldn't leave without me – but did they get so wrecked that they'd actually forgotten about *l'Anglais*?

Finally, cursing and muttering, I picked up my laptop and kit bag, stepped out into the maelstrom of sleet, rain and wind, crossed the old Pont Solferino and headed up towards Compiègne town centre. In the square in front of the grand and imposing Palais, riders huddled under the signing-on podium, while a hardy crowd lined the barriers. Start time was looming. Even so, most of Europe's top professional riders remained resolutely inside their team cars to the frustration of French, Belgian and Italian TV crews, as the icy rain continued to pelt down. I fought through the crowds of drenched teenagers, flashed my press pass at security and headed across the windswept cobbled square to the steaming, multilingual scrum of the breakfast tent.

But there was still no sign of Jacques and Pascal. With only a few minutes to go to the start, alarm bells rang out as beginner's paranoia took hold. Of course – they'd done this to me on purpose. And I knew why. My French was so poor, so utterly inadequate at dinner last night that they'd decided to leave me behind. They'd be kilometres down the road by now, laughing at my improper use of the subjunctive and my mangling of masculine and feminine, my struggle with the menu and most heinously, the way I drank a beer with the first course while they tucked into the Gigondas. They'd deliberately left me among the fans and hangers-on, cut off from Planet Tour like all the other wannabes, watching and waving as the race swept past, standing pathetically in the rain, wishing that I was at home scouring Monday's papers in search of a proper job.

Panic-stricken and drenched, I began jogging through the side-streets and alleys in search of the battered Renault Nevada, hunting in the sleet among the logo-spattered saloons and estates for the familiar scrapes and shunts that punctuated the car's body-work. One by one, cars representing the world's media, Fiats and Renaults, BMWs and Alfas with stickers bearing the names of RTL, Antenne 2, Radio Monte Carlo, RAI, *L'Equipe*, *La Gazetta dello Sport*, *Le Figaro* and *Marca* pulled away from the kerb. I watched from the pavement as the rain dripped down my neck. Across the road, the Tour's *chef de presse* stepped into his Fiat and gave me a curious look as he did so. I smiled thinly, trying to affect a disinterested nonchalance. Just as the last press car swept past and out of the square with a purposeful, racy squeal of rubber and my morale sank to a new low, my ride clattered into view. In one movement, the Nevada slid unsteadily to a halt in front of me, a door was thrown open and I was in – back *en route* for Planet Tour.

Inside the lumbering estate, our French editor Jacques – garrulous, ebullient, Parisian and married just four times at the age of forty – floored the old diesel engine and we lurched into the convoy of Tempras, Passats, Méganes and Lagunas. Beside him sat an old man in a flat cap – his father, a former

French champion – while in the back on my right, Pascal, Jacques' Belgian assistant editor, stared biliously out of the window. '*Ça va, Pascal?*' I ventured. '*Non – malade,*' he groaned in reply. But at last we were off, on the race known as the Hell of the North. Paris–Roubaix is the ultimate hard man's race, with long passages where the race rattles murderously over the treacherous cobbles of northern France. Bleak, windswept and unrelenting, it's a test of man and machine – and a test of patience, for anyone travelling in the back of this particular press car.

First stop, naturally enough, was a roadside patisserie.

'We were up drinking 'til four,' Jacques explained off-handedly as Pascal, hand clasped to his mouth, sprinted down a nearby alleyway.

'He can't handle it – typical!' snorted Jacques derisively as his assistant editor's violent hurling echoed back towards us. 'Reckons he's a big drinker but he's all mouth.'

Meanwhile, on the closed roads behind us, the 1994 Paris–Roubaix was taking shape. Out across the plains of Picardy one man had ridden clear of the bunch, bravely going it alone as flurries of snow whirled around him. It was a new Czech professional called Lom Lubos, plucked from obscurity by the Italian Navigare team, but sadly soon destined to return there.

Back in the Nevada, Pascal belched and swallowed and was clearly not coping at all well, even on the straight, flat roads through the dark forests that made up the first half of the race route. Worryingly, the worst was yet to come. The skating rink of mud and cowshit – the riders call it 'Belgian toothpaste' – covering the rutted cobbles that make up the latter part of 'Hell' still lay ahead of us. Pascal chundered his way through St Quentin and in the suburbs of Soissons, desperately burbled '*Arrêtez!*' in time only to throw the door open yet again and drop his head into the gutter. We hurtled onwards, forced to pause briefly for him at a drab industrial estate on the edge of the desolate mining town of Valenciennes. Jacques, by now warmed to the task of humiliating his hapless assistant, threw us through each and every bend with gusto while his father, oblivious to his fellow passenger's torture, produced a hunting knife and began to slice a garlic sausage into ruddy, pungent chunks.

I was undergoing rites of passage in this motley press car while out on the wide plains of north-east France, an epic edition of Paris–Roubaix was taking shape. Andrei Tchmil, a hardy Russian rider plying his trade in Belgium with national lottery-sponsored team Lotto, had set off across the muddy sleet-slick cobbles – the *pavé* – on what looked to be a futile lone escape.

In the Nevada, the race radio crackled intermittently, giving us time checks on the group of riders chasing the Russian, as the appalling conditions reduced the old race to a fight for survival. Driving ahead of Tchmil, we skated over the *pavé*, sliding through the muddy pot-holed bends with no let-up, as Pascal battled vainly to keep his stomach in check. By now, after five hours trapped in the car, recoiling from his sallow, unshaven features, my professional respect for Pascal had been irretrievably damaged. The rakish Jacques, on the other hand, was surely all that a Hemingway-esque sports writer should be: dashing, devil-may-care and full of dramatic flourishes, handling the car with the same cavalier attitude that had no doubt stood him in good stead throughout his four marriages.

Meanwhile, to everyone's surprise, Tchmil was still clear but was locked into a bitter pursuit match with former team-mate turned deadly rival, Belgian star Johan Museeuw. Museeuw came across as a cold, ambitious character determined to win Paris–Roubaix, but the race was effectively decided and his hopes of catching the Russian ended when the frame of his specially built bike snapped in two on a particularly brutal section of cobbles.

As Tchmil neared the glory of becoming the race's first-ever winner from the former Eastern Bloc, Pascal too was nearing the end of his day on the Limousin telephone just as I neared the end of my own physical and emotional tolerance – yet his most dramatic regurgitation was still to come. Minutes from the vélodrome finish in Roubaix, his stomach overpowered him once more as we approached a road junction lined by flag-waving schoolkids. Seizing the chance for one final public humiliation, Jacques carefully picked his spot. The Nevada screeched to a halt in front of the mass of cheering kids, policed gently by an ageing local *gendarme*. Pascal threw the door open with a now well-practised flourish. As the cop gaped in horror and I stared out of the opposite window in appalled resignation, he leaned well out into the street and, for the final time, held forth with feeling on to the cobbles of north-east France.

Things, as they say, could only get better. Thankfully, by the time I'd got to Dublin for the start of the 1998 Tour de France, they had.

This time at least, I had my own car.

So why Dublin for the start of the 1998 Tour de France? Why Dublin for the start of a race invented by the French and coveted by the French; a race that for decades – much more than football or tennis – has swelled the hearts of French traditionalists; a race that finishes in Paris on the Champs-Elysées, that takes in the country's two great mountain ranges, the Alps and the Pyrénées, and that every July conjures up a reassuring and unchanging image of Gallic cultural life?

What's Dublin got to do with it?

These days, the Tour, once a continental curiosity, is about as French as Mickey Mouse and Disneyland and as ubiquitously international as McDonald's and Coca-Cola. It's the only bike race that everybody has heard of. There may be other tours, but there's only one Tour and the modern race is constantly expanding, constantly on the look out for new markets. Most of us have a foggy childhood memory of the Tour, of Dickie Davies on *World of Sport* linking to a few stolen moments of the race on a summer Saturday afternoon; or of a tea bag advert, with a cast of chimpanzees, that stole its script from the Tour's brutal reputation. '*Can yer ride tandem?*' These days, you need more than a strong cup of tea to survive the modern Tour de France, as the 1998 edition of the race revealed.

For the start of the 85th Tour, Dublin would host the giant Tour caravan for the best part of four days. Although only two of those days – Saturday's prologue time trial stage and Sunday's road race through the hills of Wicklow and back into Phoenix Park – would actually start and finish in the city, many of the giant crew of officials, riders and media arrived in Dublin three days earlier.

Dublin was expecting a multilingual fête, a carnival; it was expecting the glitz and glamour of world sport's biggest roving show. It was expecting all the excesses that come as part of the Planet Tour package. But as the city readied itself for the French invasion, a bespectacled Belgian called Willy Voet was approaching the Belgian–French border at Neuville-en-Ferrain at the wheel of a car belonging to the Festina cycling team, loaded to the gunwales with performance-enhancing drugs.

We'll come back to Willy – and his car boot sale's-worth of banned blood-booster EPO – after we've dealt with the

Tour's first tense forty-eight hours – and the long queue for press accreditations in Dublin Castle.

There were, in fact, two very good reasons to choose Dublin for a Tour start. The first was Sean Kelly, a farmer's son from Carrick-on-Suir and the other, Stephen Roche, an ambitious Dublin lad. As alike as chalk and cheese, the two were thrown together in the 1980s as Irish cycling hit the heights. Kelly, the older of the pair, was the no-nonsense hard man, the blood and guts country boy, the man who ate peat for breakfast; Roche was the ambitious, chatty Dubliner, with an eye for sports cars, determined and driven to win. Roche won big races because he needed to, but Kelly won simply because he could. Nobody expected them to like each other, although outwardly they seemed to. Yet together they became Irish institutions. Kelly, who based himself in Belgium, was adored by the Flemish, in the land where granite-jawed, swarthy monosyllabic cyclists who take to muddy, cobbled roads are traditionally bred. Roche married a French girl and set about charming his adopted nation with his sweet boyish pedalling style, mastering the language in a knockabout way and chatting dreamily of winning the Tour de France. When he fulfilled that dream in July 1987, the French celebrated as if he was one of their own.

Kelly won race after race and went on to become one of the most successful riders of his generation, but he never finished higher than fourth in the Tour. Roche, a far less prolific but more spectacular winner, excelled one glorious season, winning the Tour, the Giro d'Italia and the World Championships in the space of four months. These men were two good reasons to choose Dublin from a romantic's point of view, at least; but in the grey morning light at Holyhead as I waited to board the ferry to Dublin, there was time to ponder the real reasons why Amary Group, the Tour's parent company, had decided to cross the Irish sea.

Starting the race in Ireland, aside from the fee paid by Dublin City Council and the Irish government said to be in the region of £2.1 million, had other more immediate benefits. It had been an unexpectedly fortuitous decision. Football's World Cup climaxed in Paris as the Tour, starting a week later than usual to avoid a clash with the tournament's final week, got underway. Riding a wave of opportunism and nationalistic fervour, the French national team had reached the final and were squaring up to Brazil. If the Tour's opening shots had been played out in Lyon or Le Mans, Avignon or Auxerre, they would have been swept aside by the tide of patriotism emanating from Paris as *les bleues* marched inexorably towards the Stade de France. With the World Cup holding sway in France, the Irish capital had been chosen for the attention-grabbing start of a race that allows little time for rest or recovery, privacy or solitude and barely makes time for that most sacrosanct of cyclist's moments: satisfying toilet time. It was only a couple of years earlier that Australian rider Neil Stephens said, 'I've been so busy during this bloody Tour that I haven't had time to shit, mate.'

Dublin offered the possibility of paying tribute to Kelly and Roche, as well as other Irish heroes such as Shay Elliott and lesser lights such as Martin Earley, Paul Kimmage and Laurence Roche, all of whom rode the Tour in those halcyon days of the 1980s. Best of all, a Dublin start ensured plenty of advance publicity for a free event that thrives on marketing and public relations, on achieving the seemingly impossible with a nonchalant swagger. It was the most adventurous Tour *départ* to date and set tongues wagging over the possibilities of a Guadeloupe start in the year 2000.

Ultimately, none of that mattered because, thanks to Willy Voet and the Festina team, *Le Tour en Irlande* was soon to become headline news, even as Paris partied through Sunday night and long into Monday morning following the French soccer team's dream victory over the disappointing Brazilians. Even so, a lot of the enthusiasm for Dublin, a lot of the talk of the city's great literary past and its thrusting millennial future, of the warm Guinness-fuelled welcome, of the *craic*, was driven by the Irish Tourist Board and the race organising company l'Evenement, headed by Alan Rushton.

Unlike the provincial atmosphere of other stage races, the heavyweight stature of the Tour gives it the power to close major roads well in advance, to close down town centres and villages, even banks and schools. The Tour's bureaucracy dictates that most of the Tour convoy arrives forty-eight hours before the race start, building the tension as the race start looms; but as I drove off the ferry at Dun Laoghaire, Dublin seemed strangely indifferent to the global attention soon to be focused on the city centre.

The Irish papers certainly weren't making a fuss. Thursday's dailies carried barely a column inch of news on the arrival of the world's top cyclists, or of the media invasion that the Tour sparked. Instead there were the first belligerent rumblings of complaint over road closures and traffic congestion. Only the *Irish Times*, with a special supplement shouting '*Vive la France! Vive l'Irlande!*' seemed to realise the full magnitude of what was about to be unleashed on Dublin.

Dublin's streets were thick with lunch-time traffic and I trawled slowly alongside the Liffey before the familiar Tour directional arrows came into view. At the gates of the race HQ in Dublin Castle, armed police stopped and searched the car, opening the boot and eyeing my press card carefully before allowing the Audi through the barrier. I found a parking space within the cramped, rambling confines of the Castle's walls and headed off through another security cordon at the gates of the Castle's Lower Yard in search of my press badge, press sticker for the car, radio transmitter to pick up Radio Tour and in search of the *salle de presse* itself. Radio Tour, the shortwave service provided by the race organisation's lead commissaire car, is the lifeline for those following the race in team cars and in press cars. It crackles throughout each and every day, listing crashes and attacks, retirements and punctures, in French, Italian and English.

The media nerve centre of the Tour de France is the *presse permanence*. All of the 1,500 accredited journalists working on the Tour must go through its strict vetting procedures to obtain a pass. Even though I'd been to the Société du Tour de France's events many times before, there was that same familiar frisson of anxiety that the coveted green pass wouldn't be forthcoming – that the God of Planet Tour would exclude me from the party and that I'd be left on the outside looking in.

In one of the Castle's grand ante-rooms, I stood in the multilingual, multinational queue, exchanging *ça vas* with familiar faces, smiling and shaking hands. An Irish journalist bustled anxiously alongside and immediately launched into a tirade about the city centre road closures. Ahead of us, a German journalist was edging nearer to the precipice, complaining furiously to a Tour official over the *service presse*'s refusal to give him a pass. Another wrong word and he'd blow his chances completely. The Irishwoman blustered on, listing closed streets and shutdown by-passes, restricted roundabouts and drastic diversions. I asked her if this was her first time on the race. 'Oh yes,' she gushed. 'Wonderful, isn't it?'

By now the German was swearing under his breath, as the queuing system fell apart completely following the influx of a loud post-lunch party of gate-crashing French hacks and snappers. Hands were extended through the crowd and yet more *ça vas* exchanged, while we inched forward. As the French party picked up their press badges, the Irishwoman looked wounded and bemused while the German swore loudly through clenched teeth. Suddenly, between the leather jackets and overcoats, the blazers and the T-shirts, I saw a gap, slipped into it, and moments later was walking back to the car, press pass and press car sticker in hand.

I was in – I was on board Planet Tour. I had my ticket for the roller-coaster. And the fun was only just beginning.

Across Dublin Castle garden, the usual throng of journalists and photographers were chatting, smoking and sipping coffee from plastic cups at the entrance to the *salle de presse* in the Chester Beatty Library. The crew of familiar faces from France, Italy, Belgium and Spain that follows the professional scene from the very first races of the season through to October's closing events swells each July as the Americans and the Brits, the Danes and the Germans and even the Japanese turn up for *Le Tour*. For many of them, it was far from their first Tour, but for some the excited expectancy lighting up their eyes gave them away as Tour virgins. They buzzed back and forth, picking up every available leaflet, drinking gallons of complimentary coffee and furiously chewing mouthfuls of complimentary bread and cheese, proudly wearing their crisp official Tour T-shirts bearing the Nike swoosh.

There is a Tour uniform of sorts, a casual outfit that brings together branding from the Tour's *partenaires*, or major sponsors, with a self-consciously Euro-style chic. Lacoste polo shirts mingle with Oakley shades and Nike trainers, while action sandals – stowed-away in chilly Ireland – are always *de rigueur* in France. The more adventurous throw in the odd

Mambo or Patagonia label, mixed in with a little Converse and, here and there, a classic touch of Timberland or Armani. There are the sadder cases though, those who've bought whole outfits from *le boutique du Tour*. They wander in and out of the press room, clad head to toe in Nike, Oakleys perched on their foreheads, adding the finishing touch with a Festina watch. They are so gripped by Tour merchandising that they have become walking hoardings for the global brands at the heart of the Tour's marketing pull.

Up in the *salle de presse*, a fit-looking Miguel Indurain, winner of five successive Tours between 1991 and 1995, was chatting unnoticed to journalists, while Irish heroes Kelly and Roche worked the throng, smiling and shaking hands. Oddly for the start of *Le Tour*, the French head count seemed unusually low, perhaps because many of those who normally followed the Tour from the start were planning to pick the race up in Brittany, when it arrived in Roscoff for Stage Three. But the influx of German and Danish media who'd flocked to the Tour since the victories of the Deutsche Telekom team in 1996 and 1997, more than made up for the absent French. Affable, helpful and best of all, English-speaking, the Danes had been on the race in large numbers since Telekom's Bjarne Riis overcame Miguel Indurain in the 1996 Tour. Even though he spoke fluent French as well as good English and Italian, Riis had remained a distant figure to foreign journalists since his success that July, the first win by a Dane in the history of the race. The Danish press corps had helped us unravel the enigma of the tall, balding and often monosyllabic Riis. Now we knew for sure that he could be insular and evasive – it wasn't just a linguistic misunderstanding. A year later, in 1997, Riis had endured a nightmarish Tour defence, losing his form and suffering from a virus as his young Telekom team-mate and protégé, Germany's Jan

Ullrich, rode clear to an emphatic win.

Yet as Dublin's prologue loomed, Riis, now in his mid-thirties and with Ullrich monopolising his team's attention, was either supremely confident or in a state of denial. Even though Ullrich was the champion, and in spite of half-hearted denials by his team manager Walter Godefroot, Riis had insisted during his build-up to the race that he would ride the Tour to win. So, late that afternoon we all trooped dutifully back across the Castle garden to the Telekom press conference in one of the grander reception rooms.

At the far end of the long gilded room, facing the bank of microphones and cameras, sat Riis, Godefroot and team sprinter Erik Zabel, alongside Telekom press officer Matthias Schuman. Finally, after a long wait, Ullrich joined them. Only Godefroot could force a smile of greeting. Riis, wary of the press since an extra-marital affair was outed by his own national media at the end of 1997, stared anxiously back at his interrogators. Even Godefroot, a distinguished former professional, couldn't resist a crack about Dublin's road closures, as he explained away Ullrich's late arrival. Riis meanwhile was sighing and shrugging his way through the usual queries over team leadership.

'I'm here to win,' he said disinterestedly, 'but if that's not possible then I'm happy to help Jan.'

Red hair shaven tight to his cranium Terminator-style, Ullrich sat close by, hiding his nerves by staring at his hands or at the tablecloth. He looked bored. But then we knew – and he knew – that we'd all come to look at him, not to listen to what he said. After a winter of public appearances, award ceremonies and bib-and-tucker dinners, the wunderkind had let things go. Somehow, the most valuable talent in cycling had started the 1998 season a disastrous ten kilos over his ideal racing weight.

Since his Tour victory in 1997, Ullrich had ousted Michael Schumacher and Steffi Graf as the leading superstar of German sport. Now, with the empty-handed German football team on their way home from the World Cup following defeat by Croatia, the expectations of him were massive. All spring he'd been fighting to lose those excess kilos. It had made him ill, exhausted by the painful routine of racing and dieting. The German rider had started a bucketload of races, only to abandon most of them long before the finish. He'd sweated and puffed through the first stage of April's Tour of the Basque Country, a tough Spanish stage race. It quickly became a catastrophe for him. On the second day of the race, Ullrich conceded twenty-two minutes to the stage winner; on the third day, looking like he was towing a double-decker bus full of American tourists up to Hampstead Heath, he gave up the ghost after just thirty-eight kilometres.

The Tour champion was in crisis. The press, in particular the French press, dwelt gleefully on his chubby chins and big belly. Past Tour winners rounded on him, accusing him of unprofessionalism; while the Tour's own race director, Jean-Marie Leblanc, hinted darkly that he had disgraced the yellow jersey. French sports newspaper *L'Equipe* published a full page of high-handed condemnation, and a few days later Telekom's other *directeur sportif*, Rudy Pevenage, made plain the team's displeasure, calling the press 'shits'. Sure Ullrich was fat, but all this mumbo-jumbo of 'disgracing the Tour's tradition' was over the top. Jacques Anquetil won the Tour five times on the back of cigarettes, champagne, card schools and women, his preferred schedule of preparation. *Ah, but he was French, wasn't he?*

Nevertheless, the 'Tubby Tour Champ' was a good story and, given the lack of openness on the part of Telekom, who knew full well that the young German had come close to cracking up under pressure during the 1997 Tour, it was inevitable that the media would play devil's advocate. Unsurprisingly, Telekom hadn't seen things that way and in the final weeks of his Tour build-up, during which Ullrich had followed a punishing training schedule put together by his long-term coach Peter Becker, the German team's PR machine had zealously shielded their young star from the media. Requests for interviews all had to go through the meticulous Schuman and all questions had to be submitted by fax. There was no chance of actually speaking, one on one, either to Ullrich or to Riis.

So we sat – all Pevenage's 'shits' together – staring at the elusive wunderkind while Riis fielded the questions and young Jan stared unblinkingly at the tablecloth. We studied Ullrich's face and torso for double chins and flab; we sought signs of where you could pinch more than an inch; we scrutinised the poor kid for any signs of beer belly or upper-arm wobble. We couldn't find any. Instead, Ullrich looked like a carefully primed hit man. He was mean, steely, angular and determined. There was no hint of a smile or of warmth – just a set, chiselled jaw and an impassive look of brutal invincibility.

Finally, as Riis dried up yet again, Ullrich was at last asked a question. How difficult would his troubled Tour preparation make the defence of his title? There was a long pause followed by a flurry of conferring between Schuman, Godefroot and Ullrich. And then, after weeks of silence, the wunderkind found his voice.

'I tried to prepare like last year, but I lost three weeks to illness,' he said matter-of-factly. 'So the Tour's later start has helped and I've come out of recent races in good condition.'

It was hardly gripping stuff, but at least, for a brief

moment, he'd actually spoken to us. And that was it. Mercifully, the Telekom press conference was over and they stood up to leave.

Back in the phone room, the Irish were baffled. This may have been the centre of Dublin, but France Telecom's team of technicians would only take payment for calls in French francs. I e-mailed my story, fished out some francs and headed off to find my hotel room, somewhere in the narrow streets around Temple Bar. Dublin's packed streets were crammed with rush-hour traffic and it took me an hour to crawl the quarter mile to the hotel.

After a shower, I met up with a photographer and some radio people from the BBC. We moseyed down to the Civic Offices for more *craic* at an official Tour reception. There was plenty of free Jameson's, Guinness and in my case, Harp lager – all downed on an empty stomach. Out on the terrace, an Irish band mixed traditional reels with cheery pub rock – it was a bland mix, sounding like a kind of Corrs-lite. Back in Temple Bar, young Dublin was at play. The pubs seemed to be packed with ruddy-faced teenagers, while each restaurant battled to seat lengthy queues. Finally, we found a table and unceremoniously wolfed down a plate of risotto – it had been a long day.

I woke up at two in the morning as the sounds of shouting and breaking glass floated up from the street. Through the curtains, I watched the soft drizzle glistening in the street lights as it swept across the Liffey. Paris and the grandeur of the Champs-Elysées seemed a long way away.

Day 2

I walked into the press room on Friday morning to find that we had a full-blown scandal on our hands. We had arrests and accusations, denials and rebuttals, gossip and rumour – and the race start was still twenty-four hours away. Over in the Castle there were more team medicals and press calls, but in the *salle de presse*, events back across the Channel, centring on the hapless Festina *soigneur* Willy Voet, were overshadowing all the normal Tour protocol.

Just before 6.30 on the previous Wednesday morning, Voet's Festina Tour car, issued as is the case with all other team cars by the Tour organisation itself and emblazoned with team promotional logos, had been searched by French customs as he crossed the border with Belgium. In those moments in the shabby suburbs of Lille, the destiny of the 1998 Tour de France – and perhaps of all future Tours – was changed for good. The customs officials discovered 235 doses of erythropoietin – the soon-to-be infamous EPO – syringes, batches of human growth hormone, anabolic steroids and various masking agents, in addition to a long list of other doping products, said to total 400 doses in all.

With *Le Tour* building up to its showbiz send-off, the story at first seemed far away, out of sight and out of mind, but the snowball was gathering pace and impact was inevitable. Even so, the papers fought shy of the story, wary of printing unsubstantiated allegations. For a while that Friday after-noon, the story hung in the air, the media uncertain how to play it. I rang London where the sports desk opted to hold fire and await further developments. There was no word from Festina or from the Tour organisation, although by the end of the day their hands would be forced.

Sitting quietly in the press room a couple of seats away was Paul Kimmage; the infamous Kimmage, author and jour-nalist, and with Roche, Kelly and Martin Earley, one of the Irish 'Fab Four' cyclists of the mid-eighties. Kimmage had ridden alongside both Roche and Kelly during their glory years, most notably at the euphoric World Championships in 1987 when Roche, aided and abetted by this dashing trio, had tearfully completed his triple crown. Kimmage rode the Tour three times, reaching Paris only once, but making a big contribution to the Kelly–Roche legend and to Irish cycling as a whole.

Yet Kimmage's own career was, by his own admission, far less successful as nerves and injuries took their toll. But through it all, the Dubliner kept his head screwed on. When, inevitably, he retired early from the sport, he turned to journalism and wrote *A Rough Ride*, a riveting exposé of his own *naïveté* and the ruthlessness of the professional scene. Unflinchingly, he dished the dirt – on himself and on others. He talked of rampant amphetamine abuse, even in

31

races as insignificant as criteriums, the lucrative post-Tour circuit of town centre gallops in rural France. Kimmage spoke of the shame not in taking drugs, but in being caught; and of the law of silence hanging over any of those, such as himself, who thought of speaking out. 'I WAS A VICTIM,' he wrote in capital letters towards the end of the book. 'A victim of a system that actually promotes drug-taking in the sport.'

Unsurprisingly, the book hadn't made him popular with his Irish peers. He'd broken that unspoken law of silence and spat in the soup, the 'soup' that all those with interests in the sport, athletic, professional or financial, shared. Now with *A Rough Ride* about to be reissued to coincide with the Tour's visit to Ireland and his regular column in the *Sunday Independent* also ruffling feathers, Kimmage once more stood accused of betraying his peers and tarnishing the image of professional cycling.

Chief among his accusers was the man who had once been his hero and mentor, Roche himself.

'He's using this whole thing to give himself profile,' declared Roche in the city's listings magazine, *In Dublin*. 'What he's doing is encouraging parents not to put kids on bikes, because he's making this drugs thing sound more widespread than it actually is. The Tour de France is the biggest annual sporting event in the world and all Paul Kimmage is doing is bringing it down. He's a sensationalist journalist.'

Kimmage sat working a few feet away, so I pulled a copy of *In Dublin* out of my bag, moved down the row of seats and said hello.

'What do you think of this?' I asked, holding up the mag so he could see Roche's name on the cover.

Kimmage half-smiled in recognition of the article. 'Well, what can you say?' he shrugged wearily.

★ ★ ★

Back across the Castle garden, there were yet more press conferences and medical visits. Both have now become an essential part of the two day build-up to the Tour's opening prologue time trial. Team by team, the riders come into the *permanence* and visit the Tour's medical controls. There, they are weighed and measured, have their blood pressure taken and their resting pulse rate measured. A few select photographers are allowed in to take stage-managed shots of Ullrich, Riis or Chris Boardman having a stethoscope put to their chest. The press hover outside, hoping to gauge the mood of the riders, searching for any team titbits. Camera crews descend on the likes of Italian sprinter Mario Cipollini, hoping for some unguarded comment or snippet of racy gossip.

Boardman may have been favourite for the following afternoon's prologue but the Merseysider's meetings with the press have always been something of a mixed bag. Although he is usually talkative and forthcoming, he sometimes baffles those listening with his love of sports theory and frustrates them with his tendency to stick to a script. Every now and then, listening to him expound on recent test results, on lactic thresholds and the joys of working in the lab with training guru Peter Keen, the overwhelming temptation has been to blurt, 'Chris – just *do* it!' Some believe that Boardman's mind for scientific rationalisation has actually worked against him in a sport where intelligence can sometimes hamper achievement. Every now and then, they argue, you can sense him backing off, reasoning that he is going beyond proven ground – yet isn't unchartered territory where the greatest athletes find their true capabilities? All the same, Dublin was preparing itself for a Boardman victory, but it wasn't as much of a sure thing as it once might have been. Despite his rousing ride in that spring's Prudential Tour of Britain, chinks had appeared

33

in the Merseysider's armour during the previous year's Tour. Since then, he'd shown little sign of overcoming his own doubts.

Since his first success in the July of 1994, the Tour's prologue time trial has always been the biggest day of Boardman's year. He takes on the character of a prize-fighter as the prologue approaches, chewing gum frenetically, talking a mean ride, his self-belief almost touched with uncharacteristic arrogance. But since the golden start to his professional career in 1994, when he was the most exciting and highly rated new professional of his generation, his star has steadily fallen. When he dropped out of the 1994 Tour, his first, as the race arrived at the foot of the Pyrénées, he was fired with enthusiasm for *Le Tour*, talking excitedly of coming back in the future to challenge for victory.

But perhaps his prospects as a potential Tour challenger turned on a foul evening in Brittany a year later, midway through the prologue of the 1995 Tour. Boardman, hyped up by the media and by the expectations of his own team, charged down the start ramp into the teeth of a squally storm and crashed heavily, breaking his ankle. The lure of victory in the prologue had overridden common sense. The weather had been so bad that night that most of the other pre-race favourites had taken their foot off the gas and avoided unnecessary risks. They'd kept their eyes on the long-term prize, while GAN, Boardman's sponsor, in need of a boost after a poor opening to the season, had emphasised short-term gain. As a stage race rider, Boardman has never quite been the same since, even though he has made a full recovery from that horrendous crash. The time trial stage wins and prologue successes are many, but the high placings in stage races are few.

In some ways, his 1998 Tour hopes were over even before

the race began, simply because victory in the prologue – a tough but insignificant stage in overall Tour terms – and custody of the Tour's first *maillot jaune*, had become a be-all and end-all. 'That's why I'm here,' he said bluntly. 'That's what they pay me for.' Thoughts of making an overall challenge had already been ruled out. As long as he won the prologue, thereby fulfilling his personal goals and meeting his sponsor's requirements, then the rest of the Tour was unimportant. That mind-set went some of the way towards explaining his recurring problems in the mountain stages of the race.

I was walking down Dame Street at lunch-time pondering Boardman's compromised talent when, as if on cue, he appeared on his bike in the distance. Seeing him coming, I strolled towards the middle of the closed road to wave in greeting.

'You'll get run over standing there,' he called knowingly, as he pedalled slowly past towards the prologue course. It was a glib remark, but it hid his true nature.

'How have you been sleeping, Chris?' I had once asked him after he crashed heavily during the 1997 Tour, damaging muscles in his back. 'Oh, mostly at night,' he shot back, with a sly grin on his face.

Even so, Boardman is a likeable and approachable athlete. He's self-deprecating and a little shy, but he's fought hard to overcome that, forcing himself into the deep end of the European scene at a time when most British hopefuls still witter on about missing home cooking and learning the language.

Deep down, he also harbours a bright flame of patriotic pride. During his first Tour, following that prologue success in Lille, he got a little carried away when the race arrived in Britain. Three days after his victory in Lille, the Tour staged a finish in Brighton. Boardman, hyped by the excited response of the huge British crowds, needlessly broke away from the field on the hilly finishing circuit in fruitless pursuit of Spain's Francisco Cabello. In the press room, heads shook in disapproval. What on earth was GAN's team leader doing, wasting all this energy on such a pointless attack? In hard-nosed professional terms, it was a good question. This wasn't the kind of energy-wasting move that the canny and experienced Miguel Indurain would make. Back then, though, Boardman's competitive fire ensured that he didn't care about little things like that.

Boardman didn't catch Cabello before the seafront finish, but his efforts enabled him to hold off the chasing bunch by a few seconds, as the sprinters wound up speed in their dash for the line. He crossed the line as if he was World Champion, dementedly celebrating his Pyrrhic victory, grinning like a Cheshire cat, punching the air for joy. The French press sat watching on TV, utterly bemused by the whole crowd-pleasing display. The rest of us knew that he was a Brit newcomer, overcome by excitement; a Planet Tour virgin, pumped up with Yellow Fever.

Meanwhile, back in 1998, Dublin seemed to have belatedly woken up to the Tour's arrival as the Irish papers put out their weekend previews. French national champion and world number one Laurent Jalabert wasn't convinced though.

'We arrived in Dublin on Thursday, but I haven't yet noticed much of a festival atmosphere,' said the Frenchman. 'To be honest, I prefer it when the Tour starts in France and I think most French people would agree with me.'

But by Friday evening, there was at last a keen sense of anticipation, as restaurants wheeled out Tour de France menus and shops dressed their windows with bicycles and pictures of Kelly and the ubiquitous Roche taken at the height of their powers. Even so, there were as many column inches devoted to – you guessed it – traffic congestion and parking restrictions caused by the Tour as there were guides to the riders and the route. Even Cork Airport was unhappy. The Tour convoy uses so many radio frequencies that flights into the south of the country would have been unsafe if they had continued, so for much of Sunday and Monday the airport was expected to be closed. The Dublin Chamber of Commerce got in on the act too, protesting that the weekend road closures were bound to affect Saturday trading. And this was the city of good times, the home of the *craic*? Weren't they supposed to be welcoming us with open arms? The *Irish Times* wrote a leader on the subject.

'Dublin Chamber of Commerce and Cork Airport should have the vision to see that their interests will be very considerably advanced in the long term,' it said. 'The logistics of staging such an important event will cause inconvenience for some, but the balance of advantage is to give a rousing welcome to the Tour de France.'

But then maybe the Chamber of Commerce knew something we didn't. As the *salle de presse* cleared that evening and the race drew ever nearer, Festina team manager Bruno Roussel was busy stonewalling the French press.

'I know nothing about this,' insisted Roussel, when quizzed about the seizure of the Festina car. 'We have all our personnel here,' he said, dismissing suggestions that Willy Voet's EPO-laden Fiat was on its way to Dublin. 'We're not missing a car or a *soigneur*. Everybody's asking me about this story, but all I know is what I've learned from you. There are too many rumours and not enough facts. I'm dumbfounded – to me, all this sounds like a bad joke.'

Day 3   Prologue

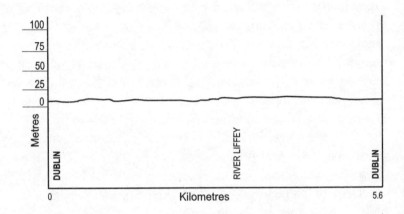

Finally, the 1998 Tour de France was about to begin, but D-Day dawned grey, with more than a hint of rain in the air. Clouds were gathering over the Tour in more ways than one. But at least by mid-Saturday morning, Dublin had finally given itself up to the Tour de France. The city centre had been closed and the finish and warm-up areas, centred on O'Connell Street and O'Connell Bridge, were awash with Tour vehicles and Tour personnel. Down at Trinity College the start village had taken over the university's graceful quadrangles, as the top half of the College's old bell tower fought for survival among the Tour village's cluster of garish tents in Library Square. The curious crowds were gathering, keen to see what all the fuss was about, even though the first rider wasn't rolling down the start ramp until shortly before half-past three.

With a few hours to spare, I turned back up Dame Street

towards the Castle and the *salle de presse*. I grabbed a coffee and picked up the papers, all of which were now giving major coverage to the Tour; although much of it yet again centred on the inconvenience the race would cause. But as the rumblings of scandal focusing on the Festina team rolled on, there was a surprising new story. Overnight, further cracks had begun to show in the uneasy Irish alliance between the nation's past cycling heroes. At Friday night's team presentation, a showy TV festival that officially opens each year's Tour, the unthinkable happened. Stephen Roche and Sean Kelly, Irish cycling's dream team, fell out – in public.

Both men had worked hard to ensure that the Irish bid to host the Tour was a success, helping to plan and front proposals put to the *Société du Tour*, as well as allowing their reputations to be used as the peg for the whole idea. But Roche was bitter about his treatment by l'Evenement, the Anglo-Irish promotional company behind the plan to lure the Tour to Ireland. The last time I'd spoken to him on the phone, about a month before the Tour began, Roche had launched into a tirade against l'Evenement, furious at his exclusion from the financial benefits that he felt his support deserved. But then Roche's life seemed full of conflict. When he was a professional there had been arguments with team managers, rival riders and even, famously, bitter spats with riders on his own team. Back then, his talent had seen him through those battles, but now he was a retired rider with a holiday company to promote and a string of bikes to sell.

So in an uneasy truce with the promoters, Roche ended up as an unlikely co-presenter of the Eurovision-RTE coverage of Friday night's team presentation. The Dubliner, fully aware that the Tour wasn't likely to come back to Ireland in his lifetime, wasn't about to pass up the opportunity. So little by little, the 1998 Tour's team presentation turned into something of a Roche-fest. We had regular mentions of Roche's holidays in Majorca, of his range of top-level bikes and of his glittering career. There wasn't much said about Kelly or Earley and even less of Kimmage, the black sheep of the family. But it was an interview with Roche, apparently filmed some weeks earlier by Eurovision rather than RTE, in which the Dubliner spoke of his disillusionment with Ireland and his intention to move back to France, that proved too much for Kelly to stomach.

'When you see so many kids on street corners, so many delinquents and especially the drink, it does frighten me,' said Roche. That was it for Kelly: he stood up and, with the unfussy decisiveness associated with his professional career, walked out.

By lunch-time on Saturday, he was mingling with the press, happy to explain exactly why he'd made such a public protest.

'I was disappointed by what they showed as representative of Ireland last night,' said Kelly, suited and looking cool, with his russet hair slicked back. 'It looked back rather than forward. It wasn't the right time or the right place. It gave a bad image of Ireland at a time when we should all be ambassadors. Personally I was disappointed because I didn't get the recognition I feel I deserved, and neither did other Irish riders like Martin Earley, Paul Kimmage and Laurence Roche.'

In the build-up to the Tour start, he had remained in the background as Roche's battles with the promoters made the headlines; but now Kelly, once renowned as a man of few words, was only too happy to talk.

'I had no problem with the way things were going until last night,' said Kelly. 'I've now spoken to Jean-Marie Leblanc and told him what I thought. Even he said he was surprised that all the other Irish riders weren't included, that he'd always wanted to see them paid tribute to. But I'm not doing any more work with RTE and I'm going to talk to Stephen and tell him what I think. I just feel that if I'd been so heavily involved in such a presentation, I'd have included him and all the others in it too.'

Meanwhile, the sports pages wheeled out their cycling specialists and gave them more column inches to fill than most of them had been offered in a lifetime. They were almost unanimously agreed on the six Tour favourites. Top of the list was the champion, Jan Ullrich, still only twenty-four; the rider who'd come in from the commercial cold of the former Eastern Bloc to lead the German-sponsored Deutsche Telekom team. Ullrich had an enviable Tour record; he'd been placed second to his mentor Bjarne Riis in 1996, in a year when many experts felt he could have won, and had triumphed over a brutal course in 1997. The podginess of the spring now gone, his recent form in both the Tour of Switzerland and the French race, the Route du Sud, had been enough to convince most pundits that he would successfully defend his title – even if there were questions over his long-term stamina.

If Ullrich faltered, then his team captain, mentor and supposed friend, Bjarne Riis, was the man Telekom expected to take over the reins. The thirty-four-year-old Dane knew the Tour so well, finishing fifth and then third before notching up his memorable victory in 1996. Tactically astute and psychologically cunning, the aloof Riis was able to relax in the knowledge that this time the pressure was on his young and immature team-mate.

French popular hero Richard Virenque, second to Ullrich in 1997 and four times the Tour's 'King of the Mountains' was touted by his national media as the people's choice of champion-in-waiting, and, backed by the strong Festina team, looked Ullrich's most likely challenger. An emotive showman, Virenque's habit was to under-perform for much of the year, then come alive in the mountain stages of the Tour. His willingness to sacrifice the rest of the season for success in the Tour had always endeared him to the French, who viewed him as a rider of the old school. Yet others, including some of his peers, have accused him of calculated histrionics, of playing to the gallery.

'He's the archetype of the attacking rider,' said Manolo Saiz, manager of the rival Spanish team ONCE. 'But he'd be better off concentrating on his results and spending less time talking to journalists.'

Spain's Abraham Olano, fourth in the 1997 Tour and the inheritor of the Miguel Indurain mantle, was the fourth of the Tour's Big Six, although his shortcomings in the mountains made final victory unlikely. But Olano's time-trialling was his forte and on a Tour route criticised by both Virenque and Italian climber Marco Pantani for lacking tough mountain stages, the 110 kilometres of racing against the clock were expected to suit his strengths. Perhaps the Basque rider's greatest worry was the burden of Spanish expectation.

'To Spaniards, I've been a substitute for Indurain,' he admitted. 'But there's no way for me to get the same results as him.'

Alongside the ebullient Virenque the Festina team also included Switzerland's quiet and bespectacled Alex Zulle, who was also eyeing one of the top three placings on the Paris podium. But Zulle was on the rebound, fighting to repair his shattered morale after a harrowing final week of the Tour of Italy – the Giro d'Italia – in June. After dominating the race – and Italian star Marco Pantani – in the first two weeks of the

Giro, Zulle collapsed in the mountain passes of the Dolomites and floundered helplessly as his overall advantage was overturned by the irrepressible Pantani. The Swiss had humiliated Pantani in the first Giro time trial in Trieste, catching and then dropping the little climber, who had started three minutes earlier, far behind. But he made a dangerous enemy in the process.

'Zulle didn't have to humiliate me like that,' said 'Pantanino' after the Giro ended in Milan. 'It made me angry – I'm happy I made him pay for it in the mountains.'

Pantani, an Italian icon since his luminescent Giro win, had done little real preparation for the Tour and arrived in Dublin with few expectations of victory.

'I'm hoping to win the odd stage or two,' he said modestly, a few days prior to arriving in Dublin, before asserting that 'it will be impossible to win both the Giro and the Tour this year. The course isn't really suited to me and I'm still overwhelmed by the reaction of Italian fans to my victory in the Giro,' explained 'Pantarosa'. 'It's been one long session of partying with the fans.'

On Saturday afternoon, at 15.25 Irish time – 16.25 French time – as a light drizzle fell on the city, Denis Leproux of the BigMat Auber team rolled down the prologue start ramp in front of Trinity College to begin the eighty-fifth Tour de France. Riders set off on the 5.6 kilometre course at one minute intervals, with the lesser lights leading the way. Ullrich, as defending champion, would ride in his yellow jersey of 1997 and, as is now traditional, would be last man off.

But there was only really one favourite among the 189 riders and Chris Boardman knew it. As the rain eased off, he warmed up on a set of rollers alongside the GAN team's mobile home, anxiously awaiting his 18.30 start time. There were other riders – Festina's Christophe Moreau and, as expected, Banesto's Abraham Olano – who set impressive times, but everybody knew that the Merseysider's ride would set the time to beat.

Out on the course, Miguel Indurain sat in a Vitalicio Seguros team car following his brother Prudencio as he raced through the wet streets. Later, the burly Eddy Merckx, another five-time Tour champion, watched his son Axel, now co-leader with Frenchman Luc Leblanc of the Italian Polti team, from the passenger seat of the *directeur sportif's* car. It made good TV, but neither Axel nor Prudencio had a hope of winning. In fact, there was only one man likely to take the first yellow jersey of the 1998 Tour – and by now, minutes before his moment of truth, Chris Boardman was wound as tight as a violin string.

It was all the hanging round, the press calls, searching for the right soundbite, waiting for the race to begin that often seemed too much for Boardman; when he finally sped determinedly away from the start, crouched low over the bike, legs pumping with a graceful and potent rhythm, his relief was almost palpable. As the roads dried out and his touch and confidence on the series of right-hand bends increased, Boardman picked up speed. He swung right, barely breaking his stride, at the end of Nassau Street as his nerves evaporated and the crowd cheered him on. Then it was right again, past St Stephen's Green and up the slight rise leading to Patrick Street. At the 3.6 kilometre check point, his was the fastest time and, as he dropped back down towards the Liffey and the last kilometre along Ormond Quay, he looked unbeatable.

In that final kilometre, as he pushed hard for the line, the crowd roared him on. For a moment the noise seemed to overwhelm him, but on the last bend, the left-hander into O'Connell Street, he went again, fighting to strengthen his advantage in the final 400 metres. There was a roar of triumph as he crossed the line, even though Pantani, Virenque and Ullrich were still out on the course. But looking at Boardman's time – six minutes and twelve seconds – and his average speed of 54.19 kilometres per hour, we all knew he'd won.

A distinctly disinterested-looking Pantani was next across the line, finishing forty-eight seconds behind Boardman in 181st place. Even for a rider whose past time-trialling performance had been weak, it was a crushingly poor result and left him with a lot of ground to make up. Next came Virenque, giving it his all as he entered the final kilometre. Shoulders bobbing, head nodding, mouth agape in have-a-go-hero agony, he was as far away from Boardman's pure and metronomic style as it was possible to be. Even so, his twelve second deficit to Boardman was a surprisingly strong ride for Virenque. Maybe this was to be his year after all.

Then, last of the 181 riders came Jan Ullrich, the champion, wearing the yellow jersey, the *maillot jaune* of Tour de France leadership. Ullrich had finished second to Boardman in the 1997 Rouen prologue in warm, dry weather. This time however, on the greasy city centre roads, he wasn't taking any chances on the bends, preferring to freewheel gently through them rather than take the risks that Boardman had diced with. Sixth place for the champion, five seconds down on the Englishman but just a second behind the more dangerous Olano, meant that Ullrich could be happy with his performance.

'It's not a disappointment,' he said coolly afterwards. 'It wasn't worth taking any risks on the corners because the Tour will be decided later.'

Even as he spoke, Boardman was exploding with joy on the presentation podium in O'Connell Street as a huge Dublin roar greeted his appearance on the winner's rostrum. He pulled the yellow jersey over his head, kissed the podium girls and grinned his broad exuberant grin, at the same time milking the applause and playfully egging the crowd on. It had been a tough twelve months, personally and professionally, since that last prologue success in Rouen and Boardman was loving every minute of it.

He was soon back at the Castle, chatting to the press, after notching the second-fastest prologue in Tour history, behind his own win at record speed in 1994.

'After all the problems I've had over the past few months and the pressure that I've been under, this is the best prologue win of my career,' Boardman said of his third success in the Tour's opening time trial. 'I don't normally dedicate my wins to anybody, but for personal reasons, this one is for my wife Sally. She puts up with my being away and often has to look after four kids on her own. So I want to say thank you to her.

'I persuaded myself before the start that all the bends were dry,' he continued. 'I'm surprised, because I really didn't expect to win. I had good form in the beginning of June, but I lost most of that a couple of weeks ago. But I was very focused today; my mental training served me well. I can remember the details of every prologue course I've ever ridden, yet I can't remember my children's birthdays without great effort,' he smiled sheepishly. 'That's pretty sad really. The atmosphere was fantastic, especially in the last hundred and fifty metres – but I wouldn't have expected anything less in Ireland. People here aren't afraid to show emotion and they really get into it.'

With the prologue over and the Tour readying itself for the first road stage, the Festina scandal again reared its ugly head. Festina's team boss Bruno Roussel had appeared live on French TV alongside Jean-Marie Leblanc during the prologue coverage, denying all knowledge of the affair. Both he and French presenter Gérard Holtz were all reassuring smiles and, with the race underway, the affair was temporarily glossed over. But Roussel was looking increasingly desperate as he made subtle changes to his story.

'I was surprised that Voet was not here by Friday after-noon,' he let slip to one journalist on Saturday evening. *Ah, but Bruno, didn't you say that you weren't missing any person-nel?* And Willy Voet, who'd been rubbing legs and looking after top professionals for more than a decade, was just the sort of experienced salt-of-the-earth *soigneur* you would miss. After all, Voet had been Virenque's personal *soigneur* for several seasons – was Roussel seriously saying that he hadn't noticed the absence of his team leader's masseur until a few hours before the Tour began?

'It has been a difficult time for the team,' said Roussel, 'but I know they have nothing to feel guilty about.'

And the Tour organisation? 'Let's calm down,' said Jean-Marie Leblanc. 'This man may have been acting on his own, without the knowledge of the team, so there is no question of penalising them. It's a doping case, but it doesn't involve a rider, it's not connected with this race – it's hundreds of kilometres from here. We'll reserve judgement until the enquiry is com-plete – we want justice, not to react inappropriately.'

It was Saturday night, the eve of the World Cup final in Paris, the eve of the first road stage of the Tour de France. French, Irish, Italian, English, Spanish and Belgian fans mingled bois-terously in the pubs and restaurants around Temple Bar. Dublin's boast of the *craic* and of its 600 pubs ensured another late night's hard drinking. But by midnight, the bon-homie had turned into another whirlwind of raucous street life. Up in my room, I listened to the din floating up from the street as the city settled into its regular Saturday night pattern. But there was much more to Dublin than just pubs and drinking, I told myself. I thought about the music and the literature; about the lyrical gilded words, tumbling down the years. I thought about Brendan Behan, Dermot O'Brien, Sean O'Casey, James Joyce, George Bernard Shaw – they're the ones who illuminated Dublin's sombre Georgian streets. But by 1.30, with the yelling and the tinkling of broken glass getting worse, I'd given up on sleep. I got dressed and went down to the street to get a closer look at the wild Dublin night. Was this the mythical and supposedly good-natured *craic*? The slurred shouts and screams of drunken teenagers filled Temple Bar, their faces flushed with the combined effects of booze and sexual excitement.

I walked up to Dame Street to buy the first of the Sunday papers, but as I turned the corner, a snarling, shaven-headed boy had pushed a girl up against a doorway and was thudding his fist into the shuttered doorway immediately behind her head, spitting and screaming obscenities into her face. Despite his terrifying rage, she had a bored and weary look on her face. She looked away disinterestedly while nearby her friends stood chatting and eating chips.

Further along, on another corner, there was a carpet of broken glass mixed with steaming urine. By a nearby bank, a boy was leaning against the service till for support as he vomited unrelentingly on to the pavement.

I was beginning to see Stephen Roche's point of view.

Stage winner: Chris Boardman, Britain (GAN)
Overall race leader: Chris Boardman
Points classification leader: Chris Boardman
Team classification leader: Festina

Day 4   Stage 1

Sunday 12 July
Dublin–Dublin, 180.5 km

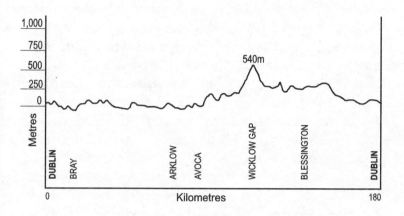

Another fresh but grey dawn on O'Connell Street with the Tour about to get on its way, but once again the Irish press had mixed feelings about the French fête that had been thrust upon the city.

'The French appear to be ignoring the Tour this weekend,' moaned the *Sunday Independent* on the morning of the France–Brazil World Cup final. 'They have bigger fish to fry. It's like we're minding their damn race for them while they've got better things to do.'

In the *Sunday Tribune*, Paul Howard continued his running battle with the Tour and professional cycling, attacking the shroud of statistics quoted by those defending the sport against accusations of widespread doping.

'In a world where the science of the cheats is ten years ahead of the science of the testers, only the careless get caught. Even when they do, they're not always punished. But

49

the sponsors have to be protected,' continued Howard sardonically. 'Sporting authorities try to defend the efficacy of dope controls which don't work and which can't really be allowed to work either. This weekend, tens of thousands of children will line the route of the Tour and will dream of doing things that aren't possible without using dangerous drugs.'

It was hard-hitting stuff, but then it was matched by the reactions of the French press to the Festina affair. 'Sports Minister Marie-Georges Buffet warned that the consequences of this affair for the 1998 Tour could be disastrous if the enquiry establishes a link between these products, their destination and a French team,' said *Le Journal du Dimanche*.

In *L'Equipe*, the controversy was considered to have left the Tour in a 'state of shock' and the paper asked for the inquiry to act quickly to lift the 'atmosphere of dread weighing down the race'. They quoted Jean-Marie Leblanc's comments of the previous day: 'This affair doesn't relate to a rider on the Tour, and it didn't take place on the Tour. In fact, it happened hundreds of kilometres from here.'

Down at the chilly *village départ*, dance music reverberated around O'Connell Street as the riders arrived for the stage start. Team cars and buses crowded into the start area as the 1998 Tour prepared for its first day on the open road. In front of the Telekom team bus, autograph hunters waited for Riis and Ullrich to appear, as riders climbed from their team cars and headed down to the presentation podium to sign the daily start sheet.

Mario Cipollini, the self-styled 'Lion King', the inimitable Italian sprinter who'd surprised everybody with eighteenth place in the prologue, was already looking forward to the finishing straight in Phoenix Park. With only a thirteen-second deficit on Boardman and time bonuses on offer over the next week of flat stages, the Italian was hopeful of picking up the yellow jersey, perhaps even before the race arrived in France. Daniel Mangeas, the Tour's official speaker, gave Cipo a big build-up as he stepped on to the signing-on podium. The coiffured Italian signed his name, scratched his stubbled chin and then turned to grin broadly at the cheering crowd. The lanky Italian and his team, who missed few opportunities for extra publicity, had hoped to pull on green racing jerseys sporting the dove of peace, after his sponsor Saeco announced its own 'peace initiative'. Not for the first time in his career, the Italian was told in no uncertain terms that any sudden change of kit was unacceptable, so he and his team-mates turned up at the start in their usual red and white.

Other riders came and went, some recognised by the crowd and cheered; while others, more often than not the more obscure Spanish riders, signed on quietly, greeted only by muted applause. Riis finally emerged from the Telekom bus and sat on the bonnet of a team car, aloofly signing autographs. I had time to say hello briefly to GAN's Magnus Backstedt, riding his first Tour and US Postal's experienced team rider Marty Jemison, before Ullrich suddenly emerged into the mêlée. As he did so, Pantani pedalled past, leaving the autograph hunters with a difficult decision. Some sprinted after the Italian, while others pushed even harder into the crush of people surrounding the startled Ullrich.

Pantani, Virenque, Olano, Zulle, Jalabert, Boardman and eventually the young German were met with thunderous roars of approval as they joined the pack of riders threading their way through the crowds and the cars to the start line, waiting for the flag to drop. Just after 11.15, the flotilla of police and TV motorbikes, guest cars and commissaires' cars rolled over O'Connell Bridge ahead of the field and *Le Tour* headed off towards the Irish countryside.

I stood among the cars behind the line, studying the maze

of graceful brown legs as the riders rolled away from me and then stepped hurriedly aside as the team cars roared into life and set off in pursuit. And that was it. They were gone and, for a moment, I felt that same fleeting sadness that I'd once felt as a roadside spectator, that same sense of having been left behind by this strange foreign whirlwind. The crowd lingered a little longer, leaning over the barriers, craning to see the last of the following team cars disappear from sight. Then quietly, they turned and strolled back down O'Connell Street towards the Liffey, as the Tour's construction crews moved in to dismantle the scene.

On the walk back up to the Castle's press room, I fell in step with a veteran Belgian journalist, setting off on his umpteenth Tour. He wasn't interested in talking about the race or about the Dublin start; instead he and his newspaper offices back in Brussels had been researching the circumstances surrounding the Willy Voet incident and the unexpected detention of the Belgian *soigneur*.

As we walked down Dame Street, he related what he had so far unearthed: that, after picking up the team car from the Tour organisation's garages in Paris, Voet had apparently headed east towards the Swiss border, even as the rest of the Tour convoy drove north towards the Channel ports. Voet crossed into Switzerland and then made a collection. After that shady rendezvous, he drove north on the *autoroutes* through Germany and Belgium, towards the ferry port at Calais.

What the *soigneur* didn't know, explained my Belgian colleague, was that, according to his sources, the French police were trailing him, waiting to pounce when he crossed the French border. They were sure, he insisted, that of course Voet had been heading for Dublin and suggested that the batches of EPO found in the car were also for riders on other teams – that it was impossible for such a large amount of

EPO to be used by just one nine-man team during the Tour. Even before Voet had been stopped by customs, he said, the French police had searched the Festina team's headquarters and offices in the suburbs of Lyon. Effectively, he was telling me that he and his paper believed that Willy Voet, the most experienced masseur behind the world's top team, could have been acting as the drugs 'mule' for the leading teams in the Tour de France.

Meanwhile, the race was rolling through the south Dublin suburb of Dundrum, heading out to Wicklow and past a monument commemorating local boy Roche's golden 1987 season. At the first sprint, on the seafront at Bray, GAN's Frédéric Moncassin did his best to look after Chris Boardman's interests, but failed to hold off Czech sprinter Jan Svorada and Telekom's moody fast man, Erik Zabel. Already Boardman's few seconds of advantage were being eaten away, but at least it wasn't Cipollini, the man most likely to snatch the leader's jersey, who'd picked up time.

The field settled down as it rolled along the main coast road towards Wicklow and it wasn't until the fifty-sixth kilometre that an attack moved clear of the field. It was led by Jacky Durand of the Casino team, formerly French national champion and a specialist in long-distance, head-down breakaways. 'Dudu', as the French call him, was joined by six other riders including GAN's young German rider Jens Voigt and burly Italian Stefano Zanini of the powerful Mapei team. Predictably enough, with so many days of racing to come, the main bunch weren't interested in the slightest, letting the group have their head until they'd built a four minute lead as they rode into the designated 'feed zone' in the vale of Avoca after 82.5 kilometres.

The riders don't stop in the feed zones; instead, they eat

on the hoof, pedalling through a crowd of anxious *soigneurs* who hold out lightweight shoulder bags – *musettes* – containing everything from bananas and dried fruit to energy bars, sandwiches and glucose drinks. As they ride down the line of *soigneurs*, they pick out their sponsor's logo, snatch the bag by the strap and wind it around their neck, whether pedalling downhill, uphill, or even chasing hard behind a breakaway. Remarkably, spillages are rare.

The break made its way to the foot of the day's major challenge, the six kilometre climb of Wicklow Gap. Up at the summit the weather had done its worst, with squalls of wind and rain sweeping over the ridge. Even so, spectators were out in huge numbers lining the roadside, although the day hadn't quite turned into the barbecue and baguette festival that the organisers had hoped for.

Behind the leading seven riders, Cipollini's Saeco team began to move up to the front of the main field and lift the pace. On the drop from the Wicklow hills, the breakaway's advantage dwindled until after 160 kilometres, with the Tour field flying back towards Dublin's Phoenix Park, they were swept up by the pursuing bunch. With the field all together and in sight of the finish, the sprinters' teams fought for control of the front of the race, battling to find the best position for their top finishers.

The Tour's opening stages, with their hectic finishes and nervy stressed riders chasing precious time bonuses, are always among the most dangerous days in the race. The sprinters, riders such as Cipollini, Zabel, Moncassin and Svorada, will risk everything to win a Tour de France stage, while the overall race favourites slip towards the back of the field, anxious to stay clear of the jostling for position, the high-speed pushing and shoving as the bunch hurtles into the final kilometre. In 1994, on the Tour's opening road stage, there was a horrendous crash – a 'stack-up' – just yards from the finish line in the narrow streets of Armentières in northern France. That afternoon, Laurent Jalabert was among the worst injured after bearing the full brunt of the impact with an inexperienced local policeman who had stepped out from the barriers – to take a photograph. At well over forty miles per hour, Jalabert, the *gendarme* and several other sprinters had been tossed high into the air by the collision before crashing to the road; in Jalabert's case, face first.

Cipollini, the undisputed sprint king, the rider with as many nicknames as stage victories, may have been absent from the fray that day four years earlier, but he was back in contention as the '98 Tour sped into Phoenix Park. At least he *was*, until a sudden touch of wheels between two of his well-drilled team-mates sent 'Il Magnifico' flying to the tarmac, just seven kilometres from the line. Cipo explained later that Massimiliano Mori had fallen in front of him after touching Mario Scirea's wheel. He was so close that there was no time to react and Cipollini went straight over the top of Mori's bike. It took more than two minutes for the dazed and bruised Lion King to get back on to his feet and in that time his hopes of wearing the race leader's *maillot jaune* vanished down Chesterfield Avenue.

'I gave everything in the prologue because I wanted to take the yellow jersey today,' he said disconsolately afterwards. 'Now that dream has gone.'

Up at the front of the race, the Telekom team, working for Zabel, were scrapping hard with the Italian Mapei team who were looking after the interests of Belgian national champion, Tom Steels. Zabel, winner of the Tour's points competition in 1996 and 1997 had won a brace of stages in each of the previous three Tours, but had suffered a little in the Tour build-up as the Telekom team sought to protect their precious leader, Ullrich.

The affable Steels, meanwhile, winner of stages in the tours of Spain and Switzerland as well as in a string of other races, had suffered the ignominy of being thrown off the 1997 Tour, his first, after a run-in with French favourite Moncassin.

Now, speeding towards the straight and slightly uphill final kilometre in Phoenix Park, Steels, Moncassin and Zabel were about to cross swords once more.

With Zabel tucked neatly into his slipstream, it was Bjarne Riis, Telekom's team captain, who led the school of riders into the final 500 metres as the figures behind him darted in and out of the leading positions. His job done, Riis pulled to one side and Zabel, wearing the white jersey of German national champion, hit the front, standing on the pedals and raising the pace even higher. But it was too much, too soon. As he sprinted into the head wind his strength faded and Steels, having judged his effort to perfection, lunged past the dark-haired German to notch a first Tour stage success.

The Belgian was euphoric, hugging his team-mates and his team manager as he celebrated his sponsor's first Tour stage success in four years of competition.

'The Tour is always the most dangerous for the sprinters,' he mused as he chatted to the press afterwards, switching easily from Flemish to French and English. 'The trouble is that there are riders who you never see contesting the sprints during the rest of the year suddenly fighting for sprints in the Tour. They're the ones who stir up trouble and force us to take risks, because the regular sprinters understand each other.'

Meanwhile, a surprised Chris Boardman, who'd successfully avoided trouble throughout the stage, was stepping up on to the podium to collect his second yellow jersey.

'I had a lot of luck today,' he smiled later. 'The breakaway helped me and so did the crash in the finale. I'm sorry for Cipollini and I hope he's OK, but it all worked in my favour.'

We were all hunched over our laptops in the frenetic press room when Sophie del Rizzo of the Tour's *service presse* walked in and announced that Bruno Roussel, *directeur* of the Festina team, was about to give a press conference in the Castle. The *salle de presse* cleared in seconds as the world's media snatched their notebooks and their cameras, stampeded back across the Castle gardens, up the Castle's grand staircase and into the press conference. We filed breathlessly into the room and waited, expectantly. Then, after a pause, Roussel appeared, unaccompanied, and sat down before us, the Tour's circular Euro-logo hovering above his head on the wall behind.

The questions started. Bizarrely, almost immediately, Roussel began admitting the truth behind some of those scurrilous media 'rumours'. Yes, the Festina HQ had been raided, he said. He'd been warned of the police presence in Lyon on Wednesday. But, Roussel insisted, he hadn't lied when saying that stories of Voet's detention were a 'bad joke'.

'That was simply because I thought they were talking about Michel Gros, our other *directeur*,' he said hesitantly, 'and he was here with us, in Ireland.'

But the more Roussel talked, the more contradictory and confused his arguments became. Under the lights and in the battery of flash bulbs, he looked grey and strained as he squinted into the glare.

'Today we are missing one of our party,' he finally acknowledged, going back on his earlier denial that any of his staff were missing from Festina's Tour contingent, 'but I'd prefer not to reveal his identity.'

Then came awkward questions over Voet's unexplained Swiss detour. 'I don't know anything about his route between the Tour garage in Evry on Tuesday morning and his arrest on Wednesday morning,' said Roussel. 'I'm looking forward to getting back to France because then I'll get more details about what happened. Right now, I don't want to put forward any theories about where these products were going, because all the information I've got to date has come from the press. We mustn't throw suspicion on riders who have always behaved properly, thinking that all their results are due to doping,' he argued defensively. 'That's pure madness.'

But would he pull the team out of the Tour if things got any worse?

'I've never imagined that we'd be excluded from the race or that we'd pull the team out,' he insisted. 'We have our place here. We're victims of injustice, because it's the name of Festina that's being dragged through the mire and that's what makes me really sad.'

The dazed looking *directeur* stood up to leave, but Roussel's uncertain performance only served to confirm the media's worst fears. By now, we all suspected that Festina would be famous for a lot more than sports watches by the time the Tour arrived back in France.

Ah, but it was still World Cup final night. I finished work and headed off to meet friends in Temple Bar's subterranean Sports Café. The streets had emptied and the match was just kicking off as I fought my way through the ruck of screaming French youngsters packing the Sports Café's interior. Somewhere, in a dark corner, my group of friends – outsiders, ordinary regular folk, not of Planet Tour's Euro-roving tribe – were sitting at a reserved table. Finally, as I fell over yet another French fan, I found them. I tumbled headlong into a seat, yelled hello and ordered a beer above the din.

The match was fascinating but one-sided. After only a few minutes it was apparent that Brazil were, as they say, all over the place. In Dublin's Sports Café, far from Paris and the Stade de France, we all watched with bated breath as the French set about the destruction of the world champions. Zinedine Zidane and Emmanuel Petit harried the Brazilian midfield and defence, while Youri Djorkaeff and yes, even Stéphane Guivarc'h, looked likely to open the scoring.

I was on to my second beer when the first goal came, and I almost lost it, as the Sports Café erupted and tables and chairs went flying. In a second, Dublin's Temple Bar became a far-flung outpost of St Denis. It was only as the euphoric crowd settled down again that I noticed the dapper, lean Italian gentleman, sitting in a sober suit a couple of tables away. Italian legend Felice Gimondi, the last rider from his nation to win the Tour de France, sat unnoticed, quietly supping Guinness and nervously eyeing his wobbling table as excited French fans thronged around him. The next goal nearly did for him, too. Zidane scored again and the chairs in front of Gimondi's table went flying across the floor as more French teenagers leapt to their feet. Indignantly, Gimondi stood up and glared, as only a true *campionissimo italiano* can, at the hysterical kids around him.

I didn't hang around for the third French goal, but I remember only too well that Temple Bar celebrated long into Monday morning. Aptly enough for the last night of *Le Tour en Irlande*, I finally fell asleep to drunken renderings of the

'Marseillaise', but whether they were French or Irish accents, I really couldn't say.

Stage winner: Tom Steels, Belgium (Mapei–Bricobi)
Overall race leader: Chris Boardman, Britain (GAN)
Points classification leader: Tom Steels
Team classification leader: Festina
Mountains classification leader: Stefano Zanini, Italy
    (Mapei–Bricobi)

Day 5   Stage 2

Monday 13 July
Enniscorthy–Cork, 205.5 km

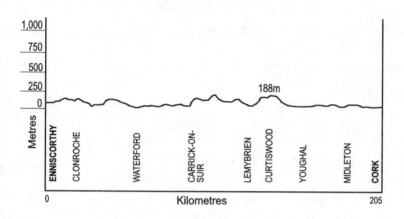

At 6.30 the next morning, in bright sunshine, I swung the Audi
out of Temple Bar on to O'Connell Bridge. After picking up
Andy, a hungover American friend hitching a ride down to
Brittany, we hit the main M7 down to Cork and the south coast.

Andy, a journalist, ski-guide and mountain biker from
Colorado, was on his third Tour of duty. When I originally
met him midway through his first Tour, he was driving a
Peugeot 406 crammed with sleeping bags, duvets and camping equipment, following the Tour around France with a
fellow American hack. That year, Andy's summer holidaying
Peugeot was the unlikeliest-looking press car on the race.
Parked alongside the shining saloons from *L'Equipe*, *Marca* and
La Gazetta, the cramped and battered 406 had a distinctly
down-home feel to it. The pair of them were on such a tight
budget that on warm nights they'd pitch camp at the roadside,
stopping half-way up a mountain pass, and stretch out under

61

the summer stars. In contrast, I inhabited a world of polo shirts and trouser presses, cable TV and buffet breakfasts.

Andy had one great story that never failed to crack me up. One night after a late finish in the press room during that first Tour, they drove off into the countryside, somewhere in the Massif Central, following the route of the next day's stage. After an hour or two, they pulled up at the side of the road, wearily rolled out their sleeping bags and settled down for the night. Andy woke first, late the next morning. The pair of them had overslept and were woken by advance vehicles in the Tour's publicity caravan. Sitting around them on plastic picnic chairs, with Tupperware and wine glasses laid out on a blanket, was a large French family, presided over by a grizzled old man, eagerly awaiting the arrival of the race. They glared disdainfully at Andy and stunned, unwashed and unshaven, Andy peered back. '*Sales journalistes,*' tutted the old man as Andy and his colleague hurriedly pulled on their shoes and climbed back into the Peugeot.

Le Tour en Irlande suffered its first casualty even before the start of Stage Two, in the shadow of Enniscorthy's Duffry Gate. Ludovic Auger of the lowly BigMat team had fractured his left forearm in the Cipollini stack-up the previous afternoon and had his arm in plaster. After just 186 kilometres and even before the race reached his native France, the twenty-seven-year-old's Tour – the second of his professional career – was over. But despite his hard luck, Auger was a happy man this Monday morning, the morning after France had won the World Cup. Even Laurent Jalabert was smiling, telling reporters how he'd enjoyed watching the game.

'I was in massage in my hotel during the first half, so I kept having to turn my head so I could see the telly. But the restaurant had a giant screen, so we went down there to watch the second half with the guys from the Casino, FDJ and Saeco teams. There was a good atmosphere – it was a great night,' he enthused wistfully. 'It was like we weren't on the Tour any more . . .'

With our ferry to Brittany leaving Cork harbour at 6.30 that evening and the stage scheduled to finish at a quarter past three, we'd opted to skip the long detour to Enniscorthy. Instead, as the stage was expected to finish late because of strong head winds, we headed straight for the finish, arriving at the press room just before lunch-time, as the citizens of Cork prepared to greet the Tour juggernaut. By then, the stage was well on its way, passing through Sean Kelly Square in the Irishman's home town of Carrick-on-Suir as the field wended its way south.

In strong cross winds and on narrow undulating roads, there were almost inevitably plenty of crashes. The anxiety among the sprinters to make the most of the bonuses on hand was one contributory factor to the chaos; but here and there the large crowds, seemingly unaware of the proximity of the riders, flirted with catastrophe as they leaned out into the road, straining for a better view. The bunch ebbed and flowed, split up here and there as the violent cross winds fractured the long line of riders on each short rise. Even though the Irish media had repeated warnings from the Tour organisation on the dangers of stepping into the road, in the heat of the moment too many fans, unaccustomed to the speed of the passing *peloton*, ignored the advice.

Then the catastrophe happened. An eleven-year-old Irish girl stepped out too far from the crowd on a wide bend and was hit by Italy's Federico de Beni, a Tour débutant riding for the Riso Scotti team. Like any good professional, Beni got up to finish the stage, but the girl was taken to Cork University hospital with head injuries. She was still unconscious as the riders boarded their plane for the transfer to France later that afternoon. Without as much as a backward glance, the Tour convoy hurtled onwards, as the sprinters' teams, keeping their eyes firmly on the yellow jersey prize, jostled for position.

Telekom's Zabel was soon making up lost ground, picking up time at the first and second intermediate sprints and as the stage progressed, narrowing his deficit to Boardman. The pace was too much for Erik Dekker of the Rabobank team, a faller in the previous afternoon's finale in Phoenix Park. He became the first mid-race abandon of the 1998 Tour, climbing off in the feed zone after 111 kilometres.

The speed wound up still further, as the bunch headed into County Cork and towards the third bonus sprint at Youghal, with Boardman's GAN team battling to prevent Zabel snatching the vital seconds he needed. Even though the Englishman understood and expected that one of the cluster of top sprinters would steal away his *maillot jaune* in the opening flat stages, he and his team-mates were still determined and proud enough to fight tooth and nail to defend the colours. So as the Telekom team led the field off Curtiswood Hill and down towards Youghal, Boardman was sitting comfortably tucked in behind his speeding team-mates, about twentieth in the long line of riders stretching across the green Irish landscape.

Moments later, the Merseysider lay battered and unconscious at the foot of a dry stone wall after one of the most dramatic crashes ever to befall the race leader in the Tour's opening stages. A touch of wheels in the group had sent Boardman, the ONCE team's Johan Bruyneel and, some said, Francesco Casagrande of the Cofidis team crashing to the road. In the press room, we'd sprung to our feet in horror at the first glimpse of the Briton's ripped and bloodied yellow jersey. Crashes had taken him out of the race in 1995 and 1997 – surely it couldn't have happened again?

Of the three or four to fall, Boardman had come off worst, slithering along the tarmac on his side before juddering head first into the wall and then bouncing off it, back into the road. His racing helmet was shattered by the impact. The helicopter television cameras hovered overhead as he lay in the road, unmoving. For a moment, as we watched, hoping against hope that he could somehow climb back on and finish the stage, we feared the worst. Still he didn't move. Then finally, as the Tour's medical team, led by Dr Gérard Porte, crowded around and the posse of motorbike photographers arrived on the scene, he stirred.

Meanwhile, a couple of kilometres up the road, Zabel was winning the third bonus sprint to seal his grip on the race lead. By then, however, it was academic as Boardman, gripping the hand of his *directeur sportif* Roger Legeay, was lifted gingerly into the back of an ambulance.

Up ahead, the race wondered what to do. With the yellow jersey wearer nowhere in sight, there was a lull as the field tried to find out whether Boardman was able to continue.

'Nobody wants to race with the yellow jersey lying bleeding on the road,' said Boardman's Australian team-mate Stuart O'Grady succinctly, after the finish.

The riders had their answer soon enough though. Guided by police outriders, a wailing ambulance hooted its way past them and ferried the erstwhile race leader to Cork University hospital.

Rumours were soon flying around the press room. Boardman had broken his cheekbone, his back, his jaw, his neck – even at one memorable moment, was said to be suffering from a 'fractured eyebrow'. I rang his agent Peter Woodworth, who was on his way back to Liverpool from Dublin on a ferry. Stranded out in the Irish Sea, Woodworth was just taking in the gravity of the news. 'It's an absolute disaster,' he groaned. Yet even he didn't know how bad his friend's injuries were.

Back out on the road, Boardman's team-mates, Eddy Seigneur and François Simon, made the rash decision to attack into a strong head wind as the field bore down on Cork. Seigneur admitted afterwards that it was a reaction to what had happened to his English team-mate – an attempt to lift his spirits. Although the pair stayed clear long enough for Seigneur to gain sufficient time to take over the race lead, the field soon reeled them in; although as they did so, Jalabert, Olano and Virenque were all involved in minor crashes.

As the tension mounted, the sprinters – Cipollini, Zabel, Steels, Svorada and Moncassin – all gathered at the front of the field as the Tour entered the suburbs of Ireland's second city. But Cipo's plans were thwarted yet again, as two of his team-mates fell shortly before the final kilometre marker. It was enough to disrupt his rhythm and the Italian lost ground as Steels, Zabel and Svorada moved forward.

After a heavy shower earlier in the afternoon, warm sunlight bathed the finish line as the Tour's 186-man field sped down the Carrigrohane Road, on the banks of the river Lee. Zabel moved to the front in the final 500 metres, but once again he was outwitted – this time by Czech national champion Svorada, who held off Australian sprinter Robbie McEwen to claim the second Tour stage win of his seven year professional career. Zabel didn't care about missing out on another stage though, because he was soon bounding up on to the podium, joyfully pulling the *maillot jaune* over his head and closing his eyes in ecstasy.

'I wish Boardman well,' he said carefully, 'but even without his crash, I'm sure that I would still have got the jersey.'

Up in the *salle de presse*, we were desperate for more information about Boardman. I rang Michel Laurent, the GAN team's frosty PR man, but his mobile was constantly engaged. So we called Cork University hospital, asked for the doctor looking after Chris Boardman and were immediately put through to the very helpful Dr Stephen Cusack. Boardman was conscious but groggy, Dr Cusack explained, and had concussion, cuts and bruising to his left wrist and his elbow and cuts around his left eye. After the impact, the doctor said, he'd been unconscious for about three minutes. They were giving him a brain scan, carrying out X-rays for a possible broken wrist and were keeping him in overnight for observation – all standard practice for such an accident. But the exact circumstances of the crash itself were still shrouded in mystery.

I walked down to the team cars lined up outside the nearby Cork Sports Centre. Inside, the riders were pulling off their sweaty kit, showering and changing into their team casuals in readiness for the flight to Brittany. One by one they came out, some nursing deep grazes on their elbows, others rolling their tracksuit legs up over their knees to allow the deep and bloody gouges on their shins to breathe. Bobby Julich, leader-in-waiting at the Cofidis team, pulled a ruck-sack out of the boot of his team car and confirmed that team-mate Casagrande had fallen heavily, bruising his ribs and sustaining cuts and bruises. The young American's *directeur sportif*, Bernard Quilfen, shrugged his shoulders in resigna-tion. 'The first week of the Tour, there are always crashes,' sighed the Frenchman. '*C'est normal . . .*'

Nearby, GAN pair Magnus Backstedt and Stuart O'Grady stood snacking on some fruit and downing bottles of mineral water.

'Chris was riding behind us because we were all working towards the sprint,' said Backstedt. 'I heard the crash but we didn't know who it was or how serious it was until a few kilometres further up the road.'

'Losing Chris is a big blow,' said O'Grady. 'He's become the nucleus of the team – he holds everyone together. It's hard to believe that he's crashed out of the race two years in a row – it leaves a big hole in the team.'

Boardman was the twelfth rider in the history of the Tour to be forced to abandon while wearing the leader's jersey. By a twist of fate, the last rider to quit the race while wearing yellow was also sponsored by GAN. In 1996, Stéphane Heulot had abandoned the Tour in tears, after a bout of acute tendinitis in his left knee forced him to a dramatic standstill on the wild ascent of the Cornet de Roselend, high in the Alps. Now Boardman followed suit, his Tour ending in the back of an Irish ambulance. It was the latest catastrophe in his roller-coaster career, which in just five years had known as many downs as ups.

We worked frantically in the press room, battling to send out stories before we left for the ferry to France. Down at the harbour, we threaded our way through the crowds gathering to give the Tour convoy an affectionate send-off.

The long transfer to Ireland was the most logistically demanding operation the Tour had ever taken on. Stena Sealink had sailed their élite cruise ships to Cork and passage was provided free by the race organisation – with a pay bar. In all, there were 1,500 vehicles to load and transport to France, with the media designated to board the 6.30 crossing. Three ships carried the Tour convoy, while three chartered flights from Cork Airport transported the riders and the most senior officials in the entourage to Brest in Brittany.

It was a beautiful evening as the *Koningen Beatrix* slid out into Ringabella Bay. On the quayside, the Irish stood smiling and waving, many of them flourishing French flags in the gentle breeze. As the huge boat turned slowly to head out to sea, thousands of blue, red and white balloons were released from the ship's top deck, sailing high into the evening sky. The Tour was on its way back home, back to France.

After dinner, I sank exhausted into my bunk, listening to the soothing distant hum of the ferry's engines as my mind buzzed with the events of the Tour's opening three days. Ireland had been a success on many levels, introducing a new generation, unfamiliar with Roche and Kelly's successes, to the magnitude and spectacle of the Tour. But on others, as the Irish press didn't shrink from highlighting, it had only served to raise the issue of doping that had already been so painfully brought home to the Irish by the controversy surrounding swimmer Michelle de Bruin. The next morning, the French, the Tour's own people, still drunk on the euphoria of World Cup success, would reclaim their race. From there on, it would be up to them to see what they would make of the already tainted eighty-fifth edition of their annual sporting monument.

Stage winner: Jan Svorada, Czech Republic (Mapei–Bricobi)

Overall race leader: Erik Zabel, Germany (Deutsche Telekom)

Points classification leader: Tom Steels, Belgium (Mapei–Bricobi)

Team classification: Festina

Mountains classification leader: Stefano Zanini, Italy (Mapei–Bricobi)

Overall standings of favourites after Irish stages:
4. Abraham Olano, Spain (Banesto), 391.7 kilometres in 10 hrs, 21 mins 24 secs
5. Laurent Jalabert, France (ONCE) 10 hrs, 21 mins 25 secs
6. Bobby Julich, America (Cofidis) 10 hrs, 21 mins 25 secs
8. Jan Ullrich, Germany (Deutsche Telekom) 10 hrs, 21 mins 25 secs
11. Alex Zulle, Switzerland (Festina) 10 hrs, 21 mins 27 secs
19. Richard Virenque, France (Festina) 10 hrs, 21 mins 32 secs
25. Bjarne Riis, Denmark (Deutsche Telekom) 10 hrs, 21 mins 34 secs
162. Marco Pantani, Italy (Mercatone Uno) 10 hrs, 22 mins 8 secs

PART TWO

Day 6   # Stage 3

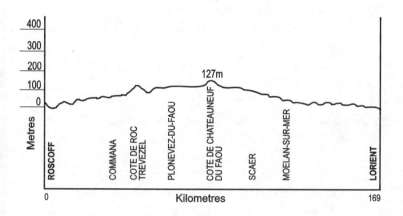

The *Koningen Beatrix* sat off the Breton coast, waiting at the gates of Roscoff's tiny Port de Bloscon as out of view, around the headland, the Tour de France hit town. We stood on the deck, basking in the warm Bastille Day sunshine, anxiously eyeing the ferry in front of us which stubbornly continued to monopolise the harbour's small quayside. We were behind schedule and the start of stage three was looming. Finally, the Stena Sealink boat ahead of us moved clear of the harbour and we coasted gingerly into dock.

Roscoff's narrow lanes were never intended for a ferry-load of stressed-out press cars arriving all at once. We got within 500 metres of the *village départ* and then ground to a halt between high stone walls as gridlock took over the start area. Even the race organisation's Fiats were having problems getting through the crush; but with a flurry of air-horns, a few choice epithets and a flash of their headlights, they made their way to the front of the convoy. We pulled up in a side road, jogged across the seafront to the start village and then joined the throng of media people queuing at the yellow Crédit Lyonnais tent, where every day the press picked up complimentary copies of the French papers.

The opening pages of *Aujourd'hui* and *L'Equipe* were dominated by coverage of the triumphant French football team's celebratory procession on the Champs-Elysées. But there, tucked in the latter pages of both papers, were the photos of a prone Chris Boardman – and the latest revelations in the continuing Festina scandal. According to *Aujourd'hui*, Willy Voet, still being questioned by Lille police, had changed his story. After first telling the police that the enormous batch of stimulants concealed in the Festina team car were for his personal use, he'd revealed that he was acting 'under orders'. The fifty-three-year-old Belgian, said the paper, had admitted that it wasn't the first time he'd taken on such a mission and that he had been expected to deliver the products to the team hotel in Dublin.

Standing a few feet away, while I took in the weight of this latest twist in the tale, was Festina's Australian rider Neil Stephens, one of the most popular and highly regarded professionals in the bunch. 'Stevo', as he is universally known, was talking quietly to a veteran Australian journalist when I approached. He looked shattered and distressed. I stopped to say hello, but he muttered only a perfunctory greeting before climbing into the saddle and pedalling away.

Out among the team cars the other Festina riders were battling their way to the start line through a scrum of journalists and photographers.

'I'm here to race – not to get involved in gossip,' blurted the team's long-haired world champion, Laurent Brochard, as a Spanish camera crew barged me out of the way.

74

Nearby, despite the chaos, Brochard's team-mate Pascal Hervé seemed disarmingly calm.

'Willy Voet is my friend,' Hervé said to the mass of microphones thrust into his face, 'and will always be my friend. I'm not annoyed – why would I be? Everything I've heard about this so far has come from the press.'

By now, the name of the judge leading the Lille-based investigation had appeared in the papers. Judge Patrick Keil was rapidly becoming a household name. And lawyers were getting heavily involved too, with Voet's side defending their client's assertions, while Roussel's Parisian brief robustly protected the Festina *directeur*'s interests in the French press.

'You can be sure that we know how to defend ourselves,' said Roussel's lawyer. 'If it does come to that, it will be very serious for all concerned.'

Roussel meanwhile, now shadowed by the press wherever he went, was again adamant that he wanted to clear the whole business up as soon as possible.

'I'm shocked,' he said yet again, and later went on to formally deny everything in a press release. 'The management of the Festina team,' stated the communiqué, 'formally refute suggestions that we asked a *soigneur* to supply substances banned by law or by the regulations of the Tour de France.'

As VIP guests wandered around the Tour's first truly French *village départ* drinking calvados and sampling the local seafood, those riders not involved in the scandal sat quietly under sponsors' umbrellas, awaiting the stage start. Across at the Maison du Café kiosk, GAN pair Backstedt and O'Grady sipped coffees and surveyed the scene. The previous night's trip from Cork to Brest and then on by road to the hotel had been uneventful, even if it had meant a late supper.

'This is where the race begins,' said Backstedt with grim certainty as he drank his espresso. 'Telekom will have to look after Ullrich from now on, because he has to get to the first time trial without any problems. Then he'll take the jersey in the time trial. I've been watching him and he looks great – from there he'll keep the jersey all the way to Paris.'

Close by, British rider Max Sciandri sat chatting in Italian and French to his team-mates, including the faltering Russian star Evgeni Berzin, winner of the 1994 Tour of Italy and once touted as a possible future Tour champion. Blond-haired Berzin, now an Italian resident and Sciandri, born in Derby of Italian parentage, were two of the leading riders with the French national lottery sponsored team, La Française des Jeux.

Anglo-Italian Sciandri opted to take out a British licence in 1995 in response to the disappointment of being repeatedly left out of the Italian national team. The change had suited him. Soon afterwards, he won a stage in the Tour and claimed a bronze medal for his country of birth in the Atlanta Olympics road race.

Yet the thirty-two-year-old resident of Tuscany had never been championed by British fans, despite winning the Leeds Classic in front of a home crowd in 1995 and a stage of the Tour itself earlier the same summer. But then Max always came across as Italian at heart. In 1996, when he had narrowly missed out on victory at Milan–San Remo, he had been devastated by the disappointment of coming so close to success in Italy's most coveted one day Classic. And even when claiming that sole Tour stage win in 1995 with the Union Jack flag stamped plainly on his race number, he sat indulgently with the Italian press for an hour or so afterwards, unwittingly snubbing the chaps from the BBC in the process. Still, he was in good spirits in Roscoff, following a successful recovery from back injuries sustained in a bad training accident the previous winter.

'A pedestrian stepped out in front of me and when I swerved to avoid them, I hit a car head on,' he recalled. 'I'm not quite back to one hundred per cent yet, but it's getting there.'

Sciandri's form was good and following two stage wins in the prestigious French race, the Dauphine Libère, he'd come to the Tour brimming with confidence.

'Yup, I'm up for it,' he beamed, and got to his feet as the bell rang to call the riders to the start line.

We ran back to the car and headed out through the back roads of Roscoff to join the race route just ahead of the riders, outside town. But as we came to the junction and prepared to roll between the barriers, a local *gendarme* appeared wagging his finger in admonition. Usual Tour convention understands that accredited vehicles can dip in and out of the race route as they wish, providing it's safe to do so and doesn't endanger the public or the convoy. Our man in blue wasn't having any of it. Maybe it was the English plates and the right-hand drive that threw him because infuriatingly, half a minute later when a flurry of French and Belgian press cars flew past us and drove straight on to the *route du Tour*, he stepped politely aside. I waited until his back was turned, inched forward to check that the road was clear, and sped off after them.

Bastille Day, a French national holiday, always draws plenty of picnicking spectators to the Tour; but the atmosphere of rapture and intoxication that enveloped France after their World Cup victory had swelled the crowd tenfold. Thousands of people lined the route, waving the *tricolore* flag or wearing it wrapped around their shoulders. Others had painted their faces red, white and blue or were wearing replica national football shirts. Some waved fake inflatable World Cups and posters of Aimé Jacquet, the national coach – most of them looked to be nursing the hangovers of a lifetime, while others had opted to carry on drinking. It would have been funny if, once or twice, it hadn't been so frightening.

Just short of the fifty kilometre mark, the route climbed up towards the wild ridge of the Monts d'Arrée on the Côte de Roc-Trévézel, where spectators virtually blocked the road. Up at the very top of the climb were the biggest and rowdiest crowds I had ever seen on the *route du Tour*. We crawled gingerly through the packed, partying throng, anxious not to crush any toes, winding up the windows as they yelled '*Allo eengleesh*', and showered the car with champagne, cider and beer.

Behind us, at the foot of the hill, the Casino team had suddenly picked up the pace, sending out their Danish rider Bo Hamburger to snatch the time bonus at the first intermediate sprint. Following him in an opportunistic move were eight other riders, including GAN's O'Grady, Willy Voet's loyal friend Pascal Hervé of the Festina team and New Yorker George Hincapie, a sprinter from US Postal, the sole American sponsor competing in the Tour. The nine moved clear of the field, with Jens Heppner, team-mate to Telekom's race leader Zabel, sitting at the back of the group, following team tactics to the letter by refusing to assist in keeping the pace high. After 100 kilometres, with Telekom opting not to defend Zabel's overall race lead by chasing the escapees, the break led by just over seven minutes. Their pace was still as fierce as when they had first slipped clear.

Driving over the race route a few kilometres ahead of them, we pulled over to snatch a *café au lait* and stood in a battered but friendly local bar watching the break's progress on a flickering colour telly. As they got closer, we rejoined the race route and then stopped again a short while later to let the riders go past us. Then, as they swung out of sight around a left-hand bend, we sped away from the verge to join the flotilla of cars and motorbikes driving behind them. I didn't often drive behind the breakaway on the Tour. I preferred to do so in lesser races with fewer cars and smaller crowds, as it was safer and less stressful. But there was something so exciting, so stirring, so damn glorious about driving behind the breakaway – the *échappée* – in the Tour de France, that I always tried to spend at least a few moments during the race savouring that unique atmosphere.

We slipped into the ebb and flow behind the break, giving way to the organisation's commissaire and guest cars. Every now and then, somewhere among the group of hunched riders just ahead of us, a hand went up as a rider called for his team car. Then, paying close attention to the spectators lining the roadside, we'd quickly move aside as a flashing, tooting Fiat rocketed towards us in the rear-view mirror. From time to time the road would become a three-lane highway as the team cars scuttled back and forth.

Some journalists chose not to sample the flavour of the race in that way, preferring instead to talk to the riders in the start village, then jump into their car, head for the *autoroute* and gun straight to the press room. Often the next time they saw the riders would be either for a few seconds on the finish line, or even twenty-four hours later in the start village the next morning. Others picked up their soundbites and back-ground information by calling the riders on their mobiles as they headed back to their team hotels. But then we all had different deadlines to work to, different audiences to cater for and different ways of working.

On the road ahead of us O'Grady looked to be the strong man of the group, sharing much of the work with Hamburger, the Dane's team-mate Pascal Chanteur and Festina's Hervé. Even though they had been riding at full extent for the best part of 100 kilometres, their speed was still frighteningly high. On flatter sections they averaged about thirty miles per hour, wavering slightly on the uphill hauls before picking up to speeds of almost fifty miles per hour on the short Breton descents.

If Zabel had hoped that his team would look after his interest in the race lead then he was disappointed, as with little more than fifty kilometres still to race, Jalabert's ONCE team took up the initiative and led the pursuit. But with so much at stake and the field finally stirring behind, the tension in the lead group was building. Provided they stayed clear of the main field all the way to Lorient, one of their number was sure to take the yellow jersey from Zabel. None of them had ever worn the *maillot jaune* before and it would all come down to time bonuses picked up along the way.

It was Hamburger who did enough to clinch the overall race lead, winning the third sprint of the day after 130 kilometres at Moëlan-sur-Mer. By then, we'd been waved past the breakaway by race director Jean-Marie Leblanc and were speeding to the *salle de presse* in Lorient, desperate to see the final half hour of the race on TV. Despite the best efforts of the field in the final approach to Lorient along the wild sandy beachfronts of the Morbihan coast, the group of nine survived into the town and Jens Heppner, who'd conserved much of his strength during the day, readied himself for a sprint to the line.

A year earlier, the thirty-three-year-old German had been controversially disqualified after a bad-tempered and laughably clumsy two-man sprint towards the end of the 1997 Tour in Dijon. This time he made no mistake, outwitting La

Française des Jeux's young professional Xavier Jan and GAN's weary O'Grady as he sprinted for the line. It was the biggest success of his eight-year career, seven seasons of which had been spent at the formerly unglamorous Telekom team. Once, a long time ago, before the advent of Ullrich and Riis, Heppner had been touted as the future of German cycling. In 1992, he'd finished tenth in his first Tour de France, a result that seemed to herald great things. But the earliest incarnation of the Telekom team had been unable to support his talents. It wasn't until the ambitious and driven Riis joined the team in 1996 that Heppner rediscovered his own ambition, developing a strong protective bond with the prodigiously talented Ullrich. It was Heppner who had been assigned to monitor Ullrich's training and focus his mind as he battled to lose weight late in the spring, with those long and punishing rides in the hills of the Black Forest.

While Heppner celebrated, Bo Hamburger looked on, unconcerned. The likeable Dane, blessed with a surname that brings a smile to the faces of headline writers everywhere, had taken the *maillot jaune* for the first time. He was ecstatic.

'I feel pretty good right now,' he grinned, as he reflected on his string of good results since joining the French Casino team from Dutch sponsor TVM. 'Things started well when I changed teams, but then when I had the third second-place of my career in the Danish national championships, I thought "here we go – the nearly man again . . ." But Sanne, my wife, talked me round and said that I hadn't come so close for nothing. She told me the best was yet to come – she was right.'

Dodgy phone lines meant that it took a while to send my story. Finally, temper fraying, I got through to London and as

81

the daylight faded, we set off into the countryside in search of our hotel. The paper headed the next morning's story *'Hamburger Relishes Change of Fortune'*.

Stage winner: Jens Heppner, Germany (Deutsche Telekom)

Overall race leader: Bo Hamburger, Denmark (Casino)

Points classification leader: Jan Svorada, Czech Republic (Mapei–Bricobi)

Team classification leader: Casino

Mountains classification leader: Pascal Hervé, France (Festina)

Day 7   Stage 4

Wednesday 15 July
Plouay–Cholet, 252 km

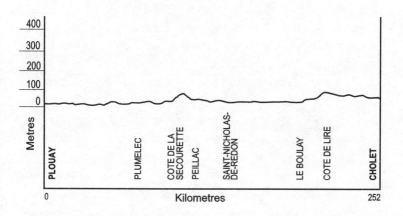

Stuart O'Grady sat despondently in the start village, the Vélo Parc de Menéhouarne on the outskirts of Plouay. Normally the freckled and red-haired Australian was cheery enough, but on this grey morning he sat in the midst of an Antipodean enclave, dejectedly mulling over the previous day's racing. The twenty-four-year-old from Adelaide was about to start stage four just three seconds in arrears of race leader Hamburger, but the prospect of missing out on the yellow jersey was eating him up.

'I got so close to the jersey yesterday,' he said quietly, shaking his head. 'I was pretty devastated, especially as it was such a good break – opportunities as good as that don't come along too often in the Tour de France. I was thinking about it loads last night so I didn't sleep too well – 'specially as they let off bloody Bastille Day fireworks outside the hotel at midnight. When Hamburger took the last sprint yesterday, I knew the chance was gone, so when we got to the finish I was thinking, "OK – go for the stage win." But when I attacked in the finale, Heppner, who hadn't done a stroke to help the breakaway the whole time, chased me down,' he said disgustedly. 'I thought, "Oh great – thanks, pal." '

Festina's Neil Stephens, sitting sipping coffee nearby, leaned across. 'Careful what yer say Stu – don't forget there's a journalist here.'

O'Grady forced a smile. Heartened, the ever-enthusiastic Stevo continued, keen to lift his countryman's spirits. 'Listen mate, ya gotta go for the jersey,' he encouraged. 'All you need is one good sprint and it's yours. Think of the old country – if you get the jersey, it'll mean jobs for all of us when we get back!'

A few yards away, America's Bobby Julich, his star very much on the rise following his solid start to the race and some promising results earlier in the year, was relaxed and chatty as he faced up to the Tour's longest stage. The self-possessed Bobby J, seventeenth overall in his first Tour the previous July, was sure to do better this year. But for the time being, with the form of the favourites yet to reveal itself, the media allowed him the space to wander relatively untroubled through the village each morning.

'It's been pretty calm so far this year,' he smiled, 'certainly a lot calmer than last year. Maybe it's because I'm better at dealing with all the hassle that comes with the Tour.'

Julich liked to talk – in fact, in his short professional career, he'd already built an affectionate reputation, even among other Americans, for his showbiz quotability. Once, an American journalist had asked him why he'd set such high goals for his career. 'Well, if you shoot for the moon at least you might hit the stars,' replied Bobby J, earnestly. Bobby J's new age soundbites didn't appeal to everybody, though. One

Brochard, Virenque and Roussel: Festina's key trio wave to the crowds at the Dublin teams presentation.

Mean machine: Jan Ullrich giving little away at the pre-prologue press conference.

A lonely Bruno Roussel faces the press after the first stage in Dublin.

LE TOUR DE FRANCE

CHATEAU DE DUBLIN

Yet more soundbites: Chris Boardman feels the pressure of wearing the Tour's yellow jersey.

Cipollini on his throne: the 'Lion King' fooling around at the race HQ in Dublin Castle.

The Tour de France hits the very Irish streets of Arklow.

Boardman takes the plaudits in Phoenix Park while Bernard Hinault looks on.

Tom Steels sprints for the line at the stage finish in Cap d'Agde.

The world's media gather on the steps of the Festina hotel on the night that the team was thrown off the race.

The morning after the night before and a lone fan waits for the Festina team at the Castel Novel hotel.

Francesco Frattini of Telekom crosses the line at the end of the stage seven time trial.

US Postal's Marty Jemison buckles up for another day in the saddle.

Max Sciandri, looking cool before the pressure took its toll.

Tour director Jean-Marie Leblanc showing the strain.

Laurent Roux embraces his wife at the party in his honour during stage eight to Montauban.

Roux's good-time band at the roadside picnic on the route to Montauban.

The Tour organisation's Sophie del Rizzo coping with the demands of the *salle de presse*.

The Tour in the French heartlands on the approach to the Pyrenees.

or two of his English-speaking peers had been seen rolling their eyes skywards as they listened to the greater excesses of his positive-thinking spiel. But at least he was open and affable and didn't hide behind team managers or stonewalling PR people. With the undaunted and unflinching Bobby J, unlike so many other top riders, what you saw was what you got.

We chatted on and talked of his compatriot George Hincapie's efforts to take the race lead the previous afternoon.

'They – US Postal – got it *all* wrong yesterday,' said Julich emphatically. 'They let Hamburger take the seconds at the sprint when they should have been fighting for them. They have to go for it today – to get that close and need only a couple of seconds. George *has* to try to take it.'

We picked up the papers from the Crédit Lyonnais stand and went back to the car. With the best part of 260 kilometres to the finish in Cholet, we skipped the race route, joined the fast coast road and headed south to Nantes. As we drove towards Vannes I scanned the papers. They made for staggering reading. In the tabloid newspaper *France-Soir*, a Swiss sports doctor, Gérard Gremion, had claimed that '99 per cent of professional cyclists take drugs'. Suddenly the papers seemed to have more revelations than there was space to print. Confessions, accusations and speculation were hitting the sport from all sides. We sped on down the *autoroute* as the race took a parallel route inland. 'Four to five hundred professionals are destroying their health by taking banned substances,' I read in the Gremion story.

Back on the course, O'Grady had recovered his morale and had set the GAN team working in the approach to the first of the long day's three time bonus sprints. But well before O'Grady and Hincapie could contest the sprint at Plumelec, the Tour lost its most traumatised rider. Federico de Beni, the

Italian rider who had collided with an Irish girl on the road to Cork, pulled out of the race after thirty-two kilometres of the stage. Since the accident in Ireland, the twenty-five-year-old Italian had been in turmoil. Riso Scotti's team management confided that his mind had not been on the race. De Beni was said to have wept when told that the girl, eleven-year-old Laura Seward, was still in a coma two days after the crash.

The Italian left the race convoy at the feed zone, hitching a lift back to the team hotel before travelling to Paris to catch a flight to Verona.

'All I can think about is the girl,' he told Italian journalists before he left. 'It's a shame to leave the Tour like this but more than anything, I hope she recovers.'

At the first intermediate sprint O'Grady, aided by his team's faltering fast man Frédéric Moncassin, took the six second bonus to leap-frog over Hincapie and Hamburger and become '*maillot virtuel*' – race leader on the road. He also won the second sprint after 102 kilometres at Peillac and took third in the final one at Le Boulay to pick up fourteen bonus seconds in all. It was an impressive day's work.

It was after the second sprint on the approach to Redon that Casino's Jacky 'Dudu' Durand made his daily bid for glory, accompanied by La Française des Jeux's Damien Nazon. 'Dudu' has always been loved by French fans and ensures plenty of publicity for whichever sponsor he rides for. He's become a fixture on the post-stage chat show *Vélo Club* hosted by French heart-throb Gérard Holtz. Dudu's break with Nazon coincided with the arrival of live TV coverage and guaranteed plenty of images of the Casino logo, plus column inches in the French press the following morning. There was also the slim possibility that the attack might stay clear. It was a gambler's move, typical of the effervescent Dudu.

Durand wasn't the only popular French rider whose name had been shortened to a childlike derivative. We had national champion Jalabert – 'Jaja'; TVM's Laurent Roux – 'Lollo'; Polti's Luc Leblanc – 'Lucho'. Even the *directeurs* weren't immune. Cofidis' greying Bernard Quilfen, team manager to Bobby J, had become 'Qui-Qui'. Every now and then the Tour's TV commentary sounded like a French surrealist's version of the children's programme *Hector's House*.

So off Dudu went, pluckily working to open up a gap on the *peloton*. The Frenchman knew that the field would eventually give chase, but if he and Nazon had a big enough time cushion on the run into Cholet, then their attack might just work. But the GAN team wanted the yellow jersey too badly and their blue and white colours moved up to the front of the bunch, setting a regular pace on the long straight roads of the Anjou region; just enough, in fact, to keep Durand and Nazon within reach. The pair were finally reeled in after 230 kilometres, when the Mapei, Saeco and Telekom teams lent a hand to the pursuit. Nazon – 'Nazzer' – and Dudu had been clear for a punishing 117 kilometres, for little or no reward.

On the fast approach to Cholet, the sprinters' teams began the usual fight for position. We were four stages into the Tour but Cipollini, the self-styled Super Mario, had yet to win. Opportunities for the Lion King to roar were steadily running out. But fate was against Cipo again. Four kilometres from the finish, as he followed the speeding bunch through the suburbs of Cholet, a group of riders fell on a tight left-hand bend, bringing the Italian crashing down once more.

Sprawled on the tarmac alongside Cipo was race leader-in-waiting O'Grady. But the Australian's luck was in. Hincapie, his closest overall rival among the sprinters, was also on the deck. He got back on his bike and luckily Magnus Backstedt was there and had waited for him. They rode the final kilometres flat out to get back to the field.

Just ahead of O'Grady, the TVM team's Jeroen Blijlevens was expertly clinging on to the slipstream of Italian sprinter Nicola Minali. Blijlevens, a stage winner in each of the previous three Tours, was benefiting from the confusion after the stack-up.

'After the crash, there was a gap in front of me,' Blijlevens said later in the post-race press conference, 'but I was able to get on to Minali's wheel. It turned out to be the right one to follow.'

As Minali closed on the line with victory in sight, Blijlevens darted to the Italian's left shoulder and thrust his bike towards the line. It was enough to snatch victory.

Nearby, in the Parc de Moine skating rink, site of the day's *salle de presse*, we were paying little attention to the Dutch rider's success. Yet again, the rumours were coming thick and fast: the latest, as French TV ran yet another action replay of the sprint finale, was that the French drugs squad were waiting for the Festina team and Roussel at their hotel on the far side of town.

We'd arrived in Cholet at midday and after setting up shop in the press room dived into the adjacent tent to enjoy a generous press buffet. We wandered back in time to see 'Dudu' and 'Nazzer' making the most of TV airtime. I grabbed a coffee and re-read the Gremion article in *France-Soir*. I wanted to know more about this outspoken doctor and his background, so I strolled over to a Swiss journalist to quiz him on Gremion's history.

As we were chatting, Tony Rominger, three-times winner of the Tour of Spain, runner-up to the indomitable Indurain in the 1993 Tour de France and one of the army of former professionals working on the Tour, appeared. The Swiss had only recently retired and was now acting as a consultant to the Cofidis team. Inevitably, Rominger had his own spin on the Gremion story.

'Ah, he's just a bitter doctor, y'know,' he said dismissively in tactless English. 'He left the Swiss Post team because it didn't work out so now he goes to the press with this story.'

Rominger's argument was the same as that put forward for several seasons by cycling's governing body, the Union Cycliste International, or UCI. In recent years, a succession of riders, some whose careers had been ended by illness or injury, others who had left the professional scene disillusioned by its demands, had accused the sport of institutionalised doping. The UCI, in particular its president, Hein Verbruggen, had always dismissed such claims as those of embittered and failed athletes. Now Rominger took refuge in the same defence, without stopping to address the damaging accusations levelled at the riders.

In January 1997, *L'Equipe* had published an investigative series of articles exploring the extent of doping in professional cycling. Among the published interviews with former professionals – confessional interviews which UCI President Verbruggen would later describe as 'so bloody cheap' – was one with Nicolas Aubier, a twenty-five-year-old French professional, who after only four years of racing had opted to retire from the sport.

'EPO is bought from dealers,' Aubier told the paper. 'He might be a team-mate or a *soigneur* – they'll sell it and take a commission. It's bought in Belgium, Holland or Switzerland. The dealers make a profit, as do the laboratories. You can even buy it over the Internet. Everybody profits from the system,' said Aubier. 'The riders optimise their performance.

The teams are more competitive and attractive to sponsors. Even in the media the slant is always about winning. Everybody knows what's going on, but nobody says a word.'

After Blijlevens' victory, O'Grady, only the second Australian ever to wear the yellow jersey, appeared for the press conference speaking via the video link from close to the finish line.

'This morning we thought that Casino would let *échappées* go, but I still needed a strong team to help me in the sprints,' O'Grady said. 'Yesterday I was really depressed to get so close. I kept thinking it over, but I knew that all it would need was one good sprint and I managed to do it.'

'I just wish Chris Boardman was here to be part of this,' the Adelaide-born O'Grady said. 'Before his crash he gave me a yellow jersey to take back to the car and said that one day soon he'd be doing the same for me. I wish him the best and hope that he recovers quickly.'

But the Australian's celebrations were quickly overshadowed. The rumours of further police intervention in the 1998 Tour proved to be well-founded. Festina *directeur* Roussel had been greeted by the police at the finish, as had team doctor Eric Ryckaert. By the time that startling news filtered through to the press room, both men were being interviewed at Cholet police station. French TV crews, sensing the gravity of Festina's – and particularly, national hero Virenque's – situation, soon turned up at the hotel, screening live pictures of the police coming and going from riders' rooms.

Then we were back in the *Vélo Club* studio as the Tour's overwhelmed administration, so used to planning for every eventuality, for every logistical detail, began to look very out of its depth. Jean-Marie Leblanc had chosen to appear live, speaking unscripted alongside O'Grady's GAN *directeur sportif*, Roger Legeay, also head of the professional team managers' association.

'As yet,' insisted Leblanc, 'this affair does not concern riders competing in the Tour. As such, it's profoundly unjust to those riders who are here. What has happened is a shame for the Tour, but we're not going to turn our back on the affair. Yet so far, everything we've learnt has been from the press, and there have been plenty of stupid rumours.'

Legeay, listening intently alongside, was more sagacious. 'There's no question of the Tour carrying on for three weeks in an atmosphere like this,' he said. 'The Tour is supposed to be a festival. This business must be resolved as soon as possible.'

Stage winner: Jeroen Blijlevens, Holland (TVM)
Overall race leader: Stuart O'Grady, Australia (GAN)
Points classification leader: Jan Svorada, Czech Republic (Mapei–Bricobi)
Team classification leader: Casino
Mountains classification leader: Pascal Hervé, France (Festina)

Day 8   Stage 5

Thursday 16 July
Cholet–Châteauroux, 228.5 km

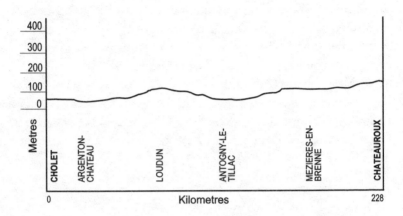

It was raining outside the somnolent Hôtel La Boule d'Or in Bressuire, a quiet rural town in the northern reaches of the Deux Sèvres region. Getting to the start of stage five in Cholet meant an hour's drive in the opposite direction to the stage finish in Châteauroux, but given the events of the previous evening, we felt sure that this was one *village départ* not to be missed. Despite the rain, the crowds had come out to see the Tour convoy move on. We were hunting for a parking place when the *caravane publicitaire* moved off just ahead of us, so we ground to a standstill behind a long queue of press cars.

When we finally got into the windswept tented village, the UCI's Martin Bruin, president of the race jury, accompanied by Jean-Marie Leblanc, the Tour's race director, was well into an impromptu press conference. We climbed on to plastic chairs and tables, craning to hear their muffled words through a crowd of cameras, baseball caps and umbrellas.

'The UCI has decided to provisionally ban Bruno Roussel from holding a *directeur sportif*'s licence,' announced Bruin. 'The UCI committee decided that the evidence is sufficient for a provisional suspension of his licence. He is banned from any function in cycling.'

Bruin paused. Leblanc, who only hours earlier had talked of 'stupid rumours', looked up with heavy-lidded eyes as we all scribbled notes furiously.

'The UCI understood the need to take urgent measures to restore public confidence,' said Bruin. 'On July 14 we asked Roussel to report to us but he has not done so. Priority has to be given to the general interest.'

But, said Leblanc, the riders themselves were unlikely to face any further action. 'The riders have committed no infractions against the UCI's anti-doping rules.'

Later it emerged that the UCI executive had sent Roussel a fax from the junior World Championships in Havana, inviting him to put his side of the story. When he failed to reply, his suspension became inevitable.

As Leblanc and Bruin stood up to wade through the media scrum, Richard Virenque and the rest of the Festina team were making their way to the start. The storm was breaking all around them, yet still they were intent on continuing. Half an hour later Virenque, together with team-mates Laurent Brochard and Laurent Dufaux, sat in the same seats, defending themselves against all accusations levelled at them.

'We're staying in the race,' insisted Virenque, 'and we have a clear conscience. We've all come here to show that we're speaking with one voice.'

Dufaux, eloquent and intelligent, looked dazed and emotional. 'We have wives and children yet we're being treated like assassins,' said the twenty-nine-year-old Swiss, his voice quavering with feeling. 'Our families have been hurt by what they're reading in the papers at the moment. We've all been shocked by the stories that have been put forward by the press.'

Virenque picked up the theme, talking of the stress of the Tour's opening few days and then speaking of his continuing hopes of victory despite the developing scandal.

'I'm here to win,' Virenque said. 'But I hope I haven't used up too much energy with this business, just at the time when I should be trying to save myself. I'm risking paying for it during the final week of the race.'

Virenque's detractors, those who accused him of playing to the gallery, of manipulating the media to maintain his huge popularity with French fans rather than concentrating on winning races, had another moment to savour as the press conference wound to a close. As the questions ended, he leaned forward deliberately towards the microphones.

'Don't turn this into a detective novel,' he warned tetchily, 'because you'll kill cycling. I want to talk about cycling and racing. *Vive le vélo, vive le Tour!*' Virenque concluded as he, Dufaux, Brochard and the rest of the Festina team readied themselves to join the Tour field for another day's racing.

Roussel and Festina team doctor Eric Ryckaert had been held overnight in custody in Cholet police station. The pair were expected to be transferred to Lille to be interviewed by Judge Keil within the next twenty-four hours. Michel Gros, Roussel's assistant, immediately took over management duties for the stage to Châteauroux while Miguel Moreno, the squad's third coach, was scheduled to fly up from Toledo in Spain. Roussel, Virenque's guiding light since the Frenchman's early professional career, clearly wasn't expected to be coming back to the Tour.

He and Ryckaert's first night in police custody had prompted confusing rumours. At first, with the media laying siege outside Cholet police station, both men had refused to co-operate with the enquiry. There was plenty of conjecture over Ryckaert's role in the affair. The doctor had been subjected to a visit from the Belgian police the previous winter.

'Nine months ago, the police came to my offices in Ghent to look at my computer database,' Ryckaert had told journalists, 'not to look for the products that have been mentioned.'

But persistent rumours linked Ryckaert and Voet to a Belgian pharmacist, who, after being investigated by the authorities over undisclosed earnings, was alleged by the Belgian media to deal in EPO.

'I'm against doping,' Ryckaert continued, 'although there are questions you must ask yourself on the definition of doping. As a doctor,' he said pointedly, 'I want to know where medical treatments end and doping begins.'

But Ryckaert and Roussel were fighting a losing battle. In further reports emanating from Lille, Voet was alleged to have said that he would pick up stocks of doping products from the team headquarters in the Rhône valley and then deliver them to Ryckaert at races.

Increasingly, reporting of the race itself was taking more of a back seat as the tidal wave of revelations threatened to engulf the Tour caravan. In *L'Equipe*'s editorial, titled '*L'Omerta*' – the 'law of silence' – the paper revealed that it had taped an interview with 'Mr X', an experienced French rider, who had spoken 'from the heart' of the culture of doping. Mr X had said that doping was rife in the *peloton*; that the dreaded EPO had been in widespread use since 1994; that the sport had arrived at stalemate because nobody among the top professionals wanted to be the first to give the stuff up. Then, hours after giving the interview, the rider, fearful of the consequences according to *L'Equipe*, had changed his mind and pleaded with the paper not to run the piece. So they dropped it.

The editorial concluded by saying that the rider had apologised to the journalist concerned. 'Yesterday I used my head,' Mr X had said sarcastically. 'Today, I'm stupid again.'

Out in the wind and rain sweeping across the southern Loire, race leader O'Grady was having a tough time. At the first intermediate sprint he could only finish fourth, missing out on vital bonus seconds. On the tortuous approach to the second sprint in Loudun after eighty kilometres, he skidded and fell heavily on a right-hand bend. Four of the Australian's team-mates also fell, along with French champion Jalabert and Svorada, Mapei's Czech sprinter, stage winner in Cork. They were all quickly back on their bikes, although soon afterwards O'Grady spent some time riding alongside the race doctor's car, having nasty cuts to his knee and thigh attended to.

While the race leader recovered and made his way back towards the front of the bunch, a lone rider set off down the long straight roads. Unsung Aart Vierhouten of the Dutch sponsored Rabobank team rode clear with the best part of 130 kilometres still to race. Within four kilometres, the twenty-eight-year-old had a lead of just over a minute, although the thought of battling alone to stay clear of the field must have been playing on his mind.

But he was in luck; willing reinforcements soon arrived in the shape of Italy's Fabio Roscioli, a solo stage winner in Marseilles in 1993 and Thierry Gouvenou, a big-hearted French *rouleur* – a strong all-rounder from Normandy. The trio worked well, building a lead of four minutes on the *peloton*; but with so many teams still looking for stage wins, their hopes of holding off a concerted pursuit were slim.

Perhaps on the day before a time trial stage or a mountain stage, when the favourites wanted to take things easy and discouraged a high pace, they might have had a chance; but not on a day like this. They were finally picked up by the speeding field after 215 kilometres with only thirteen kilometres to go. Now it was down to the sprinters, particularly Cipollini, to make their inevitable bid for victory.

Châteauroux witnessed a classic Tour finale; a crazed, manic and acrobatic sprint that left Telekom's Zabel yet again frustrated and Cipo reborn as 'Super Mario', beaming his big, cheesy smile at the photographers and podium girls. Cipollini had survived another barging and pushing match, this time between himself and Zabel, to record his seventh stage success in six Tours. But behind him, his old team-mate Silvio Martinello, now with the rival Italian team Polti, lay stunned in the finishing straight.

Martinello had been sprinting alongside Cholet's stage winner Jeroen Blijlevens and Estonian Jaan Kirsipuu of the Casino team, when suddenly all of them had clattered to the ground. Kirsipuu and Mapei's Svorada, both of whom were said to be tussling shoulder to shoulder at the time of the crash, were relegated to joint last place for irregular sprinting. But Martinello had come off worst. Even so, the thirty-five-year-old had managed to walk across the line carrying his bike before climbing into an ambulance and heading to hospital. Later, X-rays revealed that he had fractured his pelvis.

In the video link-up between the *salle de presse* and the finish line, Cipollini was his usual ebullient self, joshing with reporters and flirting with the female interpreter. Characterised by the media as a Mediterranean playboy, but in fact more of a Tuscan wide-boy, Cipo had mellowed in recent seasons following his marriage and the birth of a daughter. But four stage wins and plenty of attention-grabbing stunts in the Giro d'Italia shortly before the Tour began had rekindled his high ambitions.

'This is just the start,' he said bullishly. 'The sun's coming back and my dream is to finish in Paris with the green points jersey on my back. If that doesn't happen,' he grinned, flushed with his own success, 'then I'll go out and buy one . . .'

In contrast, the race leader was in solemn mood. 'It was a hellish day, nervous and fast,' said O'Grady, his shorts and socks stained with blood. 'I fell hard but luckily I didn't break anything, so I was able to carry on. But I'm tired. I don't think I'll be able to hold on to the lead after the time trial.'

Back in the press room, Châteauroux's Stade de Ligue gymnasium, things were hotting up. The rain had blown over and towards the end of the afternoon, rays of warm sunshine came through the skylights over our heads, picking out dense clouds of cigarette smoke. Up on the bank of television screens, French TV continued to play down the Festina affair, although they could no longer ignore the climate of scandal surrounding the race.

On *Vélo Club*, Gérard Holtz conducted a live telephone interview with Miguel Rodriguez, proprietor of the Festina watch company. Contrary to reports indicating that he would pull out of sponsoring the team, the Spaniard pledged his whole-hearted support.

'You mustn't confuse the bad behaviour and bad practices of one person involved with the team with everybody else who's involved,' Rodriguez argued.

The Spanish businessman was also less than happy with remarks made by the French minister for sport, Marie-Georges Buffet.

'She's been behaving like she is the minister for justice,' grumbled Rodriguez. 'I've been asking myself if all this isn't a political manoeuvre on the part of the French, against my company and my team. Now we have to let justice do its work. Richard Virenque, Pascal Hervé and Laurent Brochard have given so much to cycling and to France in particular. We haven't heard much talk of that. It's not up to the media to judge and condemn these men. There's no question of pulling the team out of the Tour. I believe in the innocence and good conduct of Bruno Roussel, and of our riders. They have done nothing to be reproached for.'

Stage winner: Mario Cipollini, Italy (Saeco)
Overall race leader: Stuart O'Grady, Australia (GAN)
Points classification leader: Erik Zabel, Germany (Telekom)
Team classification leader: Casino
Mountains classification leader: Pascal Hervé, France (Festina)

Day 9   Stage 6

Friday 17 July
La Châtre–Brive-la-Gaillarde, 204.5 km

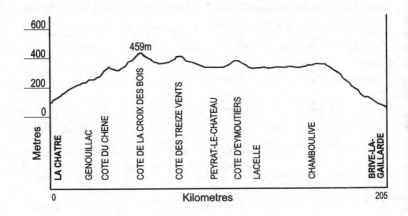

The Tour turned away from the plains of northern France and began its approach to the Pyrénées with stage six, an undulating route south, skirting the western reaches of the Massif Central before heading into the heart of the Corrèze region.

Silvio Martinello, after a night of painkillers taken to ease the agony of his fractured pelvis, was said to be preparing to start the stage; but in the end, the rumours came to nothing. By lunch-time, Cipollini's estranged former lead-out man was on his way back to Italy.

With the Festina team in limbo, the atmosphere of unreality which hung over the start village in La Châtre persisted. A quick glance at the morning's newspapers again brought home the widespread condemnation of the team for continuing to race. Marc Madiot, *directeur* of La Française des Jeux, had told the media that the team should withdraw their damaging presence from the race immediately, regardless of any legal niceties. It was an opinion that was steadily gaining ground as the scandal rumbled on.

And even as the team cars pulled up in the start village in the Place du Général de Gaulle, Roussel and Ryckaert were still in custody and were being transferred to Lille, in two unmarked cars, for interviews with Judge Keil. Although the authorities had yet to confirm it, Roussel, Ryckaert and the hapless Willy Voet were expected to meet on 24 July, under Judge Keil's jurisdiction. Yet the team stubbornly stayed in the race – for the time being. The Festina team cars were late arriving at the *départ* that morning, but just as rumours began to spread of their withdrawal, the fleet of Fiats appeared. Even so, Virenque and his team-mates were becoming increasingly isolated as the pressure on them to pull out of the Tour increased.

Out in the long convoy of press cars rolling down the undulating route towards Brive, there looked to be one notable absentee. Spanish daily *Marca*, Italian paper *La Gazzetta dello Sport*, Belgium's *La Dernière Heure* – they were all there, but where were the simple red stickers denoting *L'Equipe's* cars? Stung by hostile crowd reaction since the race had returned to French soil, France's top-selling national newspaper had removed its unmistakable logo from all of its cars working on the Tour. Before and during the World Cup, the paper had criticised Aimé Jacquet, the French football coach. Now with the Bobby Robson-like Jacquet considered a national hero, the paper was being made to pay for its strong opinions.

'We were getting a lot of abuse,' said one *L'Equipe* writer. 'People were spitting at the cars and throwing stones, yelling stuff like "*Allez Jacquet*" and "*Vive Jacquet*". Since we took the stickers off, everybody smiles and waves, because they don't know who we are,' he said.

On other matters, too, the crowd was intent on making its voice heard. Banners supporting Festina and in particular Virenque himself increased in number every day. Despite the clamour surrounding them, sanctioning Festina in any way was clearly going to be unpopular and was likely to make martyrs of the riders.

In the town of Seilhac, 172 kilometres down the route of stage six, the locals were already preparing to greet the Tour de France *peloton*. The influx of spectators and holiday-makers had been enough to double the small town's popula-tion. 'Yesterday, the camp site had twenty-two new entries,' said one local proudly, 'and nineteen of those had come to see the Tour. Everybody's here to see the race – everybody's here, standing in the street, to watch the Tour go by.'

By midday, the tables in front of the bars on the corner of the Place de la Poste were crowded with generations of local families, gathered to toast the passing of '*La Grande Boucle*'. Local policemen stood by the crowd barriers, idly chatting with spectators and extravagantly blowing their whistles every few minutes as accredited Tour cars roared through the square. The riders weren't due, even at the highest average speed, until six minutes to four; but by two in the afternoon the crowd was squeezed tight along the barriers. The most advanced commercial vehicles in the race convoy, the magazine and newspaper vendors, drove into the square in Seilhac blaring distorted music at ear-splitting volume. They lurched to a halt in front of the most densely-packed knots of spectators. Every now and then the loudspeaker on the roof would crackle into life, over the accordion or dance music, as the driver ran through yet another Tour special offer.

Just before three, the police escort for the Tour's most

infamous, loud and distinctive sight, the official *caravane publicitaire*, came into view. The slow-moving convoy, which precedes the riders along the route by about an hour, is an essential part of the Tour de France experience. Yet the commercial excesses of the Tour's inimitable *caravane publicitaire* are closer to the American culture of the Superbowl than to a European event steeped in tradition and folklore. The floats in the *caravane* give those in the exclusive Club Tour de France – the race's main sponsors, Coca-Cola, Fiat, Champion and Crédit Lyonnais – massive exposure, and also promote the Tour's *partenaires*, AGF, Nike, Sodexho, PMU, Compaq, Astra, Itineris and of course, Festina. That's without mentioning the other ten brands – Elf, France Telecom, Coeur du Lion, Locatel, Hansaplast, Lustucru, Maison du Café, Mavic, Michelin and United Savam – which provide everything from crowd barriers and presentation podiums to spare wheels and phone lines. They're all there in the wild and wacky *caravane*, all participating in the orgy of competitive leaflet and key-ring throwing, all feverishly promoting their products and services in some outlandish way or other.

Despite the arrival of global brands such as Nike, Coca-Cola and Fiat, the *caravane* remains intrinsically Francophile, a cartoonish and affectionate reflection of French culture. The *caravane* is the Tour's homage to the Citröen Dyane, to headlights that see round corners, to berets and Breton T-shirts, to baguettes and strings of onions; in a sport now dominated by the anodyne Euro-brasserie culture of sportswear, credit cards and mobile phones, the *caravane publicitaire* manages to be at the same time antiquated and contemporary.

As the *caravane* parped, jingled and littered its way through Seilhac, stage six was well underway an hour behind them on the *Route du Tour*. It was a warm day, but the sky was heavy and overcast and with the Tour's first significant rendezvous, the long time trial to Corrèze falling the following day, the stage provided a welcome opportunity for riders who specialised in long breakaways to try their luck.

One of those was Frenchman Cédric Vasseur, team-mate to Chris Boardman and Stuart O'Grady. Vasseur had sent French pulses racing in 1997 with an epic ninety-two mile solo breakaway and stage win that brought him the yellow jersey. That day, Vasseur's heroic escape had climaxed in La Châtre, starting point for this stage in the 1998 race. Twenty-seven years earlier, Cédric's father Alain had won a stage in the Tour, when riding in the same team as the Tour's current race director, Jean-Marie Leblanc. The Vasseur instinct for coincidence, heightened by the return to La Châtre, got the better of him once again and after eighty-three kilometres he was off on his own, attacking over the fourth category climb of the Côte des Treize Vents, just north of Bourganeuf.

'Maybe it was because of La Châtre that I was motivated,' said Vasseur later in the day. 'It seemed a good place to attack. I wanted to show that my win in 1997 wasn't a fluke – that I was still a good rider.'

Out of the bunch in pursuit as the road snaked uphill once more came Britain's sole remaining representative, Max Sciandri, followed by Spanish rider José Rodriguez of the Kelme team. They joined forces with the French rider and set about building a substantial lead on the field. Both Vasseur and Sciandri had serious interests in the yellow jersey, while Rodriguez, only a few seconds further in arrears in the overall standings, was hoping for a stage win. But the intricate tactical complexities of the Tour were to be their downfall.

Sciandri, who started the day one minute and thirty-nine seconds down on race leader O'Grady, steadily made up his deficit on the Australian as the trio moved clear of the idling bunch, at one point leading the field by more than six minutes. The Anglo-Italian picked up time bonuses too at the second and third intermediate sprints. It was enough to make him *maillot virtuel* – leader of the Tour on the road. Britain had sight of its second yellow jersey wearer inside the first week of the '98 Tour. But after 130 kilometres, with the break's lead still climbing, Cipollini's Saeco team were sent forward to pick up the pursuit with the TVM team. Kilometre by kilometre, as the gap closed, Max's dream began to fade.

By 180 kilometres, twenty-five kilometres from Brive, the gap had fallen to just two minutes and Max was getting anxious. So too was Vasseur, riled by instructions from *directeur sportif* Serge Beucherie in the GAN team car alongside, telling him not to co-operate with the break any more.

'I knew that the descent to the finish was tricky,' explained Beucherie afterwards, 'and that if they got there with a lead of a minute and a half, that the bunch wouldn't catch them. But equally, if they had that much time and Sciandri won the stage – which was likely – and took the winner's time bonus, he'd take the yellow jersey from O'Grady. We were on a razor's edge. In a moment, we could have lost the jersey and the stage, so I told Cédric not to co-operate any more.'

The free-spirited Vasseur wasn't happy with Beucherie's pessimism and, in response, made a futile do-or-die attack ten kilometres from the finish, as the bunch bore down on the three breakaways.

'I'm fed up that I flogged my guts out all day only to be told to stop riding twenty-five kilometres from the finish,' said a furious Vasseur afterwards. 'Maybe we should have another look at our tactics.'

Sciandri was equally disgusted. 'It was my kind of stage,' he said after the finish, 'and when we got away I really believed in it, really committed myself to it. Things were going well and then, with twenty kilometres to go, Vasseur stops working – I dunno why. It's just bad, y'know. You really believe in something and then suddenly, it's gone. I don't understand it, I don't understand those tactics.'

Just before the 190 kilometre mark, Sciandri, Vasseur and Rodriguez, ahead of the field after over 100 kilometres, slipped back into anonymity as the Tour *peloton* swallowed them up. Once again, it was down to the sprinters. The long line of riders snaked through the bends and roundabouts leading into Brive, with the Telekom and Saeco teams keeping the pace frenetically high.

Cipollini had banished his bad luck and was on a roll – and he had his clairvoyant with him. Diamantina was Cipo's muse. She had predicted his appalling crash at the Tour of Spain in 1994, when the bad blood between the 'Lion King' and his then team-mate Adriano Baffi boiled over at a stage finish in Salamanca. When he came round, after his clash with Baffi, Cipo's brother-in-law told him that a clairvoyant had called – before his crash – warning him of impending misfortune. So Cipo phoned her back and they began a strange friendship. She provided him with a lucky charm to wear around his neck. In return, he became a high profile client and invited her to watch him race. Diamantina had shown up at the season's big races, such as the Giro d'Italia and the Tour of Catalonia – Cipollini won four stages in each – and she was there as the 1998 Tour field sped into the centre of Brive, braked hard and turned sharp left for the 500 metre gallop to the far end of the Avenue Léo Lagrange.

Once out of the final corner, Cipollini was straight into Zabel's slipstream. 'He led me out again, just like he did yesterday,' said Cipo nonchalantly in the winner's press conference. 'It was a strange sprint for me.' Strange it may have been, but from the moment that the big Italian moved to Zabel's right and began pumping powerfully down the centre of the road, the outcome was inevitable.

The press tent was set up alongside the stadium in the adjacent Parc des Sports. Brive, winners of the European rugby championship in 1997, considers itself to be the home of the best in French rugby. It is also a hotbed of French amateur cycling, with more than 140 cycling clubs spread throughout the region. Foie gras, hazelnuts, truffles and wild mushrooms are all part of the Corrèze region's attractions and feature on the menus in Brive's finest restaurants.

But late in the evening, Brive-la-Gaillarde would be making headlines for something altogether more piquant.

By nine that night I'd checked into the Hôtel du Parc, twenty-five miles north of Brive in the sleepy village of Arnac Pompadour, dominated by a forbidding château. Half an hour later, the sun had dropped behind the pale stone of the château's high walls. Teenagers on mopeds buzzed noisily through the nearby square as I sat with several other hungry hacks on the terrace overlooking the hotel pool, studying an appetising menu.

It was then, just as the waitress arrived to take our order, that my phone rang. It was a contact back in Brive, still working in the *salle de presse*. Back in the Parc des Sports, they were expecting an announcement. Jean-Marie Leblanc was due to give an emergency press conference within the next few minutes. I rang the paper and told them that a big story was on its way. It was too late for the early editions, but if I could file before midnight, any news I had would make the pages. I folded my napkin, stood up from the table, went back to my room and switched on the laptop. Dinner would have to wait.

In Brive, the press tent began slowly filling up as those in nearby hotels, alerted by colleagues, left the dinner table and made their way back to the finish line. Journalists and camera crews filed back into the marquee, setting up their equipment in expectation. Leblanc had first promised to make a statement at nine o'clock and then, at the very latest, by ten. When he finally appeared, looking grey and tired, it was nearly eleven. Alongside him were the UCI's Martin Bruin and several leading figures from the race infrastructure, including the race sports director, Jean-François Pescheux, Philippe Sudres, the radio and TV liaison officer and John Lelangue of the Tour's *service presse*. Leblanc sat alongside Bruin. The others, in their Société du Tour de France blazers and ties, stood behind him.

'Gentlemen,' began Leblanc, 'it's ten to eleven. You have a difficult job to do. So do we sometimes, because the information we've received during the Tour on the Festina affair has come only from the press. There have been sometimes rumours, sometimes contradictions and interpretations.

'A week ago in Ireland, we said that we should wait for confirmed facts before taking a decision over the Festina affair,' continued Leblanc. 'Since then the Union Cycliste International has taken the decision to confiscate Bruno Roussel's licence. This evening at 6 p.m., we were informed of various further facts emanating from Lille.

'Bruno Roussel's lawyer,' said Leblanc, 'made a declaration during the day and I quote it in full:

' "Bruno Roussel has explained to the inquiry the conditions under which a co-ordinated supply of doping products was made available to the riders, organised by the team management, the doctors, the *soigneurs* and the riders. The aim was to maximise performance under strict medical control, in order to avoid the riders obtaining drugs for themselves in circumstances which might have been seriously damaging to their health, as may have been the case in the past." '

Leblanc paused before continuing.

'This statement seems terrible to us, because it reveals a classic case of institutionalised doping within a team. This is sufficient for us, the Société du Tour de France and the sporting authorities of the UCI to exclude the Festina team from the race. Sporting ethics and the Tour's morality are first and foremost among our general principles. That is why, after having been informed of this news we have decided to exclude the Festina team from the race.

'It was a difficult decision,' concluded Leblanc, 'because we thought a great deal about the riders; but it is a decision which seemed unavoidable. It is one which we hope will be salutary for the Tour and for cycling in general. It is also one which we hope puts an end to the pernicious climate which has overshadowed the Tour since the race started in Dublin. The Festina team have been informed of our decision.'

Back in my room in the hotel, I put down my mobile and started typing. I wrote that Festina, the world's top-ranked professional team, had been thrown off the Tour de France and that Roussel and Ryckaert had been charged with the 'importation, transport and use of doping products'. I wrote that the Tour had lost Richard Virenque, runner-up in 1997 and one of France's most emblematic sporting figures; that Alex Zulle, twice winner of the Tour of Spain and cycling's highest-paid rider, together with world road champion Laurent Brochard and Swiss star, Laurent Dufaux, fourth in the 1996 Tour, were also out.

I quoted Hein Verbruggen, the canny but non-committal president of the UCI, who was now telling journalists that the sport's governing body had been watching Festina's activities for several months.

'We had certain doubts about the Festina team,' Verbruggen had said. 'We think it's not only the rider who is responsible but also his environment. This affair has confirmed that it wasn't just the problem of one *soigneur*.'

When it was done, I went back to the dinner table and finally downed a glass of wine. It was only then that I realised how close we were to the Festina team hotel.

Shadows and fog settle on a river bank. In the dark night, the Tour's old ghosts come home, across the sombre plains and mountains, swirling in the trees overlooking the gothic towers of the Domaine de Castel Novel hotel. Such a strange eerie night, when it seemed anything could happen; that a line had been crossed, and that we could never go back now that the law of silence had been broken. Men with cameras snooped through the dark undergrowth, drunk on scandal, tramping clumsily through rhododendrons, hoping perhaps to stumble upon a hidden ice box or a discarded bin bag, stuffed with EPO and bloody syringes.

It wasn't a dream. I was there that surreal night, a bit player in the drama that poisoned the Tour. It was The Night That Changed Everything; the night that Virenque, Brochard, Dufaux, Zulle, Hervé, 'Stevo' – even good old Stevo – all of Festina's dream team – were thrown off the Tour de France.

It was almost midnight as we swung the Audi out of our hotel car-park and headed back towards Brive. In the shadows under the plane trees, a group of old men were playing *boules* by street-light. We followed the deserted road through the dark villages of Vignols and Objat, dropping down through woods to the banks of the river Loyre, where swathes of fog hung over the lush meadows.

Ten kilometres north of Brive, we turned right up a narrow lane, squinting through the fog as we searched for the lane leading into the grounds of the team's secluded country hotel. We came upon it suddenly and as we turned left between the old iron gates, a figure in a white shirt, with a shock of white hair, loomed menacingly through the murky darkness. It was Patrick Lefevere, manager of the Mapei–Bricobi team, watching bemusedly as the Tour's media circus descended on his team's hideaway hotel at one o'clock in the morning.

We parked half-way up the gravel drive, at the back of a long line of press cars. Through the trees and rhododendron bushes of the landscaped gardens loomed the floodlit gothic outline of the Domaine de Castel Novel hotel. A surreal scene awaited us. Thirty or forty journalists, watched uneasily by the hotel's stunned security guards, milled around the terrace. Some crouched over car bonnets, downloading stories from their laptops to their mobiles; others were simply mingling, canvassing opinion and gossip. Nearby, Tony Rominger, so sure of the misrepresentation of Gérard Gremion only two days earlier, stood chatting to one of the Festina personnel, a *soigneur* who had worked with the Swiss rider at the height of his own career.

Fresh from his stroll in the dark, Lefevere reappeared, happy to chat and explain his interpretation of events.

'We must think about organising a round table, with the UCI, the teams and the press to reflect on what measures should be taken,' said the Belgian, as journalists gathered around him in the darkness. 'But we have to wait until the end of the Tour and let the riders get on with the race. We must let justice do its work and not draw hasty conclusions.

But one thing is clear – nobody is above the law.'

A few yards from Lefevere, the Castel Novel's quiet annexe of rooms occupied by Virenque and his team-mates was shrouded in darkness and protected by an anxious cordon of *gendarmes* and hotel staff. Outside the low, barn-like building, Festina team vehicles huddled together. We stumbled through the bushes further down the sloping gardens and studied the line of balconies fronting each room. One or two had Festina racing jerseys hanging over the balustrades, drying in the warm night air. Other journalists passed close by us in the dark, whispering into their mobiles, describing the scene. Above the row of balconies, a line of roof lights indicated another floor of rooms. Most of them were in darkness, but a single light shone in the window of a top floor room.

We watched in silence, until shortly before two, as the moon stole from behind scudding clouds, the light was finally extinguished.

Stage winner: Mario Cipollini, Italy (Saeco)
Overall race leader: Stuart O'Grady, Australia (GAN)
Points classification leader: Erik Zabel, Germany (Telekom)
Team classification leader: Casino
Mountains classification leader: Pascal Hervé, France (Festina)

Day 10   Stage 7

Saturday 18 July
Meyrignac-l'Eglise–Corrèze, 58 km: individual time trial

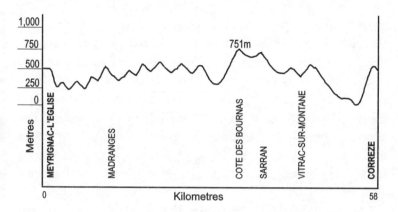

I woke with a start at half-past seven and then remembered the night before: the fog on the river, the dark, towering hotel, the sense of unreality. We were out of the Hôtel du Parc by nine, driving through the upland lanes of Corrèze to the tiny village of Meyrignac-l'Eglise, tucked away somewhere in the green Limousin countryside between Limoges and Brive. Hosting the start of a Tour time trial was the biggest thing ever to happen to little Meyrignac, with its population of just fifty-three. The fortified village, perched on a wooded promontory, was the smallest town ever to host the Tour and had set up a website on the Internet only two days earlier to celebrate its coup.

The presence of the Tour in this rural backwater had a lot to do with Jacques Chirac's wife, who was president of the Corrèze Tour de France 1998 Association and also sat on the departmental council for the region. On this sunny, calm day,

Mme Chirac and her husband were both expected to turn out to watch the race – even after a week of scandal that had threatened to overshadow the continuing celebration of France's World Cup success.

Historically, the Tour's time trials have always revealed the likely contenders for the final yellow jersey in Paris. All the Tour's legendary champions – Fausto Coppi, Jacques Anquetil, Eddy Merckx, Bernard Hinault, Greg Lemond and Miguel Indurain – have been masters of the *contre-la-montre*. The time trial is a lone test of strength and determination; a test from point A to point B against the clock, rather than against other riders. It's aptly known as the race of truth. In the race of truth, there is no hiding behind the strength of others, no hanging on to the coat-tails of the pack.

In 1996 and 1997, Jan Ullrich had demonstrated his form against the clock, winning a time trial in each of those years. Even so, after his difficult winter, the Tour champion came to sleepy Meyrignac needing a decisive victory to finally silence those who doubted him.

'I still haven't fully tested my condition in this race,' said Ullrich the night before, 'so I don't know how things'll go. I'll try to take the jersey but some of the others, Olano and Jalabert particularly, look strong.'

The route, a technical and twisting fifty-eight kilometre loop through the lanes to Corrèze, demanded far more than pure speed. Most of the favourites such as Ullrich, Riis, Olano and Jalabert had already taken advantage of a gap in their spring schedule to train on the route, months before the Tour began. They would have taken mental notes of the climbs, the descents and the tight bends. Some of them would have tried different bikes, different gearing, maybe different tyres and even taken the time to closely study the vagaries of the road surface. It wasn't pernickety professionalism. In the time trial, every second counted.

In 1989, the Tour had developed into a gripping battle between American Greg Lemond and French rider Laurent Fignon. That year, the race finished with a time trial stage climaxing on the Champs-Elysées. Fignon went into that final time trial seemingly assured of victory. But the Parisian underestimated Lemond's aerodynamic nous, not to mention his sheer speed. After three weeks and 3,285 kilometres, Fignon lost the Tour by a mere eight seconds. The French-man had animated the race throughout, riding with panache and aggression in the toughest stages, yet Lemond had finally outwitted him. In front of his home crowd, the devastated Fignon stood on the runner-up step on the Champs-Elysées podium and wept.

Inching our way by car through the crowds milling around the leafy lanes surrounding Meyrignac, we saw a smiling Max Sciandri, apparently recovered from his disappointment of the previous afternoon. Even though it was still only mid-morning, the heat of the day had become stifling. We turned into the car-park alongside the *village départ* and headed towards a distant tree, casting a sharp shadow on the bleached ground. We were just walking away from our shady parking spot, when a puffing steward from the *comité locale* jogged over and insisted that we park in line with the other press cars, baking in the sun nearby. I climbed reluctantly back into the driver's seat and parked in the long row of saloons. As we strolled through the heat towards the tented village, I looked back. The same steward was waving one of the white *L'Equipe* Fiats into place under the shady tree.

As soon as we arrived in the start village, it was clear that there was trouble. At the far end, in the enclosure reserved for the Tour organisation and its officials, another media scrum was developing. Through the crowd, I could make out Jean-Marie Leblanc in intense conversation with Joel Chabiron, the Festina team's logistics and public relations manager. Even though we couldn't hear their conversation, Leblanc's body language, despite Chabiron's insistent stance, was clear enough: Festina were out of the Tour – there was to be no last minute reprieve. After a few moments, Chabiron turned abruptly on his heel and stormed off, pursued by a stumbling posse of photographers. Meanwhile, the wan Leblanc shrugged and took refuge in the most private area of the Société du Tour's enclosure.

Back at the Castel Novel, the Festina team were trying to come to terms with the previous night's dramatic events. Virenque and his team-mates had emerged into the bright sunlight at seven-thirty. As they made their way into the old château's grand dining-rooms, the Frenchman, cursing photographers who got in his way, had a few brief words with the press.

'They're trying to put this all on us, to make us go so that it takes the blame away from the Tour de France,' he said in a truculent aside to French journalists.

The team's legal representative, Mme Lavelot, was also taking a defiant stance.

'There's no question of quitting the race,' said Lavelot. 'If someone tries to stop us riding the time trial, we'll call bailiffs. The affair that has provoked all this has not yet been to court, and under French law nobody has the right to throw us off the race.'

Down at the Festina team bus, the team mechanics were busy preparing time trial machines for the riders, as they would on any other day. Just before nine, soon after Virenque and the rest of the team had demanded to speak to Jean-Marie Leblanc, a helicopter appeared over the château and settled down nearby. Out stepped UCI judge Bruin and race director Jean-François Pescheux. In a brief conversation with the pair, Lavelot, speaking on behalf of the riders, requested a legal document signifying the race organisation's decision. Watching the scene was Mapei *directeur* Patrick Lefevere.

'This is the best hotel I've stayed in during the sixteen years I've been on the Tour and I didn't sleep a wink,' he said, an ironic smile on his face.

The big Belgian looked on as Virenque, pursued by hordes of journalists, appeared on the hotel terrace and made his way down to the Festina team cars.

'This is unbearable,' said Lefevere as he watched Virenque go by. 'We're still two weeks from the end of the Tour and I'm already wishing we were in Paris. I'm sorry for whoever wins the Tour this year – his name will be less important than the scandal.'

Moments later, Miguel Moreno, the Festina team's third *directeur sportif*, fresh from his flight from Toledo in Spain, took matters into his own hands.

'Put the bikes on the cars,' he snapped at the mechanics. 'The first rider to start is Meier, so we have to be there at ten-thirty. We're going to ride,' insisted Moreno. 'I want Leblanc to tell me to my face that we've been thrown off the Tour. Has he thought of all the careers and lives that could be broken by this decision?'

Michel Gros, Festina's remaining French *directeur* following Roussel's arrest, was equally shocked.

'Emotionally and physically, we're at our limit,' said Gros. 'Last night we only slept a couple of hours, if that. Some of the guys didn't sleep at all.'

More rumours began to circulate. The first, that the race

organisation would allow them to ride the time trial as a valedictory gesture to their loyal fans, was quickly scotched. The second, that Festina's legal team were planning to sue the Société du Tour de France if they prevented the team from starting, was soon equally discredited.

As the morning wore on, it became clear that the riders' resolve to defy the Tour's unprecedented ruling was steadily weakening. Faced with the prospect of arriving at the start line only to have their way barred by *gendarmes* and Tour security guards, their early morning bravado slowly evaporated. Armin Meier, the team's twenty-eight-year-old Swiss rider, was the first to throw in the towel, saying that he was no longer psychologically capable of racing for fifty-eight kilometres. Then at one o'clock, with the time trial long since underway, the riders were finally on the move, driving off from the Castel Novel hotel in a convoy of team cars.

'Jean-Marie Leblanc promised them official notification of the decision, but it still hasn't arrived,' said ex-professional Pello Ruiz Cabestany. 'So they're going to look for him.'

So four Festina team cars joined the slow-moving stream of camping cars and caravans crawling up the N89 towards the time trial stage finish. They pulled off the main road at Gare de Corrèze, just a stone's throw from the finish line, in an area crowded with snack bars and spectators. In front of a bemused crowd of onlookers, Virenque led his team-mates into the cramped confines of the nearby Chez Gillou *bar-tabac*. Nobody, least of all the bar owner, was expecting to see France's most popular and now controversial cyclist walk in; soon, a large crowd of spectators, mingling with journalists and photographers, had squeezed into the small room. Virenque, Brochard, Hervé and the others sought further refuge, moving into a tiny, closed-up room in the back of the building. At two o'clock, they were joined by Jean-Marie Leblanc.

After about ten minutes, a chastened-looking Leblanc emerged and spoke briefly to the press.

'It was only natural,' said Leblanc, 'that instead of sending the communiqué promised them, the director of the Tour de France would come to say goodbye one by one to Virenque, Dufaux, Brochard and all their team-mates. It was very moving. I'm fully aware of the distressing nature of this but equally aware of the moral arguments involved too.'

As Leblanc walked back through the crowds to his red race director's Fiat, Virenque, his voice trembling, was making one final statement to the media.

'We wanted to see the boss of the Tour,' Festina's leader explained. 'When such a situation arises, it's the boss who must explain himself. Under pressure from all sides, and in the interests of cycling and for the good name of the Tour de France, we have taken the decision – which I personally have found very difficult – to withdraw from the race.

'This is tough,' he went on, 'above all, on the day before a time trial for which I was feeling really motivated. I wonder how the race will manage without us, without the Festina team who've given so much to the Tour in the last few years. But,' said Virenque, his voice cracking, 'we'll be back next year. We have a lot of things to prove.'

With those final words, the tears came. As camera shutters clicked around the tiny room, the Frenchman fell into the arms of his team-mates. Finally, wiping his eyes, he got to his feet and headed out into the bright sunlight and the waiting crowds. Yet the tears and the hugs, the appreciative crowds and the jostling photographers, all gave the scenario the whiff of a stage-managed exit and many questions remained unanswered. Why had Virenque and the rest of the team not given a statement in the press room, away from the public eye; or, as they had decided not to race, at their hotel? Why here, so close to the crowds surrounding the finish line area, yet far enough from the Tour organisation's offices in the race *permanence*, to make Leblanc come to them? Was it because Virenque's tearful final walk back to his team car, through crowds of supportive and outraged fans, guaranteed martyr status? They'd made Leblanc come to them and then left him, among the hostile crowds, watching anxiously as the Festina cars, still pursued by photographers, finally disappeared into the heat of the afternoon.

Even as Virenque was climbing back into his team car, Jan Ullrich was readying himself for his biggest moment since winning the 1997 Tour – the fifty-eight kilometre race of truth.

Earlier in the day, we'd driven over the twisting course behind Marcelino Garcia, a promising young Spanish rider with Laurent Jalabert's ONCE team. Garcia had won the 'mini' Tour de France, the short stage race Criterium International, in March 1997. Since then there had been other less significant successes, but at twenty-seven, Garcia still had time to make his mark. We followed him as he sped away from the start house out of the saddle, battling his bike up hill and down dale, tackling the series of rises and descents on a course that had only eight flat kilometres.

In the first few kilometres, Garcia swooped into the descents, taking the quickest possible line through each bend. He stamped powerfully on the pedals, attacking each little climb, and rode with fluency and confidence on the few flat sections. Then, little by little as the stage wore on, his rhythm began to fade as the effort of maintaining an average speed of forty kilometres per hour on such tortuous and undulating roads took its toll.

An hour went past and Garcia's tempo stuttered still further. His head dropped between his shoulders as he swayed up each climb and then flung himself wearily down the descent on the far side of each short rise. Under normal circumstances the final climb, a three kilometre drag from Corrèze town up to the finish line, would have held few fears for most of the Tour *peloton*. But now, on this hot afternoon, after fifty-four kilometres of unrelentingly difficult solo racing, the short hill up to Gare de Corrèze became something of a torture rack.

Garcia wasn't the first rider that day to feel the pain on that last climb. Lassitude seeped into his lean frame as he fought to maintain his speed, to sustain a pace which had posed him no problems earlier in his ride. Exhausted, he hauled himself over the crest of the final rise and into the final kilometre of his race of truth. As he crossed the line, his angular back and shoulders shadowed by the glaring sunlight in his sweat-soaked jersey, we swung off into the *salle de presse* diversion and pulled up alongside the press tent.

Garcia's ride was over by lunch-time, while tucked away in the Corrèze countryside, Ullrich was still building up to his own mid-afternoon start time. The German had woken at seven-fifteen, breakfasted quietly in his hotel and then headed off to ride over the course one last time, an hour or so before the stage actually began. While Garcia was struggling up that final hill, Ullrich was resting in a shady country house close to Corrèze that had been taken over by Telekom for the day.

At twenty-six minutes past three, the wait was finally over. The defending Tour champion rolled down the start ramp and headed off east, down the D26 towards the village of St Augustin. The next hour and a quarter would be crucial to Ullrich's Tour defence. Any signs of weakness after his long winter of discontent would encourage his rivals, but a show of strength would silence those who still doubted his fitness.

At the first time check at Madranges, after thirteen rolling kilometres, Ullrich was already twelve seconds ahead of the next-best ride, that of American revelation Tyler Hamilton. When he powered to the top of the stage's only classified climb, the Côte de Bournas, in front of an unruly pro-Festina crowd, he'd stretched his lead over Hamilton to thirty-six seconds. But thirteen kilometres from the Gare de Corrèze finish, Ullrich began to show signs of flagging. His lead over the American, rather than growing further, had slightly diminished and was now only thirty-five seconds. In the sweltering press tent, we studied the TV screens, wondering if the red-haired champion had over-estimated his own strength. But the steady descent towards that final heavy climb up to the closing kilometre allowed him to recover a little. He picked up his pace and opened up the gap again to beat Hamilton by a minute and ten seconds.

'I said I'd be ready,' asserted the defiant Ullrich after picking up his first leader's jersey of the year. 'I've based my year on this race. I know that some people thought I couldn't do it because of the way my season started, but I always knew that I'd get here. The road surface wasn't very good but I didn't make any mistakes in the bends and didn't have any punctures. The choice of bike was important but it was my legs that made the difference.

'Now I've got the lead, but that doesn't mean that the Tour is already won. We're still a very long way from Paris. Four minutes on Pantani,' he said tellingly, 'is nothing in the mountains.'

Yet it wasn't the crushing display of superiority that might have been expected and it lacked the authority of Ullrich's time trial wins in 1996 and 1997. Three riders, two of them now rightly considered strong contenders for victory, had finished within a minute and a half of Ullrich's pace. Just behind Hamilton came the effusive Bobby J, proving that his strong ride in the Dublin prologue had definitely not been a fluke. His fearless, swaggering confidence and eager, hard-working team gave Ullrich cause for concern. Then there was Jalabert, one minute and twenty-four seconds down to his German rival and yet again given fresh hope of a successful Tour challenge. Virenque was long gone, thought the French, but now perhaps 'Jaja' could save their honour.

But Jaja didn't want the pressure. 'The Tour started properly today,' he shrugged, in his non-committal way. 'I'm happy with my ride – it was nothing dramatic. Now I'll have to try to resist attacks in the mountains.'

Abraham Olano, though, could only view sixth place as a failure. 'I was hoping to do better. It's a lot of time to lose to Ullrich, but not so much to my other rivals,' conceded the Basque.

Olano's time looked poorer still when compared to that of Pantani, who was roundly dismissed as a poor time triallist. The shaven headed *Pirata* had lost only four minutes and twenty-one seconds to the champion, but significantly was little more than three minutes behind the Spaniard.

'I didn't ride full tilt,' the Italian explained, 'because I didn't want to pay for my efforts later on. But my form's getting better, day by day.'

There were other big losers. Riis's limitations were cruelly brought home as the Dane lost the best part of four minutes to his young team-mate. Effectively, the 1996 champion was transformed from contender to has-been after his disappointing 'race of truth'.

And Marcelino Garcia? His strenuous efforts out in the

123

wooded hills of Corrèze brought him 119th place on the stage, seven minutes and forty-three seconds behind Jan Ullrich, the 1998 Tour's new *maillot jaune*.

Stage winner: Jan Ullrich, Germany (Telekom)
Overall race leader: Jan Ullrich, Germany (Telekom)
Points classification leader: Erik Zabel, Germany (Telekom)
Team classification leader: Telekom
Mountains classification leader: Stefano Zanini (Mapei–Bricobi)

Overall standings of favourites after one week:
1. Jan Ullrich, Germany (Deutsche Telekom) 1,303.7 kilometres in 31 hrs, 24 mins 37 secs
3. Bobby Julich, USA (Cofidis) at 1 min 18 secs
4. Laurent Jalabert, France (ONCE) at 1 min 24 secs
9. Abraham Olano, Spain (Banesto) at 2 mins 12 secs
20. Bjarne Riis, Denmark (Deutsche Telekom) at 3 mins 51 secs
43. Marco Pantani, Italy (Mercatone Uno) at 5 mins 4 secs

(Festina's Alex Zulle and Richard Virenque excluded from the race prior to stage seven.)

PART THREE

Day 11   Stage 8

Sunday 19 July
Brive-la-Gaillarde–Montauban, 190.5 km

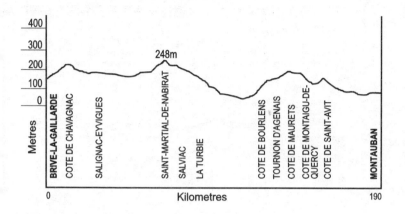

Even with their beloved Richard Virenque expelled from the race and his Festina *confrères*, including French favourites Laurent Brochard and Pascal Hervé, heading back home, the French crowds were out in force for the first '*après-scandale*' day of the 1998 Tour. Defending champion Jan Ullrich was comfortably ensconced in the yellow jersey and, if Magnus Backstedt was to be believed, was now the favourite to hold on to the race leadership until the bunch pedalled wearily into Paris. But in so many ways, it was a day like no other. The Tour had lost Virenque, Zulle and Dufaux, all favourites for a top three finish; now, somehow it had to cope with life without three of its outstanding stars: with life after Festina.

The summer heat of central France had settled on the Tour. We drove into Brive, parked up close to the start village and stepped out into the warm heavy air under unbroken blue skies. The plane trees lining Brive's Avenue de Paris offered little shade as the cicadas, the first sign of the Tour's proximity to the south and the Mediterranean, buzzed noisily in the shadows.

After the first week's shadow boxing and in the aftermath of the tricky time trial in Corrèze, the overall classification was beginning to shape up. Ullrich stood at the top of the heap, although with the temperatures rising, there were doubts over how hard his Telekom team would work in the stages before the mountains to protect his lead, with two weeks of the race still remaining. Most expected the German to let the leader's jersey slip away, providing it didn't fall into the hands of one of his main rivals, confident in his ability to make up time in the Alps and in the final time trial on the last Saturday of the race.

Hamburger, in second place overall and Casino's best-placed rider, was a strong climber but was already in unknown territory. If he kept his nerve he could become a force in the mountains but the pressure, especially from the Danish media, was building.

Even so, he was in feisty mood. 'My chances for a top three finish are the best they've ever been,' he told Danish TV. 'I'm in the form of my life.'

It was Julich – the irrepressible Bobby J – who posed the greatest threat to the defending champion. Tucked comfortably in third place, the American from the surprisingly strong Cofidis team was already dreaming of the *maillot jaune* as he sat in the shade in Brive's Place du 14 Juillet.

'If Ullrich doesn't want to hang on to the jersey, maybe he can give it to us,' he grinned, as he chatted to a film crew from ABC Sports.

A few minutes later, he expanded on his positive thinking to a group of English-speaking journalists.

'Wearing the yellow jersey would mean the world to me,' Bobby said flamboyantly. 'It's the Holy Grail of cycling. Not too many people drink from that cup – just to take a sip would mean the world to me . . .'

Had he thought about the possibility of winning the Tour?

'I've thought about finishing in the top five. That's a real goal for me. But maybe I could finish on the podium – why not?'

A few yards away, Stuart O'Grady, who'd fought so hard to snatch his time in the yellow jersey earlier in the race, was adjusting to normal life after three days leading the Tour.

'Yup,' he smiled, wryly. 'It's back to normal life in the bunch again. I won't be getting the special treatment you get when you're wearing the yellow jersey and leading the Tour de France. My family's been up partying every night this week watching the race on TV. I know there's been quite a fuss at home. From now on, I'll be working for Vasseur. He's our main man now. I'm not as tired as I was, so I'll be looking out for him.'

Over at the Telekom cars, the daunting presence of Bjarne Riis and Erik Zabel was pulling the crowds. Riis stood fiddling with his cap and sunglasses and steadfastly cold-shouldering those around him. Zabel, meanwhile, pushed his way grumpily through the journalists and autograph hunters desperate for a moment of his time, before slumping sulkily in the passenger seat of a team car. Zabel, always happy when winning, had been in a mood since the first French stage start, when he'd cold-shouldered the media, perhaps understandably preferring to sit impassively behind his shades, holding hands with his wife. But his moody display in Brive didn't go unnoticed. Riis, ever the big brother to the team's younger riders, leaned in, grasping Zabel's shoulder and offering words of encouragement. Whatever the reason behind the sprinter's pique, the tall Dane's consoling words seemed to ease his team-mate's black mood.

I wandered on, working my way through the hacks and snappers, the groupies and the hangers-on hovering claustrophobically around the team cars. Over the heads of the crowd, I caught sight of the unmistakable Magnus Backstedt and made my way towards him. But I checked and stopped when I saw him reach his long arms over the crowd barrier to hug an older, even taller man standing on the other side. The big Swede was saying a poignant goodbye to his father who'd been travelling with the Tour, supporting his son for a few days. Now he was going back to Sweden. For a moment, the brush with the outside world, with home and family left him uncharacteristically subdued. We stood chatting in the heat of the midday sun, his morale wobbling as he spoke.

'I crashed two days ago,' he said wearily, 'and I'm suffering from bad tendinitis in my left knee.'

Flummoxed by his falling spirits, I looked for reasons to be cheerful, pointing to the warm weather, the girls in bikinis, the fact that the nerve-wracking sprinters stages were now almost over.

'Yeah, but we've got the mountains to look forward to now,' Magnus said gloomily. 'I just hope it's a quiet day today, so I can sit in the bunch and recover from the time trial.' Out on the road, the sky fused with the land, shimmering in the heat haze. It was one of those archetypal Tour days, a Sunday afternoon in the French heartlands of the Lot: families picnicking at the roadside, the inevitable girls in bikinis waving at the caravan and, later, the riders rolling past, their skin turning brown in the glare. The *peloton* crossed the Dordogne, climbing the endless succession of short rises as the route took them into the undulating farmlands of the Garonne.

It was a special day for one rider – Laurent Roux of the Dutch TVM team. Stage eight passed right through Lollo's home territory. It made him the *regionale* for the day as the race came within two kilometres of his parents' home west of Cahors. Surprisingly for a Frenchman, Roux had spurned the attentions of French sponsors, opting to ride for TVM's multinational band of riders gathered from across Europe. And his 1997 results had vindicated that choice. It had been a good year for the twenty-five-year-old – he'd won the Tour de l'Avenir and the Classique des Alpes, both significant wins on his climb up the professional scene's slippery slope. The l'Avenir – thought of as a junior Tour de France for younger, inexperienced pros – was a prestigious success. Now after several years of promise in the lower ranks, he was ready to move up into the big league.

Most importantly, this hot, wearying afternoon, he was the local boy, so as is the Tour's tradition, he slipped just a few moments ahead of the field to stop at his family's roadside picnic at Frayssinet. He kissed his wife Isabelle and fifteen-month-old son Corentin, hugged his mum Thérèse and, watched by his hundred-year-old grandmother, waved cheerily to the massed ranks of the Laurent Roux Supporters Club, swaying drunkenly under shady branches on the opposite side of the road. An accordion player, backed by a raucous band made up of an eclectic combination of folksy and beatnik type locals, competed with a crazed bandana-wearing saxophonist on a trailer stage nearby.

We'd stopped at the Roux family's *sauvage* barbecue-picnic an hour or so earlier on our way to the press room, knocking back a glass of red wine and chewing on a bloody steak sandwich as we did so. The family and supporters club had been there since ten in the morning, manning the '*halte Laurent Roux*', offering those who paused on their way to the finish foie gras, Rocamadour cheese and wine from Cahors. They hadn't cared who we were or where we came from – in

131

the heat of that long afternoon, they simply wanted to celebrate their son's part in the Tour's unchanging tradition.

'I only stopped for a moment but it was magical,' said an overcome Roux after the stage finish. 'To see my fans, to race on the roads I've always trained on – even if I didn't feel that strong today, it was still too much.'

But not everybody in the crowd was feeling so cheery. We hadn't gone far down the race route when the first angry and disapproving banners appeared in support of the expelled Festina team.

'*One team thrown out – what should we do with the 20 others, all doped up?*' said one, proving that Virenque and his team-mates had, almost inevitably, achieved martyr status.

'*Festina, victims of the system – we're with you,*' said the next hastily knocked-up placard, a few kilometres further on down the road. '*Give us back our Festina,*' implored another.

Support for Festina and Virenque, its emotionally volatile leader, was everywhere, in spite of the continuing bad press that the scandal was attracting. Despite the team's expulsion, Festina's cars in the *caravane publicitaire* were still sure to stay in the convoy. Their outlandish publicity vehicles, topped off with giant sports watches, were getting huge cheers as they drove through towns on the stage route. But then the Spanish watch company and the Société du Tour de France were still inextricably linked. Festina had an agreement said to be worth about five million francs a year to provide the Tour's timing system until 2003.

In *Aujourd'hui*, Patrice Bouillon, one of the doctors in the Tour's own *service medical* gave a surprisingly frank interview in which he attacked professional cycling's 'great hypocrisy'.

'For the health of the riders,' argued Bouillon, 'it's less damaging if the doping comes through doctors than through anybody else, but ethically, it's still indefensible.'

And Jean-Marie Leblanc's aside to reporters from *L'Equipe* after the time trial in Corrèze had come back to haunt him.

'I'm no longer sure that the Festina riders are the only ones who deserved to be thrown off the Tour,' Leblanc admitted with understatement, 'so I'm a little troubled.'

Bernard Kouchner, the French government's secretary of state for health, was far more frank in his appraisal of the situation.

'We're all accomplices in this great hypocrisy, because everybody knows that doping reigns on the Tour de France,' said Kouchner. 'Taking into account the spectacle demanded, the financial stakes – how could it be otherwise? Festina are certainly not the only team under suspicion.'

Kouchner's words cut through the still, hot air of the Dordogne and echoed ominously across the pastoral landscape.

Meanwhile, Jacky 'Dudu' Durand was at it yet again. Like a hyperactive child in a toy shop, the bandana-wearing Dudu hadn't been able to resist the chance to try his luck one more time. The Casino rider led a breakaway move after seventy-six kilometres taking with him three others, including Laurent Desbiens of the Cofidis team, a stage winner by default in the 1997 Tour.

The previous year, Desbiens had been in a breakaway with TVM's bouffant blond Russian, Sergei Outschakov. The pair had sprinted into the Perpignan stage finish with Out-schakov first to cross the line, but with a hint of an irregularity to his otherwise straightforward sprint. The over-zealous UCI judges had ruled the Russian's sprint illegal and handed the stage win to a stunned Desbiens. As the Frenchman climbed on to the winner's podium to accept his bouquet and kiss the pretty girls, an enraged Outschakov had to be restrained from accosting Tour race director Leblanc. This time though, Desbiens was after a bigger prize. He was the best placed overall of the escapees and knew full well that with the Pyrénées drawing closer, now was his chance to snatch the race lead from recuperating race leader Ullrich.

A group of fourteen riders slipped away from the field in pursuit of the leading quartet, while race leader Ullrich and his Telekom team showed barely any interest in picking up the pursuit. But why should they? None of the riders ahead of them would perform well in the mountains and all of the German champion's most dangerous rivals – Julich, Jalabert, Pantani and Olano – were clustered around him. Telekom were quite happy to let 'Dudu' and Desbiens pull away into the shimmering light, to allow them to fry slowly in the still, deadening heat of the afternoon.

Between unmoving avenues of plane trees and inert fields of sunflowers the break ploughed on, Desbiens now joined by his hard-working team-mate Philippe Gaumont, and tireless Italian national champion Andrea Tafi. The break had grown to seven riders in total and as they built a lead of nine minutes on the main field, Desbiens became *maillot virtuel* – leader on the road. The question now was whether Telekom would chase to protect Ullrich's jersey.

At the front of the break Durand worked tirelessly, with Tafi and Gaumont his willing accomplices. As they got closer to Montauban, the short hills multiplied and with Gaumont's strength waning, Tafi, the crown cut out of his racing cap to cool his head, sought to take advantage, attacking intermittently in an effort to break up the group. Lotto's Joona Laukka, the Tour's only Finnish competitor, made a do-or-die move in the final five kilometres only to be chased down by Tafi, who then quickly reeled in another desperate move by his compatriot, Eddy Mazzoleni of Mario Cipollini's Saeco team.

It all played perfectly into Dudu's hands. When the time came and Tafi slid ahead of the others in the final 300 metres to the finish line in the *Avenue du 10ème Dragon* on the banks of the Tarn river, Durand was ready. The Italian champion, so deserving of victory after his efforts to bring back those late attacks, faded in the closing metres as Dudu, with an expert's cunning, stole past Tafi's shoulder to take the third Tour stage win of his career and the first for the home nation in the '98 Tour.

While the French media broke into joyful hysteria, the breathless Desbiens studied the clock. He'd started the day four minutes and thirty seconds behind Ullrich – now he had to sit and wait. A little under eight minutes later, a discontented-looking Erik Zabel sprinted home at the head of the main field containing Ullrich and all the other favourites, as on the presentation podium Desbiens pulled on the first *maillot jaune* of his career.

It was thirty-seven degrees outside in the dusty streets of Montauban but it was even hotter in the *salle de presse*. We huddled in groups, sitting as close to the propped-open fire doors of the Salle des Fêtes as possible. Every few minutes, a faint breeze wafted through the doors moving the thick, smoky air a little and temporarily drying the film of sweat on our faces. Up on the TV screens Desbiens appeared, smiling through a hug and embrace from 'Qui-Qui' – Bernard Quilfen, his Cofidis *directeur sportif* – and a hearty slap on the back from 'Dudu' himself.

'This is a much better feeling than in Perpignan last year,' admitted Desbiens. 'Because deep inside, I've always regretted winning a stage just because Outschakov was disqualified. At least with this yellow jersey, it's not thanks to the UCI commissaires that I'm wearing it.'

But there was a timely twist to Desbiens' win. Two years earlier he had tested positive for nandrolone, an anabolic steroid, after winning the Vendée International Classic.

'Once that was shown to be the fault of someone I took to be a friend, the best way to prove that I wasn't a cheat was to come back and win races,' Desbiens said.

Sadly, even though the French press battled to turn Durand's victory and Desbiens' race leadership into a glory day for French cycling, their successes only served to highlight the scent of corruption hanging over the Tour. Desbiens wasn't the only rider in the day's breakaway to have suffered at the hands of supposedly unscrupulous advisers. His loyal and hard-working team-mate Gaumont had also tested positive in recent seasons, escaping with a brief ban, while 'Dudu' himself, in spite of his cheeky chappie demeanour, had come close to the brink, escaping the threat of a long ban for steroid abuse on little more than a legal technicality.

But, whatever else happened, the mild-mannered Desbiens knew that with the Pyrénées just forty-eight hours away, his days in the *maillot jaune* were numbered.

'I am not a climber and I'm going to suffer in the Pyrénées,' he said. 'We've ridden the climb to Plateau de Beille a few times. *Bouf!* What a finish that's going to be!'

Stage winner: Jacky Durand, France (Casino)
Overall race leader: Laurent Desbiens, France (Cofidis)
Points classification leader: Erik Zabel, Germany (Deutsche Telekom)
Team classification leader: Cofidis
Mountains classification leader: Stefano Zanini, Italy (Mapei–Bricobi)

Day 12   Stage 9

Monday 20 July
Montauban–Pau, 210 km

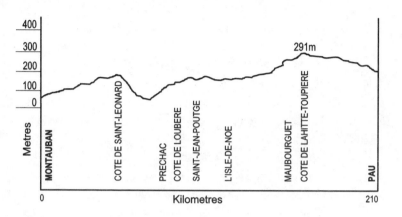

In my beige, burgundy and chrome hotel bedroom on the Toulouse *peripherique*, I tossed and turned through the dawn, struggling to catch another hour or two of rest before it was time to get up and get going. But with the window open, it was too noisy to sleep as heavy trucks trundled past over a nearby flyover, their air-brakes hissing in the still air. And with the window closed, it was so hot and claustrophobic in my Gerry Anderson-style modular room that I fought for breath, growing tense as the sweat pooled on my brow. In the end I gave up, switched on the TV and then shuffled blearily under a lukewarm shower, desperately trying to wake myself up.

An hour later we drove south from Toulouse, skipping the stage start in Montauban and jumping straight on to the A64 *autoroute* heading west through the Garonne and down to the foothills of the Pyrénées. The sun glinted off the high snow-fields of the Pic du Midi to our left as we sped on past St

137

Gaudens and Tarbes towards Pau, gateway to the mountainous uplands between France and Spain. Somewhere in
among the distant knot of peaks and valleys were the Col
d'Aubisque, the Col du Tourmalet, the Col d'Aspin and the
Col de Peyresourde, all on the route of the following day's
first mountain stage to Luchon. Before that, though, the
riders had one more day in the flatlands, one more day
through the sunflower fields and vineyards, one more day
frying slowly in the stifling heat.

By now the crowd's rage against the expulsion of Virenque
and the Festina team was becoming even more pronounced.
The previous evening, Belgian race commissaire Marc
Vandevyvere had told journalists from *Het Volk* newspaper
that he'd never been so scared in his life.

'The crowd was yelling abuse and when I put my head
through the sun-roof, I thought that they were going to start
throwing things,' he said. 'I understand people being disappointed at losing the Festina team, but I hope by the time we
reach the Pyrénées, that reason prevails.'

Not everyone was missing Virenque, though. GAN's
victory-starved sprinter Frédéric Moncassin, from nearby
Toulouse, spoke for many riders in the *peloton* when he sav-
agely attacked Virenque in French regional paper *La Dépêche*.

'I'm not moved by what happened to Virenque,' said
'Fredo'. 'Virenque is an asshole – and you can quote me. In
the mountains you wouldn't believe how he cracks me up. He
never stops showing off.'

And Moncassin was fearful of the repercussions of the
Festina affair, resentful of the entire professional bunch being
tarred with the same brush.

'Don't put us all in the same boat,' he warned. 'People
want to believe that we're all doped, but in fact it's Festina

who got caught. This affair is destroying our image.'

The route to Pau, although peppered with short climbs, appeared to offer the sprinters who'd come close but so far missed out – fast men such as Moncassin, and his rivals Zabel, McEwen and Minali – their final opportunity for a stage success before the mountains took their inevitable toll. But the most illustrious sprinter of all would be absent from the 'bus' – the group of non-climbers who always band together at the rear of the field when the mountain gradients begin to bite. 'Lion King' Cipollini was struggling his way through the day as the combined effects of the heat and a stomach bug sapped his strength. Finally, forty kilometres from the flat wide boulevards of Pau, and long since dropped by the main field, he climbed off his bike and got into a Saeco team car.

'Since yesterday, I've been suffering in the heat,' Cipo explained. 'I had a fever during the night, a stomach upset and I couldn't keep anything down.'

At least Cipo's abandon prior to the mountain stages was true to his unerring consistency in the Tour. In his six starts, the media's playboy sprint king, despite annual protests of determination to reach the Champs-Elysées, had quit the race all six times.

'Of course I'm disappointed,' Cipollini insisted. 'My condition has been really good since the start in Dublin and I really thought that this year I'd get to Paris for the first time. But I've won two stages, so I'm still quite satisfied.'

Cipollini had got out just in time. Ahead of him, dropped by the main field on the rolling run-in to the finish, Minali; Mapei's stage winner in Cork, Jan Svorada; and GAN's former French champion Eddy Seigneur were dying a thousand deaths in the searing heat. They were joined by a desperate Jaan Kirsipuu, the Casino team's Estonian sprinter. Kirsipuu had been weaving across the road on each little climb, hunting out pools of shade and grabbing bottles of mineral water from spectators as he did so. Further behind, Moncassin, in trouble since midway through the stage, had been on his own for the best part of twenty kilometres. The Toulousian, racing almost in his own back yard, was resigned to battling alone to make it into Pau inside the elimination time limit.

Kirsipuu's group was a sorry sight, red-eyed and red-faced, their lips blistered and their faces encrusted with dried salt from their own sweat. Mouths agape, searching for fresh air, they battled on up each incline, abandoned by their team-mates as the speeding *peloton* moved further ahead.

Up at the front of the race, the eight-man break that had come about after only forty-five kilometres had been whittled down to just four riders – Moncassin's German team-mate, Jens Voigt, Massimiliano Lelli of the Cofidis team, Rabobank's *rouleur* Leon van Bon, bronze medallist in the previous year's World Championships, and Casino's Christophe Agnolutto, unexpected winner of the Tour of Switzerland in 1997.

Van Bon was easily the most accomplished finisher; although Voigt, a second year professional who had led the Dauphine Libère stage race for several days in June, was no slouch himself when it came to a sprint. But with a three minute lead over the *peloton* as they rode into Pau and Agno-lutto dropped on one of the day's last sharp hills, the remaining trio started to bluff each other, knowing that a decisive attack from any one of them would ensure the stage win.

Lelli, team-mate to race leader Desbiens, had unsurpris-ingly opted to sit at the back of the group for most of the stage and posed a serious threat. He was easily the freshest of the three and both van Bon and Voigt were desperate to avoid pacing him to victory. So desperate were they that the resulting bout of foxing and freewheeling saw their lead over the field plummet. The three minute advantage they held as they entered the final ten kilometres had tumbled to under half a minute as they soft-pedalled into the final kilometre.

Their slack pace gave Agnolutto the chance to catch up with their coat-tails, and as he did so, the Casino rider put in a sudden lurching attack that only Voigt was able to chase down. But the bluff and counter-bluff was in vain. Van Bon, who later said that he'd drunk six litres of water during the stage, easily outpaced the German rider as he lunged for the line, racking up his first Tour stage win – a mere twelve seconds ahead of the speeding bunch led by the frustrated Zabel, who came agonisingly close to engulfing the tired breakaways in the last few metres of the finishing straight.

But the real drama was played out back down the road as Moncassin, Kirsipuu and company limped wearily towards the finish. By now they were being shadowed by Tyler Hamilton, US Postal's time trial revelation of just two days earlier. Johnny Weltz, US Postal's Danish *directeur*, had been sure back in Meyrignac that the Massachusetts-bred Hamilton would be one of the surprises of the race.

'Tyler's a great bike rider,' Weltz had said unequivocally. 'He's got the legs to finish in the top ten in Paris.'

But now the big surprise was that the young American was riding on his own, almost twenty minutes off the pace, in a state of near exhaustion. His team-mates Marty Jemison and Frankie Andreu had dropped back in a desperate attempt to encourage him. But dehydration, a long-standing stomach bug and the debilitating heat had slowed him even further. Finally, as the bunch disappeared down the road, Hamilton had waved Jemison and Andreu away, insisting that they save themselves. Even the pleas of his second *directeur* Mark Gorski, to stop before he made his condition any worse, went unheeded.

So Tyler, for his own reasons, rode on alone through the heat haze, for how many kilometres – maybe forty, maybe fifty – honouring his pledge to the Tour and sticking by his determination to finish what he had started. As he crossed the line, Tyler was in a state of near-collapse; but by now the French press, who'd scoffed lightly at his performance in the time trial, dismissing it as a one-off, knew exactly who this undaunted young man was. As Hamilton lay in the shade beyond the finish line, he had achieved a pyrrhic victory – his semi-delirious solo ride through the hellish heatwave qualified him, far more than the dilettantish Cipollini, as what the French would call a 'man of the Tour'.

Five kilometres from the finish line, in Pau's towering Palais des Sports, the latest twist to the Tour's doping scandals was spreading through the press room. The fall-out from the Festina shambles rumbled on, but now the talk between the long rows of laptops and mobiles was of the affair of the '*caisse noire*'. It was no less shocking than the revelations that preceded it, and, as Festina's team doctor Eric Ryckaert spoke through his lawyer in a desperate bid to shift the blame, racing again took second place to scandal.

'Festina's riders were forced to put part of their prize money into a fund which was used to buy doping products,' Ryckaert's lawyer told journalists in Lille. 'The products purchased in this way were kept at the team's headquarters in Lyon.'

There was more. Festina's detained *soigneur* Willy Voet, the lawyer claimed, had been transporting 'nearly enough EPO to give to all the teams in the Tour de France'.

Increasing speculation about the TVM team brought an immediate denial from the team's appalled head *directeur*, Cees Priem. 'I've never had anything to do with doping in twenty-five years' involvement with cycling,' he insisted as the furore around his team grew.

But whatever Priem said was drowned out – the TVM story was snowballing. A French journalist broke the latest development. On 4 March 1998, a TVM team mechanic's truck carrying bikes and equipment had been stopped and searched by customs officials on the A26 *autoroute* near Reims. According to reports 104 syringes of EPO were found, although elsewhere it was reported that doping masking agents were also hidden in the van. At the time, a file had been opened on the discovery, but no prosecution entered into. Yet that didn't explain why, on an anonymous stretch of French *autoroute*, the customs officials had swooped on an innocuous Dutch van carrying bicycle frames and wheels.

It was all getting too much for the besieged Tour organisation and the avalanche of negative media reports was beginning to overwhelm them. Bernard Hinault, wearing both his hat of five-time Tour champion and that of the Tour's public relations officer, insisted bluntly that 'it was possible to win the Tour on mineral water'. But nobody was interested in rebuttals any more. Things had gone too far: pretending that the affair was little more than a blip only insulted the public's intelligence.

Stage winner: Leon van Bon, Holland (Rabobank)
Overall race leader: Laurent Desbiens, France (Cofidis)
Points classification leader: Erik Zabel, Germany
  (Deutsche Telekom)
Team classification leader: Cofidis
Mountains classification leader: Jens Voigt, Germany
  (GAN)

Day 13   Stage 10

Tuesday 21 July
Pau–Luchon, 196.5 km

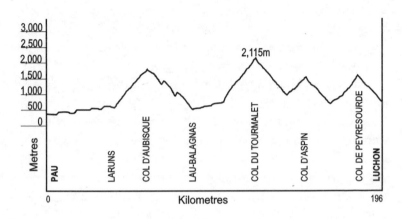

More than the prologue or the first days of searing heat, more even than the first time trial, the mountain stages of the Tour de France reveal the truth. The Alpine and Pyrenean climbs test physical and mental resilience; they tell us who has the nerve and the ambition to risk everything for success; they reveal who among the Tour's top stars is a real challenger for final victory and lay bare the failings of those who have hidden behind the strength of others. Every rider has a different story of his crossing of the Tour's mountains – even in the modern hi-tech Tour, all the sports science and meticulous preparation falls away just as it always has done, and leaves the athlete alone on his bike on a wild mountain road, battling to overcome his limitations.

Success in the time trial prompts admiration and respect, but a lone triumph in the mountains, against their dramatic backdrop, engenders some kind of love – a sense of gratitude

144

for keeping the pact with the Tour's tradition, for honouring its hopes and dreams. The great climbers are always more fondly remembered. Even when Miguel Indurain was at the peak of his five successive Tour wins, there was a frisson of resentment over his defensive loss-limiting tactics in the mountains.

OK – so he's great at time trialling, but why can't he attack more? Why won't he thrill us in the Alps and Pyrénées?

I stood in the drizzle sweeping over the start village, surveying the swirling clouds hanging over the Pic du Midi d'Ossau. Usually the panoramic view from the raised terrace of Pau's Boulevard des Pyrénées extended towards the Spanish border, but on this wet Tuesday the green slopes of the mountains rose gently into the murky gloom, their peaks hidden from view. One by one, riders pedalled to the foot of the signing-on podium, autographed the start sheet, waved perfunctorily to the crowd huddling under umbrellas on the far side of the barriers, and headed into the village in search of a coffee. For some of them, this was sure to be their last day on the 1998 Tour as the fatigue and ennui of the race finally overwhelmed them. It was a day for the contenders to show themselves and for the sprinters and team helpers to fight for survival.

A smiling Magnus Backstedt appeared out of the crowd and shook hands. 'I'm a bit nervous,' he confessed, 'because I know that today will be like that.' He pointed to the underside of his jaw with his index finger. With his tall frame and big build, Magnus knew that the steep climbs would take him to his limits. In his first Tour, with ten days of racing already under his belt, he was heading into the unknown.

'My knee is better today, but I don't like this weather much – it doesn't exactly help your morale. I suppose I'll just sit in the laughing group – and laugh,' he grinned.

The Pyrenean passes require different climbing skills to the Alps and, unlike the versatile Pantani or the departed Virenque, not every specialist climber enjoys success in both mountain ranges. Luc Leblanc, world champion in 1994, fourth overall in Paris in 1993 and *maillot jaune* when the Tour crossed the Pyrénées in 1991, was a case in point. Leblanc had emerged through the mist to win at the Hautacam ski station in 1994, but apart from a stage win at Les Arcs in 1996, had often failed to perform in the Alpine passes.

'I feel more at home in the Pyrénées,' he said. 'The first mountain stage is on my terrain. I'll be finding out just where I stand.'

And the volatile Leblanc, who had suffered enough disappointments in previous Tours, breaking down in tears at the roadside on more than one occasion, had some words of warning for the defending champion. In the 1994 Tour, Marco Pantani had been ten minutes behind the race leader at the foot of the Pyrénées, yet had still finished the Tour in the top three placings.

'This time he's only five minutes down,' said Leblanc. 'If Ullrich lets him go, he's taking an enormous risk. When Pantani turns it on, he can take a quarter of an hour – and do it again the next day. And there's nobody capable of following him.'

It was Cédric Vasseur, team leader of the GAN team in the absence of Chris Boardman, who got things going, attacking into the mist enveloping the final kilometres of the first climb, the Col d'Aubisque. As he had been on the road to Brive, Vasseur was gallantly willing to go it alone; but he soon had riders following in pursuit as Casino's Italian pair, Alberto Elli and Rodolfo Massi gave chase through the gloom.

Behind Vasseur, as he crossed the summit of the Aubisque, climbing alone at the front of the Tour *peloton*, the mountains were already weeding out the weak and weary. First to go was Philippe Gaumont of the Cofidis team, so supportive to Laurent Desbiens just two days earlier in his bid for the race lead. Gaumont had been suffering from tendinitis since the time trial in Corrèze and his morale finally deserted him after just twenty kilometres of the stage. Gaumont wheeled calmly to a halt and awaited the arrival of the 'broom wagon', the van sweeping up defeated riders and ferrying them to the finish. Normally the broom wagon is a small mini-bus, but some days, when the Tour meanders endlessly through the mountains, there aren't enough seats so a coach is laid on instead. The *voiture-balai* – the broom wagon – first appeared on the Tour route in 1910. It was the same year that the race climbed into the Pyrénées, crossing over the unmade road of the Col d'Aubisque for the very first time. Eighty-eight years on, the old mountain pass was proving just as ravaging as it had in the Tour's formative days.

Further up the road, Laurent Roux – 'Lollo', the diminutive bleach-haired climber who'd been greeted with a returning hero's welcome in Frayssinet only forty-eight hours earlier – was struggling. Roux had dropped far behind the main field and was lost among the ones and twos of stragglers. Left behind by his TVM team car and now desperate to end his misery, he begged one of the police motorcyclists to drive ahead and ask his *directeur* to wait for him. After fifty-one kilometres, suffering from acute knee pain, he finally climbed off and stepped gingerly into a waiting ambulance.

The short drop and climb from the Aubisque to the next peak, the Col du Soulor, is undemanding; but at speed, in the mist, rain and poor visibility, it proved to be one of the turning points of the Tour. Suddenly, as the field dropped through the clouds shrouding the Aubisque, the race radio crackled into life, reeling off a long list of crashes and abandons. '*Chute, Casagrande!*' came the first frantic crash announcement. Then '*Chute, Magnien!*' was quickly followed by '*Chute Moncassin!*'

In the mist and frenzy, Italian rider Francesco Casagrande, co-leader with Bobby Julich at the Cofidis team, crashed heavily on a bend; while Emmanuel Magnien of the La Française des Jeux team missed a right-hander altogether and tumbled off the road, falling into space. Moments later, Moncassin, who had battled so hard to finish in Pau, slid off on another treacherous corner, his bike skittering across the road to the edge of the precipice as brakes squealed and burned all around him.

A little further down the descent towards the Soulor, race leader Laurent Desbiens fell without serious injury; but on hearing of his team leader Casagrande's misfortune, he opted to wait and see if he could help pace the Italian back to the front of the field. Only when Casagrande, weeping with pain, gave up the ghost and climbed into a team car, did Desbiens, ever the dutiful team man despite having the *maillot jaune* on his back, decide to continue.

A near-hysterical Magnien meanwhile, his fall luckily broken by trees and bushes, had somehow climbed, bleeding and trembling, back up to the roadside. One of the Tour's medical team was trying to calm him down but the French sprinter was finished. Still shocked, he climbed into an ambulance and was taken to Luchon for X-rays.

While the favourites concentrated on staying upright, Vasseur pressed on, over the top of the Soulor and down towards the dry valley roads passing through Argelès-Gazost. Massi and Elli caught up with him soon afterwards in the feed zone at Lau-Balagnas.

Riding far behind the leading trio and the rest of the field, a cut and bleeding Moncassin pedalled into the feed area and snatched his snack bag, then slowed as he watched his last remaining companion, Casino's faltering Jan Kirsipuu, climb wearily from his bike. Moncassin had fought to stay in the race for the best part of two days, but was demoralised by the thought of climbing and descending another three mountain passes alone. Finally, the hapless French sprinter abandoned the Tour.

'Since yesterday, things have been going badly,' said Moncassin. 'Now I've hurt my hip and my ribs – I couldn't face riding alone over those three cols.'

With the leading trio well ahead, the front of the field regrouped, took a deep breath and began the long, murderous ascent of the immense Col du Tourmalet. Twelve kilometres from the summit, race leader Desbiens was in trouble and began to drift to the rear of the diminishing field, along with Italian champion Andrea Tafi and points classification leader Zabel. But all eyes were on the front of the field, with Ullrich, Julich, Pantani, Jalabert, Leblanc, Olano and the increasingly impressive Dutch champion Michael Boogerd all riding at the head of the group. With Elli the best placed of the breakaway trio and Ullrich riding about seven minutes behind him, the hard-working Italian became race leader on the road.

In front of the Tourmalet's old summit café, Elli led Vasseur and Massi over the top and began the long drop to the foot of the next climb, the Col d'Aspin. With the day's toughest ascent behind them, the three riders could start thinking about stage victory. They held on to their advantage over the top of the Aspin, where Jalabert produced the first of a series of tentative attacks in the hope of testing Ullrich's resolve. But the defending champion was having none of it and pedalled impassively to Jaja's shoulder, quickly dispelling any doubts over his strength.

During the 1997 Tour, Richard Virenque had managed to

destabilise Ullrich in the vertiginous Alpine descents. Now, on the narrow drop from the Aspin to the final climb, the Peyresourde, Jalabert, no doubt with the German's supposed weakness in mind, tried again. But Ullrich's Telekom team were quick to react, stringing out the group, leaning acrobatically into the hairpins and powering out of the saddle on the long, plunging straights into the next sharp bend. Their fierce pace reeled in Jalabert and had the effect of distancing one or two others even more. Desbiens was now long gone after struggling over the summit of the Tourmalet; while Spanish favourite Olano, suffering from the after-effects of his own fall on the Aubisque, was battling to hang on.

So when Telekom maintained that high pace as they began the gradual climb of the Peyresourde, the Spaniard was in crisis. Half-way up the climb, as up ahead Massi attacked decisively from the leading trio, Ullrich moved to the front and, gripping his handlebars purposefully, turned the screw that bit further. One by one, as the Tour champion dictated their fate, exhausted riders fell away until, two kilometres from the summit, the group had dwindled to fewer than a dozen. Olano and Jalabert had been dropped but, unexpectedly, Riis, Julich and US Postal's Jean-Cyril Robin had hung on alongside the specialist climbers such as Pantani and José María Jimenez, Olano's Banesto team-mate.

Pantani, though, had plans of his own. As Massi, scenting the biggest win of his up-and-down career, approached the summit of the Peyresourde, Pantani broke free of Ullrich's metronomic pace and suddenly attacked. In the two remaining kilometres of the climb, the Italian opened up a forty second advantage on Ullrich's group. Tucked low over his handlebars and using just one hand to steer while tucking the other behind his back, Pantani dropped from the summit like a stone. Even so, he was unable to catch Massi before he entered Luchon's genteel streets. The small group behind them, panicked by Pantani's violent attack, chased hard all the way into the finish, reducing the Italian's lead to just twenty-three seconds at the line. Thirty-two-year-old Massi was exuberant, while Ullrich, who reclaimed the race leader's yellow jersey after its two-day loan to Desbiens, was simply relieved.

'Taking the jersey today feels better than it did after the time trial,' he admitted later. 'Ideally, I'd like to keep it to Paris, but I'm not obsessed by that. There are still tough days to come.'

But the star of the first mountain stage was definitely the mercurial Pantani, who had unwittingly flagged himself up as Ullrich's greatest threat.

'I didn't really want to attack today,' he said. 'I just wanted to see how my legs were going. I've felt ill for a couple of days,' *Il Pirata* explained, 'probably because of the heat. I've been drinking up to ten litres of water a day and my stomach couldn't take it. So I wasn't sleeping well and this morning at the start my legs felt like cotton.'

Those thrilling two kilometres had made the press room buzz with excitement, giving rise to the hope that there might be more to the fate of this Tour than simply Ullrich's predictable and methodical racing. Yet Pantani himself, now increasingly seen as the 1998 Tour's salvation, was one of his own greatest doubters.

'I can win if Ullrich has one bad day, as Alex Zulle had in the Giro,' said the Italian. 'But Ullrich's not Zulle.'

Bobby Julich, confirmed as Ullrich's other principal rival following his climb to second place overall, fully recognised Pantani's growing menace.

'He's the danger,' said Bobby J. 'His attack today was scary. Ullrich is going to have his work cut out to stop him.'

★ ★ ★

I walked across from the press room to the lines of team cars and buses parked beyond the finish area. The big name riders were already in, towelled down and changed, hidden behind the tinted windows of their giant air-con buses. But on a stage like this, the stragglers would be coming in for the next forty minutes or so. Over at the GAN mobile home, Fred Moncassin was explaining his capitulation to the French press and signing autographs.

He was still talking as Magnus Backstedt and his team-mate Jens Voigt rolled to a halt alongside. By then Massi had crossed the line, arms raised, half an hour earlier, and was nearing the end of his stage winner's press conference. Voigt was bloodied but smiling, with a cut to his ear and nose and a broad, raw graze extending from his hip to his left thigh. The fabric of his shorts, soaked with blood and meshed with torn skin, had dried fast to his sliced leg. His *directeur*, Roger Legeay, looked him up and down and winced.

Magnus, meanwhile, was almost nonchalant. 'I'm OK – really. I just stayed out of trouble and followed the right wheels,' he shrugged. 'The Tourmalet was tough, but I got over it OK. After that we just made sure we got here within the time limit.'

Over at the yellow and black ONCE bus Laurent Jalabert, only twenty-third on the stage, had already climbed aboard; but his burly and outspoken team boss, Manolo Saiz, was again complaining over the logistical demands put upon his riders by the Tour organisation.

'I'm not going on about recovery for fun,' stated Saiz to a huddle of hacks, 'but all the transfers are killing us. Tonight, from Luchon, we have to drive another sixty kilometres after the stage to get to our hotel. And in Ireland, because of all the transfers, some of the team went without massage for three days. That sort of thing,' concluded Saiz, as more bloodied stragglers pedalled wearily past, 'can make a big difference to the outcome of the Tour de France.'

Stage winner: Rodolfo Massi, Italy (Casino)
Overall race leader: Jan Ullrich, Germany (Deutsche Telekom)
Points classification leader: Erik Zabel, Germany (Deutsche Telekom)
Team classification leader: Cofidis
Mountains classification leader: Rodolfo Massi, Italy (Casino)

Day 14   # Stage 11

Wednesday 22 July
Luchon–Plateau de Beille, 170 km

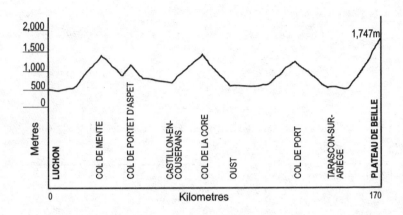

We woke up across the border in Spain, under clear blue skies, in a hotel built on the banks of a mountain stream. Reluctantly, after breakfasting lazily in the sun on the hotel terrace, we picked up our bags and climbed back into the car. No fewer than seventeen riders had abandoned the previous afternoon in the mist and rain hanging over the route to Luchon, but now the hot weather had come back to the Tour. The Pyrénées glinted imposingly in the sunlight as we drove on valley roads to the foot of the first climb, the Col de Mente.

Stage eleven, unlike the previous day's razor-tooth route, did not have such a back-breaking profile. All the day's passes fell well below the one and a half thousand metre threshold, but there was a vicious sting in the tail. The sixteen kilometre climb to the ski station finish at Plateau de Beille was steep and, in the signal words of one American rider, 'mean and hurtful'. If Pantani wanted to upset Ullrich's applecart still further, there was no doubt that this was the place.

We drove on over the leafy Col de Port, dropping down into a picture-postcard mountain landscape of green meadows and log cabins, echoing with cow bells and waterfalls. The next climb, the short but steep Col de Portet-d'Aspet which first appeared on the *route du Tour* in 1910, had recently acquired a new and melancholic significance. In 1995, the race had plummeted down the Portet-d'Aspet in the opposite direction to the one in which we were now climbing it, on its way to the ski resort at Cauterets. The hero that day had been Richard Virenque, who climbed to a solo stage win, exchanging high fives with team manager Bruno Roussel as he rode ecstatically into the finishing straight.

Yet by six o'clock that afternoon, Virenque's tub-thumping victory was long forgotten. Descending the Portet-d'Aspet at high speed at the rear of the field, former Olympic champion Fabio Casartelli had clattered to the road, sliding across a vicious camber before colliding head first with a concrete post. The Italian had suffered appalling head injuries. He lay crumpled in a pool of blood, while race doctor Gérard Porte struggled to save him. The Tour's medical team did what they could but Casartelli, one of the brightest talents in the sport, was dead by early afternoon, even as Virenque continued his lone ride to glory. In the confusion, the shock of his death brought extreme reactions. Virenque, who insisted he knew nothing of Casartelli's accident until much later in the day, joyfully celebrated his stage win on the presentation podium. Even after he stepped down from the podium, the rest of the heavily sponsored ceremony went on unhindered.

Among the team cars clustered around the finish area at Cauterets, riders broke down and wept when told the news. Tony Rominger, then in the twilight of his career, stood puffy-eyed and close to tears on the steps of his team bus, raging against the race organisation for continuing with the stage and cursing French TV for heartlessly repeating slow-motion replays of the Italian's crash. Motorola, Casartelli's respected and popular American team, was devastated. Its Colombian climber, Alvaro Meija, lay sobbing across the back seat of a team car, his face buried in his hands. In the press room, the enraged Italian media dipped their pens in vitriol and set about debunking the Tour myth, bitterly attacking the organisation for putting commercial concerns above respect for Casartelli's life. The Tour was heartless, they said; worst of all, it had pandered to the crowds, indulging their French stage winner and showing little thought for Casartelli's fate.

The next day, the teams arrived in the market-place in Tarbes, supposedly to tackle that year's second Pyrenean stage. But the riders were having none of it. As they gathered and talked quietly in small groups, it became clear that they were in no mood to race. Finally, when the Motorola cars swept into the square, mournful black ribbons hanging from their roof aerials, the Tour organisation bowed to the inevitable. The stage would be neutralised and all prize money donated to a fund set up for Casartelli's widow.

Bravely, the Motorola team came to the start line. Around them, their professional peers stood, heads bowed, for a minute of silence. Lance Armstrong, Motorola's rising Texan star, his face pained and twisted with sorrow, stared ahead. Then, jadedly, they rode away from Tarbes at touring pace, on a long mountainous haul that became a race of remembrance.

Much later the same day, the whole field entered the final kilometre in Pau as one, with the Motorola team ushered forward in the last few metres. In the long shadows of early evening, the American team's riders fanned out across the road in an intense and moving tribute to Casartelli.

Two days later, the unwavering Armstrong who, during the latter days of that year's Tour had become the race convoy's emotional touchstone, rode away to a poignant and cathartic stage win in Limoges. He said afterwards that he felt like he had the strength of two people.

Just below the spot where Casartelli had crashed two years earlier, we stopped for a few minutes at the strange, white memorial to the Italian that had been unveiled a few months after his death. The riders, out of respect, were sure to do the same when they passed by later in the morning. Racing to win was one thing but solidarity with a fallen colleague was something else again.

We'd had two scandal-free days since the *'caisse-noir'* revelations emanating from Dr Ryckaert's lawyer. The police raids behind the race's climate of paranoia left many in the press room speculating that the 1998 Tour's two Pyrenean days had been the cleanest mountain stages for years. Out under the hot sun, the riders rode untroubled to the foot of the Portet-d'Aspet, where they halted at the Casartelli memorial to pay their respects. A few minutes later they were off again as Massi, wearing his King of the Mountains jersey with pride, led them over the top and down the other side towards the third climb, the Col de la Core.

By the top of the climb, Roland Meier, Bobby Julich's Swiss colleague at the Cofidis team, had broken clear, with José Javier Gomez, a little-known Spaniard from the Kelme team for company. They were pursued down the descent by Italian champion Andrea Tafi, making his umpteenth bid for glory, and Stéphane Heulot, the shy Frenchman from La Française des Jeux. The hesitant Heulot, ninth overall, posed a threat of sorts to Ullrich but with the long drag to the summit of the Col de Port still to come and the biting gradients of the final climb weighing on their minds, the race leader and his Telekom team opted to let them go.

While Meier and Rodriguez sped through the feed zone in Oust, the little village within sight of the Spanish border saw Abraham Olano's Tour challenge come to an end. Miguel Indurain's designated successor had crashed heavily on the Col d'Aubisque the previous afternoon, along with GAN's Jens Voigt, ripping what his team management described as a 'golf-ball sized hole' in his right thigh. The Basque star had fought bravely to limit his losses at Luchon, but after a painful and sleepless night, he was immediately in trouble once the pace picked up following Meier's attack. As the speed increased, so did Olano's pain until, barely able to sit in the saddle and pedal, he slowed in the feed zone and reluctantly called it a day.

'I came to the Tour with high ambitions,' he said later, 'and I was ready to fight to get on to the podium. Crashes are part of racing and you have to accept that. I wasn't going to give up without good reason, but I'd reached the end of my tether.'

Olano wasn't the only rider struggling to hold on over the relatively innocuous Col de la Core. Russia's Vladislav Bobrik, once, like his compatriot Evgeni Berzin, a star at the mighty Gewiss team of the mid-1990s, was left behind as the field accelerated. Bobrik had surprisingly won the Tour of Lombardy in 1994, but since then there had been nothing to write home to Novosibirsk about. As Olano was driven back to his team hotel, the Russian, making his Tour début at the age of twenty-eight, also climbed off and abandoned the race.

Up at the front Meier, after surviving a spectacular but

cushioned tumble into the hedgerows, dropped Gomez on the long gradual climb to the top of the Col de Port, forging on alone over the summit. Ahead of him lay the green valley of the Ariège river and in the distance, the final haul up to the Plateau de Beille cross-country ski station. The ruddy-faced Swiss pedalled on, down through Tarascon-sur-Ariège and past campsites and hotels, heading out on to the flat valley road leading to those final sixteen kilometres of climbing. A tourist steam train running on tracks laid alongside the main road came by, tooting its whistle before slowing respectfully to allow Meier to pull ahead.

Back in the main field the climbers were moving to the front, readying themselves for the inevitable skirmishing at the foot of the climb. Ullrich warily monitored Pantani and Julich, while the Telekom guard clustered around him. But two kilometres from the beginning of the climb, as ahead of him Meier rounded the first steep hairpins, the race leader shot his hand skywards in panic, calling for his team car. Fatefully, Ullrich had punctured just as Pantani and Julich were readying themselves to attack. By the time a Telekom team car pulled alongside the frantic Tour champion, Pantani, Julich and the other leading contenders were well into the first sharp inclines. A slow and fumbled wheel change only set Ullrich's heart pumping faster and betrayed his very evident fear of Pantani's climbing prowess. Telekom's leader set off again, adrenaline rushing through him, setting such a fierce pace that the riders he passed appeared stuck to the road. Snarling in competitive rage, he flew up the hill, speeding past the entire field as he chased determinedly after his Italian rival. But the champion's panic did little to impress watching Telekom team manager Walter Godefroot.

'Instead of climbing steadily back to the front, he accelerated so hard that nobody in the team could follow him,' complained Godefroot that evening. 'At the bottom of the hill he had five guys from the team to help him and if he hadn't gone so hard, some of them would have stayed with him much longer. Instead, he put in a useless effort which could have really cost him. It's a lesson to learn and we'll be talking about it tonight.'

But in spite of Ullrich's worst fears, Pantani, following the gentleman's code of the sport, hadn't sought to take advantage of his misfortune.

'Normally, I always attack at the bottom of the last climb,' said *Il Pirata*, 'but this time, I waited for Ullrich to get back into the front group before I did it.'

In fact, Pantani waited another five kilometres as a breathless Ullrich, looking frantically over his shoulders for signs of his team-mates, realised what he had done. And when, twelve kilometres from the finish, gentleman Marco suddenly accelerated away on the right-hand side of the road, the exhausted champion was unable to respond.

'When Pantani attacked,' said Bobby J at the finish, 'I didn't even think of trying to follow him. Ullrich wanted me to help him chase, but I still had a team-mate up ahead so there was no question of me doing that.'

Further up the road, Bobby J's fading team-mate Meier had got wind of Pantani's pursuit. His head dropped in dismay as the information filtered through; but then he fought back, crouching lower and pushing the pedals around as hard as he could against the nine per cent gradient. But the stealthy Pantani soon reeled Meier in, until six kilometres from the finish, on one long and steep right-hand incline, they rode alongside each other, forcing themselves onwards and upwards. For a moment, as Pantani struggled to pull ahead, it looked as if he'd dramatically misjudged his own strength. But then, he somehow found new impetus and picked up his tempo once more as Meier receded into the background.

Ullrich's group, now dwindled to six riders, had already shed Riis, Leblanc and Jalabert. The Tour champion had been forced by Julich and his Cofidis team to chase alone for most of the day's final forty-five minutes of racing, and Pantani's advantage still grew.

Yet Julich, with Meier still riding tenaciously between him and Pantani, refused to take advantage of Ullrich's obvious fatigue. The American could have tried to break clear of the Telekom rider within those final kilometres, even perhaps to have stolen the *maillot jaune*. Instead he sat doggedly on Ullrich's shoulder right to the finish, refusing to betray Meier's lone effort to hang on to second place on the stage.

Pursued by ecstatic Italian fans, Pantani rode into the finish to climb to the fifth Tour stage win of his six year career and his fourth victory at a mountain summit. Meier held on to a worthy second place while Julich, chased by four others, accelerated clear of Ullrich by a mere seven seconds to move up to second place overall. While the champion and his team crossed the line in disarray, Pantani and Julich, both of whom had previously been too respectful of Ullrich to think of defeating him, began dreamily to entertain thoughts of final victory.

'Before the Tour, I said that it was Cofidis' time,' beamed Julich in an interview with American TV, after being told that his team now had four riders in the top twelve placings. 'I don't think Ullrich or his team is as strong as they were last year – everyone else has come up a level now.'

Pantani was even more circumspect. 'It's going to be difficult to beat Ullrich,' he mused. 'I don't believe for a minute that he was really put in trouble today, but we'll see. I don't want to think about the overall classification – after all the stress of the Giro d'Italia, thinking about it makes my head hurt.'

And there was the first hint of sour grapes from the usually diplomatic Tour champion, as he realised that both Pantani and Julich were now very much out to get him.

'It was very hard for me today,' he complained tetchily to the German press. 'The others took the chance to attack me when I punctured, which isn't very fair. Maybe I won't win this year's Tour after all, but I'm still young – I'll stay cool.'

Across the other side of the finish area, the jubilant Bobby J was still talking. 'I've felt strong in the Pyrénées,' he enthused, as his partner Angela looked on. 'If I feel at the same level in the Alps, well, then I'm going to try to win this thing . . .'

Stage winner: Marco Pantani, Italy (Mercatone Uno)
Overall race leader: Jan Ullrich, Germany (Deutsche Telekom)
Points classification leader: Erik Zabel, Germany (Deutsche Telekom)
Team classification leader: Cofidis
Mountains classification leader: Rodolfo Massi, Italy (Casino)

Leading overall standards after stage eleven:

1. Jan Ullrich, Germany (Telekom) 2,070.6 kilometres in 52 hrs, 42 mins 25 secs
2. Bobby Julich, America (Cofidis) in 52 hrs, 43 mins 36 secs
3. Laurent Jalabert, France (ONCE) in 52 hrs, 45 mins 26 secs
4. Marco Pantani, Italy (Mercatone Uno) in 52 hrs, 45 mins and 26 secs
5. Michael Boogerd, Holland (Rabobank) in 52 hrs, 45 mins and 54 secs

PART FOUR

Day 15   Rest Day

My methodical, painstaking pre-Tour build-up, free of sports doctors, nutritionists and laboratory tests had paid off – thankfully, my stock of socks and boxer shorts had made it through to the rest day – the Tour's official wash 'n' brush-up day. At least, that's how the 'rest day' used to be, until one or two top sponsors decided a few years ago that it would be a good day to hold press conferences for their leading riders, most of which ran predictably enough along the lines of 'it's half-time, Des, and I may be fifteen minutes down on Pantani, but if the team does good, there's still everything to play for.' Pretty soon, once the top sponsors had opted to milk that chance to steal yet more publicity, the Tour organisation had little choice but to set out a press room, supplying the papers, the phone lines and the press releases, just like any other day on the race. As for the riders, most of them used the rest day not for shopping in town or swimming in the hotel pool, but for sticking to their usual routines. They would ride perhaps seventy-five or even a hundred kilometres in the morning, have a massage and light lunch, usually followed by a long afternoon nap and, later on, spend a few stolen hours with their wives and families.

But GAN duo Stuart O'Grady and Cédric Vasseur, the team's most high-profile riders in the absence of Chris Boardman, faced a particularly hectic day. The French insurance company were to cease sponsoring the team immediately after the Tour ended, with an abrupt handover to the French high street bank, Crédit Agricole, whose colours would adorn the riders from 3 August onwards. Such a sudden handover allowed little time for advance publicity, so O'Grady and Vasseur were to parade the new colours at a 'mini' team launch at the GAN hotel in the afternoon. Their kit may have been different, but some things at the team didn't look likely to change. Even though GAN had always had a very high percentage of English-speaking riders, the team's creaking PR machine had always been disinterested in the Anglophone media. Unsurprisingly, as O'Grady and Vasseur pulled on their new green and white colours and smiled for the French press, barely any of the English-language media were there to witness the event.

Out on the far side of the Col de Port, our secluded little *auberge* was beyond the range of mobile phones and had no TVs in the rooms; but then on the rest day, we'd counted on there being little breaking news.

So after a busy morning with the travel wash, we left at lunch-time and headed over the pass, back towards Tarascon. But as we strolled into the picturesque Parc Pyrénéen de l'Art Préhistorique a couple of kilometres outside Tarascon, site of the rest-day press tent, we didn't know that far north of the Pyrénées the wheels of scandal were turning once more.

Earlier in the day, in the Rhône valley city of Lyon the Festina team, hidden behind their Oakley shades, had nonchalantly arrived for what they had assumed would be informal interviews with French police officers pursuing Judge Keil's investigation.

All nine riders had perhaps naïvely expected to face brief interviews before being released; but they had seriously underestimated the authorities' determination to make an example of them. Within minutes of walking into the police station they were all detained for questioning, and faced the possibility of being held for a forty-eight-hour period. Even though they were dealing with national heroes, the French authorities pursued their investigations. Reputations no longer counted for anything. Riding the wave of outrage and scandal surrounding Virenque and his team mates, the police set about humiliating the 'Festina Nine'. They put the riders in individual cells, stripped them naked and subjected them to internal searches. Zulle, Virenque, Brochard – three of the most illustrious names in cycling – riders who'd dreamed of Tour de France glory only days earlier, were now being treated as if they were no better than red-eyed drug smugglers. Virenque, who'd started July as the French nation's golden boy, their favoured hope for Tour success, was now debased by the authorities. They left him alone in a cold prison cell, far from the hot sun and the worshipping partisan crowds he so adored.

By late afternoon, news of the arrests had filtered through to a stunned press room, creating a mood of confusion and disbelief. We were shocked, not because we didn't think that the Festina team may have been guilty of doping, but because this treatment of them went too far. Even if they had been more than economic with the truth and even if they'd cheated their way to sporting success, this brutalising wave of righteous moral rage was more than Virenque, Zulle or Brochard – or any other naïve, shell-suited and immature athlete – deserved for succumbing to the extreme demands of the sport.

We sat in the press room, documenting their downfall, their final mundane humiliation. Those in the *salle de presse* who'd been hanging on to Virenque's every word at the start of the Tour in Dublin turned the full force of their indignation against him and his team-mates. Even though most of us, including myself, had privately suspected the presence of doping among the professional élite years earlier, we joined the chorus of outrage. Circumstances made us all hypocrites: the law of silence – that fear of 'spitting in the soup', the soup that we all shared – had ensnared us all. Now, happy as we'd been to share a coffee and joke with Virenque, Dufaux, Stevo and all the others, we were only too willing to wring our hands in weary condemnation while hanging them out to dry.

But there were notable exceptions. While some of the media, wary of losing their own place on the gravy train by tainting the sport's image, had turned a blind eye to what they had known was going on, some, shocked by what they had uncovered, had stuck their necks out two or three years earlier. Belgian newspaper *La Dernière Heure* could hold its head high, even if, after printing allegations of positive test cover-ups by the French cycling federation, it had, under intense legal pressure, printed a retraction. And *L'Equipe* itself had spent a week in the winter of 1997 delving into cycling's drug culture, printing a series of hard-hitting interviews with named professionals who revealed the damning extent of doping abuse, much to UCI President Verbruggen's scorn.

Sadly, though, too many of the rest of us were too used to

dealing in fanzine fantasy, compromised by our closeness to the riders and our fear of being ostracised, of being expelled from Planet Tour's inner circle. As for the long line of ex-pros now busy working for TV and other news media – well, they were hardly going to tell it like it was in their day.

The French police had disrupted the calm of the Tour's only rest day much earlier on, long before Virenque and his team-mates found themselves thrown in the cells, when officers from Reims raided the TVM team hotel in Pamiers at breakfast-time. Over the previous couple of days, the Tour convoy had been lulled back into its old rhythm, thinking wistfully of the Pantani–Ullrich battle that was sure to dominate the Alpine stages. By lunch-time on the rest day, that comforting bubble had burst yet again. Cees Priem, TVM's team manager and Andrei Mikhailov, their Russian team doctor, were taken away for questioning. The riders' possessions were searched and further ominous bin bags, rumoured to contain steroids and masking agents, were taken away. TVM sprinter, Jeroen Blijlevens, stage winner in Cholet, was outraged by the police action.

'It's scandalous,' he said. 'Why have they left us alone for five months and now suddenly decided to start on us during the Tour?'

John Lelangue and Sophie del Rizzo of the Tour's *service presse* had shed, as is rest-day custom, their official outfits and strolled around the press tent in relaxed casuals. But by late afternoon, as the TVM and Festina snowballs gathered pace, *le dopage* again had the Société du Tour furiously back-pedalling. Jean-Marie Leblanc, sought out for his perspective on the TVM affair, stuck to a tried and tested line of argument.

'I've learnt everything from the press,' he protested to

French journalists, 'and while I'm not ruling anything out, at the moment it's out of the question that we would punish TVM.'

Caught between the riders and the authorities, Jean-Marie ploughed a lonely furrow in an increasingly hostile no man's land. The riders were angry with him, the fans were angry with him, and the press were quick to condemn him. Yet he soldiered on, even if some of his comments smacked of naivety.

'When I discovered that some of the riders were using masking products to hide their doping, I was dumbfounded,' he'd told a French radio station just a couple of days earlier.

In his previous incarnation as a leading French sports writer, Leblanc had been at the forefront of the professional scene's critics.

Gracious and good-humoured, Leblanc had started working for the Tour race direction in 1989 and became director-general in 1994. An accomplished and eloquent ex-professional – he rode the Tour twice – he had a sound and balanced, if conservative, reputation. Yet he was essentially a fan, a lover of the sport, given a dream job. Now, as the brickbats came flying in, he found himself almost alone manning the battlements. 'The Tour isn't finished,' he insisted time and time again, as he fought to limit the damage done to the race's reputation.

Business, such as it was, carried on as usual. While we waited for further news of the Festina detentions and wondered if Priem and Mikhailov would return to the race, the apparently unflappable Bobby Julich strolled into the airy tent to give a scheduled press conference. Unsurprisingly, Bobby J didn't want to talk about police raids, doping scandals or strip searches. He wanted to talk about his dreams of Tour glory and his hopes for a podium placing in Paris. Pointed questions on a disgraced Tour from an outsider – a British newspaper man unused to cycling's cosy conventions – were given short shrift and the American was soon back on the subject of his seemingly limitless Tour ambitions. It wasn't Bobby J's fault – the impression was that he knew little of what was really going on away from the race; yet his impressionable words jarred uneasily against the awful reality of events far away in Lyon.

By five in the afternoon, the rumour mill was running into overdrive. More raids were on the way, we were told. Camera crews and photographers had already been despatched to team hotels across the Ariège valley in anticipation of more arrests. On the word of a reliable source that the highly successful Casino team (home to former yellow jersey wearer Bo Hamburger, stage winner Jacky Durand and King of the Mountains competition leader Rodolfo Massi) might be the next team visited by the French police, we jumped into the car and sped off to the supermarket-sponsored team's hotel in Ax-les-Thermes. But when we got to the spa town, woken out of its geriatric atrophy by the arrival of the Tour's noisy caravan, the Casino hotel was calm. We peered around the lobby and examined the team sheets posted up on the wall by the elevator. Contrary to our information, everything seemed normal. Team personnel sat quietly sipping beers in the bar, and chatting with French journalists.

On the way back to the climb up the Col de Port, as other press cars hurtled past us on their own wild-goose chase in Ax-les-Thermes, I rang the paper and topped up my story with another hundred words, based on the increasing media speculation surrounding the Casino team. Retired professional Frédéric Pontier, who had ridden for Casino manager Lavenu in 1997, had set the cat among the pigeons still further with a brief but implicatory interview that had stunned his former employers.

'It's true that I took EPO, but I never used any other doping products,' Pontier had said. 'Doctors assured me that using EPO would raise the level of my performance. I began my first course in May 1996, over three months.'

In 1997, Pontier continued, he had taken two more courses of EPO, but 'in moderation'. The Frenchman explained that he had monitored his red blood cell count, his haematocrit level, with a machine. 'In the end it didn't bother me, because the others are doing the same,' he asserted, 'so that takes the guilt away. I'm not saying that they're all doped, but a large number are.' It was the usual system, Pontier concluded, saying that it was unfair only to point the finger at Festina. 'They were just unlucky in that they got stitched up by their *soigneur*.'

Meanwhile, up in Lyon, the 'stitched-up' Festina Nine, under increasing pressure to reveal all to the police, were looking forward to a night in the cells. But at least one sponsor had apparently realised the gravity of the situation. Following their early morning visit by the Reims police, TVM had abandoned their usual 'mussels party', the lunch-time buffet open to VIP guests and selected journalists traditionally hosted by the Dutch team on the Tour's rest day.

Day 16   Stage 12

Friday 24 July
Tarascon-sur-Ariège–Le Cap d'Agde, 222 km

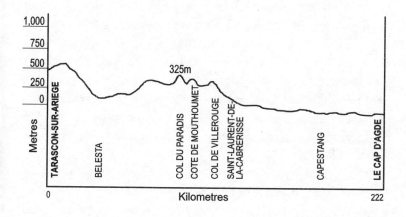

Sweat dripped steadily from my forehead on to the laptop keyboard in front of me, as thirty-nine degrees of heat smothered the Gymnase Molinie in the heart of the Mediterranean resort town of Cap d'Agde. The unmoving air hung impenetrable in the press hall as a haze of cigarette smoke and sunlight filled the room. Sitting at tables behind me, the local council's army of helpers noisily scoffed the remainders of the buffet, put together by the comité local. Sophie del Rizzo, already well aware of overcrowding and unseemly squabbles over power points, watched anxiously as a group of sweating Dutch journos piled in through the swing doors and searched irritably for a place to sit. In the end, they brusquely swept the trestle tables free of brie and breadcrumbs, setting out their mobiles and laptops among the debris of paper plates and spilt red wine. An eddy of intrigue wafted around the room, as the final hour of hot and furious racing filled the TV screens. The media corps was rife with speculation; would the TVM team be thrown off the Tour? Would the race stop, as no less a paper than *Le Monde* had implored it to, here and now, in this nondescript Mediterranean beach resort?

Outside, the sticky, blistered tarmac along the finishing straight awaited the arrival of the Tour *peloton*, something that only a few hours earlier had looked increasingly unlikely as they bickered and protested their way east from the Pyrénées. But then, after an acrimonious and shambolic start to the day, it was a miracle that the twelfth stage of the 1998 Tour de France had started at all – let alone made it to the finishing line.

Under humid cloudy skies hanging broodily over the Pyrénées, the Tour buckled up and made ready to hit the road again after what should have been a restorative thirty-six hours in Tarascon-sur-Ariège. But the events of the previous day – the TVM arrests, the brutal Festina 'interviews' and the tabloid reportage of one French camera crew – had all helped to heighten the atmosphere of tension. That unease was palpable in the start village, perched in the Place St Michel, at the top of the old town's medieval walls. Tarascon, like so many other towns before it, had innocently anticipated a sporting and cultural carnival, but what it got was a war.

The arrests of Priem and Mikhailov, not to mention the horror-stories emanating from Lyon of Festina riders being strip-searched and left to cry through the night in dingy police cells, had sent a wave of outrage and panic through those riders still in the race. As I walked up the hill to the start line, I said hello to Max Sciandri and Marty Jemison, but their greetings were cooler, more distant than usual. When I got further into the crowds cramming the tiny start village, I found out why.

Not only had *Le Monde*, perhaps France's most respected and influential national newspaper, concluded that *'il faut arrêter ce Tour'* – that this Tour must be stopped – but three Festina riders, world champion Laurent Brochard, Armin Meier and Christophe Moreau, had, according to their lawyers, admitted their guilt. They had been released at midnight the night before, while the other six continued to protest their innocence. With more accusations rolling in, the straw that broke the camel's back was a sensationalist report on France 2, ironically the TV channel providing most live coverage of the race. Three days earlier, a France 2 camera crew had rummaged through bins at the Asics team hotel in Pau. The film, shown on French network TV the previous evening, had shown a find of pharmaceutical products, some of which the programme claimed were banned. On one or two vials and bottles were stickers, bearing the names of the Italian team's riders. They'd interviewed Asics' team doctor Max Testa in search of an explanation, but he'd fumbled his way through the conversation.

An anxious Testa was in the village the next morning, looking for journalists to put his case to. I joined a group of other hacks as in halting but clear English, he battled to explain how the film had twisted his words.

'We want the Tour de France to know what happened. The interview was supposed to be about how we prepare the riders, but then they started to ask me about all the products we use,' he explained. 'Then they asked me about the products they said they'd found in the bins, saying that one was banned, but that's wrong – it's not a banned product.'

Testa went on. 'We don't use EPO – we use vitamin B12,

177

iron and folic acid, instead of EPO,' the Italian insisted. 'When I saw the film it had changed what I said, but they can come and check everything we use and they won't find any banned products.'

By then, with the start looming, it was time for us to get in the car and leave. We drove off ahead of the field, stopping off for petrol and mineral water, heading over the few small climbs before the route dropped down towards the flat, sunflower-lined roads of the Mediterranean. We'd been driving for about an hour, out of range of the race radio, when the mobile rang. It was a photographer friend who was still at the start line in Tarascon, shooting roll after roll of chaotic scenes as the Tour degenerated into farce.

The roll-out had been scheduled for 11.30 and most of the French riders, as well as the Telekom team, had pedalled dutifully away from Tarascon. Behind them, though, the disgruntled Spanish and Italian teams stayed on the line, with Pantani and Jalabert the biggest stars among the group refusing to race. It wasn't so much an organised protest as a shambolic breakdown, a very public loss of faith in the Tour itself. But they still free-wheeled, arguing and debating with each other and race officials as far as the *départ réel* – where the flag officially drops each day to signify the real start of the race. There, with their morale broken by two weeks of scandal, things finally ground to a halt as most of the riders climbed from their bikes and sat in groups on the road.

Some wanted to get on with it, though. Bjarne Riis impatiently led the Telekom team forward and stared disdainfully at those arguing with race officials, while other riders took the opportunity to vent their spleen over long-standing grievances. 'Nobody asks us about anything,' said one. 'They design the races without consulting us, they install blood tests and we're the last to know. The Tour is a circus and we're the clowns.'

They were there for the best part of an hour and a half, some laughing and disinterested, others huddled in conspiratorial groups. One or two, like Jalabert and Sciandri, appeared on the verge of quitting the race for good. Tempers were running high and ONCE's *directeur* Manolo Saiz, enraged by the attitude of the French media, soon found himself in a heated argument with Jean-François Pescheux, the Tour's sports director. Only when things became dangerously overheated were the pair separated by onlookers. Saiz's leading rider Jalabert, meanwhile, was in conversation with Jean-Marie Leblanc, and in the end almost pulled the race director's Radio Tour microphone out of his hand in order to make an impromptu announcement.

'Since the start of the Tour de France,' blurted Jalabert, 'nobody has talked about cycling – only about the "Festina Affair". The Tour has taken a back seat and us with it. We're sick of it. They've treated us like dumb animals, so we're going to behave like dumb animals: we're not racing today.'

But some of the riders, like Casino's Mountains King, Rodolfo Massi, had had enough debate for one day and, followed by several team-mates, rode slowly off down the road, watched darkly by the likes of Sciandri and Pantani. Solidarity with his peers, it seems, doesn't always come easily to a professional bike rider.

'We need to stick together,' said Sciandri later. 'But when you try to get everybody together to do something about what's happening, they won't do it.'

Those instigating the protest, such as Jalabert and Saiz, presented it as a *cri de coeur*; a heartfelt protest against media victimisation, against the over-zealous French police, against the powerlessness of the race organisation. In truth, it was probably more of a confused act born out of indignation, as they faced up to the threat of more police raids and arrests and further doping and medical tests being introduced by the UCI before the Tour even ended.

Finally, Leblanc, faced with the Tour breaking down before his very eyes, rescued the situation and persuaded the riders to start the stage. 'They owed it to the public,' he said. 'If they'd failed to start, the public would have turned their back on them.'

When they finally left almost two hours after the scheduled start time, Jalabert was incandescent with rage at his peers' lack of solidarity. He spoke to Saiz and they both agreed: ONCE should go ahead and, as one rider put it, 'kick everybody else's arse'. Saiz felt that after everything they'd had to put up with, ONCE had to show what they were made of.

The stage eventually got going after sixteen kilometres but exploded at the first bonus sprint when Jalabert, joined by his younger brother Nicolas and Bart Voskamp of the TVM team, launched a vicious and fiery attack that stunned the rest of the Tour caravan. There were still almost two hundred kilometres to race and the temperature was climbing higher and higher – especially under Jalabert's racing cap – as they sped out of the hills and down towards the Golfe du Lion. Jalabert senior set the pace, riding like a man possessed, until after almost ninety kilometres he'd made up his deficit on Ullrich and had become race leader on the road. His brother, although sponsored by the rival Cofidis team, assisted the pace-making enthusiastically while Voskamp, well aware that he might represent TVM's last chance of glory, gave as good as he got.

At the feed zone, the trio led by five minutes and

Jalabert, still racing in a semi-demented fashion, was in the race lead by a comfortable two minutes. It was enough to set Ullrich's Telekom team chasing, and as the hot roads began to take their toll, the break's lead steadily slipped. Forty kilometres later, Jalabert, aware of the approaching bunch, sat up from his effort and waved Voskamp and his brother ahead. They fought to stay clear for a few more kilometres but by now Telekom, angered by Jalabert's defiant ride, were equally motivated and the German team swept up the last breakaways with thirty kilometres still to race. There was more to come, of course – the inevitably futile solo attack by Jacky Durand, who, as the sprinters burst into life, was caught within sight of the finish line; and a desperate lunge for the line by Telekom's Erik Zabel. Unsurprisingly, however, Mapei's Tom Steels, the fastest sprinter in the race with or without the presence of Cipollini or Zabel, took his second stage win. Afterwards, the expectant media crammed into the press room, anxious to hear what Jean-Marie would have to say after another tumultuous day.

The clock ticked on and deadlines fell away as the sultry evening wore on. Still Jean-Marie didn't appear. In the smoky sauna that the Gymnase Molinie had become, a forest of TV cameras and boom microphones sprang up, surrounding the platform on which the race director was to speak, craning to hear how he proposed to address the dire crisis. The news, confirmed by the Reims prosecutor, that doping products and masking agents had been found in the TVM hotel during the rest-day search, had heightened expectations that a second leading professional squad was about to be evicted from the Tour. But as Jean-Marie finally appeared, we were in for a surprise. Accompanied by other officials from the race, he

stepped on to the platform, sat down at the bank of microphones and began to speak.

'In the aftermath of a stage ridden at more than forty-
eight kilometres an hour, first allow us to say thank you to the
riders,' he began, 'who this morning were very upset. The
riders were battered, and maybe we were too, because for
ten days now, everybody has spoken more of doping than
they have of the race. They wanted to show their anger,' said
Leblanc, 'with the way that you, newspapers, radio stations,
TV stations, have reported this Tour de France.'

'This morning,' he continued, 'we told the riders that if we
cancelled the stage, that would have been still worse for their
image. If the stage had been cancelled, then maybe the 1998
Tour wouldn't have carried on. Contrary to what some
intellectuals and Paris newspaper editorials suggest, the Tour
must continue. The riders want it and, notwithstanding this
crisis, the public are still loyal.'

Even a question from the floor, asking if he had any
contact with the police investigators in Lille or Reims,
brought a non-committal response as Leblanc explained
that he had no direct contacts with the French authorities.
With that, Jean-Marie stood up, and flanked by his colleagues stepped out of the smoke and heat into the fresh
evening air.

We filed back to our desks, stunned, almost without
exception, by what had been said. There was no mention of
TVM, the arrests of their *directeur sportif* and team doctor or
of the repercussions of the Festina investigation. Instead,
Leblanc seemed to lay most of the blame for the darkest
hours in the Tour's history at the doors of the press. The Tour
organisation, fearful of legal action by expelled riders and their
sponsors, may have been keeping their collective head in the
sand; but they were also playing with fire. TVM's continued

presence surely left the Tour's damaged credibility hanging by a thread: if any more scandal developed around the Dutch team, then that would surely be the end, both for them and for the 1998 race.

Stage winner: Tom Steels, Belgium (Mapei–Bricobi)

Overall race leader: Jan Ullrich, Germany (Deutsche Telekom)

Points classification leader: Erik Zabel, Germany (Deutsche Telekom)

Team classification leader: Cofidis

Mountains classification leader: Rodolfo Massi, Italy (Casino)

Day 17   Stage 13

Saturday 25 July
Frontignan la Peyrade–Carpentras, 196 km

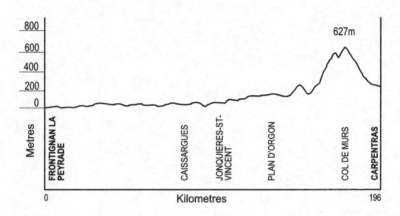

In spite of everything, I was happy. We were heading towards my own French heartlands – not somewhere that I claim any connection with through family or blood, but a place that always takes me back to the source and reminds me of my own initial love of cycling. The thirteenth stage took the Tour from the seafront at Frontignan la Peyrade, just a few kilometres south of Montpellier, and then headed eastwards and inland, skirting Nîmes and the Bouches-du-Rhône region before climbing into the Provençal hills of the Vaucluse.

The final kilometres of the route passed within the shadow of one of France's most bizarre and fearsome features, Mont Ventoux, a giant hump of calcified limestone rising from the Vaucluse plateau. A relentlessly steep road climbs up from the base of the mountain through thick forest and scrub before emerging into a barren and immense landscape of bare white rock as it grinds towards the summit. The mountain holds a fascination for me – I've slept on it, hiked on it and cycled on it, savouring its wild, other-worldly atmosphere. This year, the Tour, although passing close by, was giving it a miss; but its unmistakable outline cast a daunting shadow over the race and its history.

The gradient climbing to the top offers virtually no respite for twenty-one and a half kilometres before it turns viciously on to a narrow platform, housing a small car-park, a meteorological and telecommunication station and a tacky gift shop. From the summit you can, on a particularly clear day, see the glaciers of Mont Blanc, the hills of the Cevennes and, according to some locals, the Spanish Pyrénées. Over the top of Ventoux's humpback ridge, the road snakes across an even steeper scree of white rock before dropping back down towards the villages and lavender fields. In the myths and legends of the Tour de France, the mountain is infamous. In 1955, the Provençal heat almost brought the stage over the Ventoux from Marseille to Avignon to a standstill, as rider after rider neared a state of collapse. Breton rider Jean Mallejac, who had started the day ninth overall, fell victim to sunstroke and collapsed unconscious on his way up the climb. And a Belgian rider, Richard van Genechten, gasping for air, zigzagged his way up the mountain before falling to the verge, on the brink of asphyxiation.

Average speeds were slower back then. In 1955, long before the advent of EPO, blood doping or the use of growth hormones, the Tour was won by French legend Louison Bobet at an average speed of 34.4 kilometres per hour. In 1997, the average speed of the Tour was well over 39.2 kilometres per hour. In the fifties and sixties, amphetamines were known to be part of the professional scene; the riders, well-used to 'looking after' themselves, hardened themselves to the brutality of the sport and became accustomed to almost riding themselves into the ground. They flirted with doping, some more than others, and thought little of the potential consequences. This cavalier attitude to pain and doping undoubtedly shortened some life-spans.

The race came back to the Ventoux's brooding slopes in 1958 and 1965, but it is the events of the 1967 stage over the mountain that have become forever linked with the Tour's reputation for brutality. Britain's Tom Simpson, winner of a series of major races including the World Championships in 1965, was an ambitious and well-established rider. He was well placed when that year's stage began in front of Marseilles' old port; but the bluff, slight Yorkshireman with an impish sense of humour was about to become inextricably linked to the evils of doping.

Simpson was fiercely determined to do well in the 1967 Tour, led, as it squared up to the challenge of Ventoux, by France's Roger Pingeon. That day, as the temperature climbed beyond forty degrees at noon, the riders sweated through Apt and Roussillon before climbing the Col de Murs and dropping down to Carpentras, hosed down as they went by sympathetic spectators. Others at the roadside passed up drinks or pointed the way to the nearest fountains. Those who live in the region know how fearsome a climb the Ventoux becomes in the summer heat. From Carpentras they rode into Bedoin, a cool, airy village of plane trees and sleepy cafés, from which the climb to Ventoux's exposed summit really begins. On any day between March and October, hundreds of cyclists pass through, emulating Simpson's fateful final pedal strokes.

As they rounded the first vicious hairpin, eight riders detached themselves from the field and climbed clear, with Simpson and the rest of the favourites among them. But as the climb went on and the others rode away from him, Simpson looked strained and his eyes became glassy as he fought not to lose more ground. By the time he emerged from the forested slopes and tackled the final steep inclines to the summit, it was clear that he was in a state of near-delirium. He fell for the first time as he ground his way towards the summit but is said to have told those who rushed to his aid to 'put me back on my bike'. In fact, he simply barked, 'Get me up.' A further two kilometres from the top, his head wobbling as he zigzagged slowly across the incline, he collapsed again on to the rocky verge.

There are a few seconds of grainy film of Tom Simpson's last moments, of his nodding head and slurred pedalling. There is a glimpse of his brown and slender frame stretched out on the unforgiving rocks at the roadside while the Tour's doctor at the time, Dr Dumas, and another onlooker frantically gave him mouth-to-mouth resuscitation. Finally, the footage shows him being airlifted to hospital, but by that time it was too late. The autopsy confirmed the presence of amphetamines and alcohol in his blood, evidence which was backed up by the discovery of doping products in his bags and racing jersey. The cocktail had combined with the awful heat, the murderous gradient and his own fierce ambition to take him beyond his natural limits.

'With hand on heart,' said his old team-mate and rival Eddy Merckx in his biography, 'I can say that Tom was not the pill-taker he's been made out to be. That day on Ventoux, he was the victim of his own uncurbed ambition. His ambition knew no bounds and he ended up paying for it.'

Before the stage began in Frontignan and in the wake of the Tarascon farce, there had been a crisis meeting held behind closed doors between Daniel Baal, head of the French

Federation and vice-president of the UCI, and several prominent riders, including Laurent Jalabert, Marco Pantani, Luc Leblanc and Bjarne Riis. When they emerged into the sunlight from the cool depths of the Hotel Mercure at Balaruc-les-Bains, 'Jaja' and Riis smiled broadly for the cameras, as if the whole dire situation had been swiftly and easily resolved. Verbruggen's promised tests were to be postponed and instead an uneasy truce was called, as both the riders' representatives and the UCI agreed that further, more comprehensive medical controls would be introduced in time for the 1999 season.

'It was a good meeting,' said Riis as he squinted into the bright sunlight, 'but we weren't able to draw any real conclusions in an hour. We'll have to sit down again in the autumn to further reconcile all the problems.'

It was all positive stuff, but they had made one crucial omission from the guest list – they'd forgotten to invite the French police. The UCI's climbdown, although couched in terms that made it seem merely a necessary compromise, sent the wrong signals – as did the images of a grinning Jalabert sharing a private word with an uncomfortable looking Daniel Baal, vice-president of the UCI. But then in the face of the admissions of doping emanating from the Festina riders now running scared in Lyon, the UCI had every reason to feel aghast. As the race turned towards the Alpine foothills, the very public statements made by the likes of Alex Zulle and Armin Meier were dominating the French media.

'I told the police I took EPO,' Meier admitted on French radio. 'I told them how I took it and why I took it and then they let me go. It wasn't easy admitting it but I needed to confess and now I feel better that I have.'

The Swiss rider, shocked by his experience, revealed that he had been stripped and left in a cell for more than two hours. 'They took my clothes, my watch, my car keys and my belt,' he said.

Worse still was the treatment meted out to the shocked and frightened Zulle. Known for his frail temperament, the bespectacled double Tour of Spain winner had been left alone in a cell for the night.

'They took everything,' said Meier, 'even Zulle's glasses. And I had to bend over so they could search me internally.'

Meier admitted that he had continued to maintain his innocence, at least until the police produced documentation relating to the team's systematic doping. 'Then I understood,' conceded Meier, 'and I cracked.'

Following his release, the mild-mannered Zulle spoke to the Swiss press. 'I had good results without doping,' he said, 'but I was under pressure from the sponsors and pressure from the team. I'm sorry I lied, but there was nothing I could do. I have made a mistake and I regret disappointing my fans. But it's like when everybody's speeding on the motorway and you're the only one to get caught.'

Laurent Dufaux, their affable team-mate, seemed to have been equally moved by the experience and hoped that his confession would bring about change. 'Yes, I did take EPO,' said Dufaux, 'but it didn't make me win races. I hope the authorities can change things – it would be a shame to put the lid back on.'

Only three riders, Hervé, Virenque and Neil Stephens, stuck to their guns and continued to protest their innocence. While most of the English speakers working on the race were horrified at the popular Australian's predicament, few of them felt much sympathy for Virenque's situation. Yet he remained the public's darling, and played up to his image as French cycling's housewives' choice. The truth was that he had hardly won any major stage races and rarely performed in events other than the Tour de France. When he did stick his nose in front of the field, he became prone to theatrical, crowd-pleasing rides that sustained his popular image of thwarted hero. Now, he'd claimed the moral high ground, asserting that he was the victim of a smear campaign. Meanwhile Willy Voet, the man who'd started the whole thing off, was getting ready to publicly question Virenque's version of events.

Out in the hills of Provence, a six-man group of riders had slipped away from the field as the Tour headed towards the Plateau de Vaucluse. Frazzled by the heat, I'd driven on open roads to Avignon and then cut across country to Carpentras, where the finish-line crowd wilted under the fierce sunlight. Under the taut blue sky, the break of six rode into the picture-postcard village of Gordes, overlooking the green slopes of the Luberon valley. In the attack were Italian champion Andrea Tafi and his team-mate Daniele Nardello, Stéphane Heulot of the La Française des Jeux team, Vicente García-Acosta from Banesto, Rabobank's Koos Moerenhout and US Postal's American rider Marty Jemison. With the hardships of the Alps looming, all of them were keen for a stage win.

I was excited that Marty was in the break. His wife Jill, working on the Tour for US Postal in a public relations capacity, was a friend and Marty was just one of the army of selfless team riders, the *domestiques*, who made up the greater part of the Tour field. He hadn't had an easy Tour, but after spells with several other sponsors, he had proven himself to be a survivor. As Nardello picked up the pace on the early slopes of the Col de Murs, Marty clung to the Italian's back wheel and grimaced in pain. He'd ridden strongly for most of the year and had come close to wins in a series of lesser races.

Now he was little more than twenty kilometres from the possibility of a Tour stage win – a victory that would be the biggest moment to date in his long and often uncertain professional career. After years spent fetching and carrying for a succession of highly paid team leaders in races across Europe, Marty was at the front, in contention for his own slice of glory in the biggest race of all. A Tour stage win would ensure that he was never again just a name on the start sheet.

On the rocky, winding route to the top of the Col de Murs, the six leaders attacked and counter-attacked, testing each other's resolve. It's not a steep climb but the rough, bumpy surface and the oppressive heat made it tough going. Once over the summit, the break settled down as behind them, Luc Leblanc, taking a leaf out of the absent Virenque's book, chose to jump clear of the Telekom-led field. But Riis, keeping his promise to the team to watch over race leader Ullrich, reeled the Frenchman in on the long descent to the valley.

Back in the press room I watched the finale intently, captivated by the tactical quandary facing Marty Jemison. I could sense that compared to the two Italians, he was aware of his limitations as a sprinter, and was already entertaining thoughts of attacking before the finish in the hope that a lone break would succeed. But Tafi was keeping a close eye on any rider with visions of stealing clear and, as the group rode into the shadows of the plane trees lining the Avenue des Platanes in Carpentras, Nardello was in pole position.

Unwittingly, as Tafi expertly set up his twenty-six-year-old team-mate, Heulot found himself ushered to the front as the sextet rode into the finishing straight. Marty, after expertly tracking the crucial moves throughout the day, was boxed in as the riders around him sprinted for the line. It was Nardello, after struggling to weave his way through the wheels in front of him, who clinched Mapei's fourth win of the Tour while Marty, despite his best efforts, could only manage fifth. Seconds later, Jemison, the oldest American rider in the race, stood breathless, grimy and sweat-streaked, beyond the finish line. We closed around him as he stood gasping for air, barging through the local kids pushing autograph books under his nose, eager to hear his story.

'I was there, but I was really hurting,' he admitted. 'And when it started to split up, I thought, "*Oh God . . .*" '

Somehow, he'd found the determination to race alongside Tafi and Nardello as they powered towards the finish, even though ultimately all it amounted to was another near miss for the US Postal team.

'When we stayed together over the hill and all the way in to the finish, I was feeling better and better,' he said. 'I stayed at the back and felt really calm – I know there are better sprinters but I gave it everything. I took it all the way to the line and gave it one hell of a sprint.'

Stage winner: Daniele Nardello, Italy (Mapei–Bricobi)

Overall race leader: Jan Ullrich, Germany (Deutsche Telekom)

Points classification leader: Erik Zabel, Germany (Deutsche Telekom)

Team classification leader: Cofidis

Mountains classification leader: Rodolfo Massi, Italy (Casino)

Day 18   Stage 14

Sunday 26 July
Valréas–Grenoble, 186.5 km

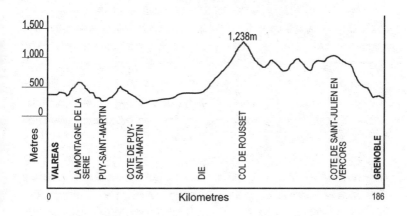

Jean-Marie Leblanc's hopes that his defensive statement in the steamy heat of Cap d'Agde had defused media criticisms of the race proved futile, as the French press continued to deride the 1998 Tour. One by one, the sports pages of Europe picked the race to ribbons until the alias 'Tour de Farce' had become stuck fast to the event. The newspapers took the culture of the Tour apart, ridiculing the need for non-stop spectacle, for showcased French scenery and for superhuman effort, putting much of it down to the Tour's close commercial ties with television.

France 2, the French national TV station transmitting the race, whose rubbish-rummagings had provoked the riders' strike in Tarascon, took more flak than just about anybody else. The station was described by one newspaper as 'schizophrenic' in its attitude towards the Tour. It was a justifiable accusation: in the afternoons, France 2's hyperbolic sports commentators gloried in the exploits of the riders and in the beauty of France; but by night, its news reporters hung around the back of team hotels on out-of-town estates, rifling through bin bags under the cover of darkness.

Gérard Holtz's cosy post-race chat show, *Vélo Club*, broadcast live on France 2 after the race ended each day, had been subject to a boycott by the riders; an action viewed by most French papers as demonstrating the professional élite's lopsided and hypocritical world-view. It was one thing, the media argued, to talk about how great the riders' athletic achievements were, but quite another to question how they had achieved them.

By now we had all realised that the 1998 Tour would do its damnedest to get to Paris, no matter how crippled it became. There was too much at stake for the race to be called off, too many commercial obligations to be fulfilled. Yet the *Société du Tour*'s leading figures repeated their assurances, insisting that they were shocked by the scale of the scandal and that they had only discovered the names of doping products through the press.

Over the weekend, Bernard Hinault, five-time Tour champion and one of the Tour's most outspoken and confrontational defenders, had argued that just because syringes and banned products were found at the TVM team's hotel, it didn't necessarily follow that the Dutch team were doping themselves. Meanwhile, the French press were quick to point out that at least one profession involved in the Tour scandal was now a booming growth market. Sports lawyers, they pointed out, had never had it so good.

Valréas, *ville départ* for stage fourteen, is a pretty town, set around an old papal village with a large and spectacular château overlooking lavender fields and olive groves. It isn't really the gateway to the Alps as the town of Gap, about a hundred kilometres to the east, has that honour; but even so, it has the feel of a final outpost of hazy Provence prior to the upland landscape of the Drôme region. Soon after leaving its shady, somnolent streets, the roads climb through the Drôme before snaking up to the buttresses of the Vercors plateau, south of Grenoble. And although there were no particularly tough climbs on the route of stage fourteen, there were enough hills on the way to Grenoble and the towering Alps to worry those riders running on empty.

I strolled into the start village, only to be waylaid by one bleary-eyed French hack who could barely contain himself as he talked of the previous night's sexual adventures. 'I got talking to her in a bar and then later on, after midnight, we went outside to a park bench,' he recalled dreamily. 'She had such legs – beautiful, brown legs . . .'

It was a rare day, one when I was alone in the car. Andy, who'd been with me since Roscoff, had gone back to England, while my next passenger, Stephen, had yet to arrive. For once, as I headed out of town past the crowds lining the start line, I was left to my own thoughts.

Like everyone else, like the riders, the fans, like Jean-Marie himself, the events of the 1998 Tour had confused and battered me. I wasn't on the race because it was a good story or because an opportunistic editor had sent me hunting for a scoop. I was there because I'd always wanted to be there, covering what I'd always thought was the world's most exciting and romantic sports event. I'd been to the Tour and to plenty of other races for the previous five years, becoming gradually aware that doping was a part of the sport. I'd interviewed big-name stars in their hotel rooms and seen the *soigneur* or team manager slam a suspicious-looking case shut as I walked through the door. I'd known that doping was there – I didn't need riders to tearfully admit it, or Bernard Hinault to vehemently deny it, to realise how much a part of the sport it had become.

But my judgment had become blurred by that fear of spitting in the communal soup, by an understanding of how ruthless a sport it had become, and by the knowledge that the riders – misguided, self-indulgent and sometimes naïve though they may have been – were really the victims in the whole saga. It was their attitudes towards the revelations that gave them away. Alex Zulle, for example, had bizarrely compared EPO use to a fondness for strong coffee. But I realised as I drove into the Drôme foothills, the truth was that they had become desensitised, that their moral compass had lost its bearing. 'We're not junkies,' insisted those riders under suspicion – and in comparison with sallow, hollow-eyed teenagers, desperately chasing the dragon in a squat, they were right. Yet they were still taking their fix, not merely to win, but in some cases just to get through the day, just to hang on to their job. If they could take it or leave it, why were so many of them willing to risk being caught red-handed by the police? Why had the TVM team apparently opted to hang on to their 'gear' despite the presence of French drugs police on the race, something realised by most of the other teams long before the rest day?

On the other hand, it was equally naïve to expect single-minded athletes, cosseted by club coaches in the depths of rural France or Switzerland since their early teens, to have a highly developed sense of altruism. Most of them had spent a third of their lives training on their bikes and when they weren't out on the road, they spent their time eating and sleeping, being primed for professionalism by the sport's old hands. It was no wonder that so many of them seemed to have difficulty relating to the outside world. Yet if there was an argument for doping, if it was justifiable and if society was prepared to accept its existence, why did they and their allies lie? If there was a moral case for doping, then why deny it so vehemently when suspicion fell upon them? They knew, just like every sports lover knows in his heart, that doping is a betrayal and that every dose of steroids, of EPO, of growth hormone, is the action of a defeated cynic. It stained their own characters; but far worse, as Paul Kimmage, Gilles Delion and Frédéric Pontier had come to realise, it threw the whole sport into doubt. How could those at the roadside keep the faith once they knew the truth? And what exactly was the truth? Who was clean and who was doped – how could we believe in any of them any more?

But many fans were still keeping the faith, turning out on the sunny roads of the Drôme to cheer on the Tour *peloton* as it passed by. As I drove up to Crest and prepared to head across country towards Valence and the A49 to Grenoble, huge crowds lined the verge. Not all of them were supportive, though. Every day, more came to the *route du Tour* to gloat over the decline of an event seen by many to symbolise much of the worst in French tradition. They held up sarcastic banners such as '*Vive le Tour d'EPO*' and every now and then hastily graffitied syringes appeared in whitewash on the hot tarmac.

I turned left off the route into a queue of stationary traffic, blocked by the closed roads and impatiently awaiting the passage of the Tour. A group of jeering teenagers leaned against a battered Renault as I squeezed past. One of them raised a single finger in derision while the others yelled abuse. '*Le Tour – c'est fini!*' I heard them yell, as I accelerated away.

The ninth stage to Pau had taken the riders to the foot of the

Pyrénées. The fourteenth stage of the 1998 Tour deposited the field at the foot of France's other great mountain range, facing two daunting days of giant Alpine passes. The undulating route to Grenoble offered the all-rounders in the *peloton* a final chance to make their mark before the passes of the Croix de Fer, Télégraphe, Galibier, Cucheron and Madeleine took their toll.

After a frantic flurry of attacks in the first hour of the stage, six riders moved clear after 106 kilometres, tackling the biggest climb of the day, the Col de Rousset, as a group. GAN's reliable Australian Stuart O'Grady was one of them, as was Leon van Bon, the stage winner back in Pau. They were joined by yet another US Postal hopeful, Denmark's Peter Meinert-Nielsen, former yellow jersey wearer Laurent Desbiens of Cofidis, Banesto's Orlando Rodrigues and ageing Italian Guiseppe Calcaterra of the absent Cipollini's Saeco team. Under overcast skies, they moved far ahead of a disinterested main field, most of whom had their minds on the bigger climbs awaiting them the following day. The break's lead peaked at twelve minutes over the top of the Rousset, but with Telekom making a semblance of a pursuit behind them, it had dropped to nine and a half minutes as they closed on the wide streets and boulevards of Grenoble.

Desbiens, who knew that he had no hope of winning a six-man sprint, tried to break clear; but with only five kilometres still to race, O'Grady determinedly pulled him back. Then Meinert-Nielsen took the option that had eluded Marty Jemison the previous afternoon, sprinting ahead over the tram lines and pedestrian crossings with the finish line almost in sight. Yet his move lacked belief and O'Grady, sensing that the others did not have the strength to break clear, readied himself for the dash to the line. O'Grady knew that he and van Bon were the quickest riders in the breakaway, but his biggest threat came from an unexpected source – the greying Calcaterra.

Suddenly, the Italian was at the front of the group as they hurtled into the final one hundred metres with O'Grady's rival van Bon fading away. Alarmed by the Italian's unexpected speed, O'Grady battled to catch the Saeco rider. When he began the sprint, the Australian was quick to get behind him, but there were only a few centimetres in it at the end. As the pair drew level, Calcaterra, seeing his rare chance for glory slipping away, leaned across into the GAN rider's path to try and block his sprint. It earned him relegation by the race jury to sixth place, but it wasn't enough to prevent the twenty-four-year-old O'Grady from thrusting his bike across the line to sneak the first Tour de France stage win of his career.

'The Tour's like Disneyland,' the Australian enthused afterwards. But then, after wearing the coveted yellow jersey from Cholet to Châteauroux and winning the stage to Grenoble ten days later, O'Grady, who had quickly become a household name back in the old country, had every reason to feel that his début Tour had been one long fairy tale.

As the construction crews moved in, the weather changed. Outside the press room, the temperature dropped and a strong breeze stirred the trees in Grenoble's Parc des Sports. I tried to crystallise the thoughts I'd had earlier in the day, took a deep breath, and wrote my story for the newspaper.

I talked of the insularity and arrogance of a sport that finds it hard to acknowledge the values of the outside world and criticised the Tour organisation, the French media and the athletes for being 'paralysed by doubt and fear'. I wanted to choose the right words at the right time and they seemed to touch a nerve somewhere along the line. When I got back home, well after the Tour had ended, a testy letter in a crisp, white envelope arrived for me from Mr Hein Verbruggen, President of the UCI.

Stage winner: Stuart O'Grady, Australia (GAN)
Overall race leader: Jan Ullrich, Germany (Deutsche Telekom)
Points classification leader: Erik Zabel, Germany (Deutsche Telekom)
Team classification leader: Cofidis
Mountains classification leader: Rodolfo Massi, Italy (Casino)

Day 19   Stage 15

Monday 27 July
Grenoble–Les Deux Alpes, 189 km

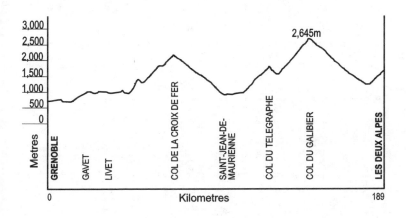

Thunderstorms hovered over Grenoble through the night. It was still raining the next morning as we stepped out of the ill-named Hôtel Splendid in the city centre and climbed into the car to drive to the stage start. Stephen, an English journalist living in Italy, had arrived by train the night before for his first taste of the Tour. From Grenoble, he was to travel with me to the Tour's end, until we finally reached the Champs-Elysées in Paris. With the rain falling in the street outside, we were slow to leave the breakfast table and found ourselves running well behind schedule. In our panic we got badly lost, driving around Grenoble's gridlocked one-way system, jumping kerbs and making illegal U-turns in an effort to find the start village. Finally, we made it on to the race route, only to find ourselves heading out of town in a convoy of press cars, unable to turn back towards the start.

Ahead of us lay the route of the key stage of the 1998 Tour

de France, a 189-kilometre ride over some of the Tour's legendary battlegrounds. The Col de la Croix de Fer, a 2,067 metre pass in the Haute Savoie, land of *raclette* and cow bells, was the first ascent of the day. It was here in 1986 that Greg Lemond from Nevada broke the mould and became the first native English-speaker to win the Tour, introducing an era of corporate sponsorship, high salaries and multinational teams. Lemond had sealed his success over the Croix de Fer, breaking clear of the rest of the field in the company of his celebrated team-mate and mentor, Bernard Hinault – the same Hinault who now acted as one of the Tour organisation's PR team.

In the 1985 Tour, Lemond had sacrificed his own hopes of victory in favour of a struggling Hinault, who was seeking his fifth Tour win, on the understanding that the Frenchman would return the favour the following year. But when the 1986 Tour reached the Pyrénées, Hinault had taken the race by the scruff of the neck, snatching the *maillot jaune* with a remarkable and unexpected attack. It left the American, obliged by team conventions not to chase the Breton, desolate and confused. But not for the first time, Hinault had overestimated himself and the following day, after an epic stage in the heart of the Pyrénées, the Frenchman lost almost all the time he had gained on the American as Lemond declared war on his team-mate.

Their battle for control of the race and of their own La Vie Claire team was a bitter affair. Their sponsoring company was owned by the infamous entrepreneur Bernard Tapie, who after his flirtation with cycling and later with French politics, was dragged through the courts in the Marseilles football club match-fixing scandal. Back in 1986 the marriage of Hinault, the tempestuous but charismatic French 'man of the soil' with Lemond, the blond-haired, blue-eyed child of the New World, perfectly represented Tapie's modernising ambitions. Supported by a combination of highly paid French, Swiss and North American riders, Tapie's two superstars made La Vie Claire the most powerful team in cycling. But as the 1986 Tour headed into the high Alps, the rift between Lemond and Hinault had brought Tapie's dream team to the verge of collapse. Instead of the usual team togetherness, Lemond and his English-speaking team-mates found themselves separated from Hinault and his French clique at meal times. By the final week of the race, the American's paranoia gripped him so deeply that he had begun to suspect his own team mechanics of tampering with his bike.

However, on the narrow road over the Croix de Fer that year, Lemond and Hinault resolved their differences, working together to distance the rest of the field. Even so, despite riding side by side for several hours, the pair barely spoke until they reached the final kilometres of the stage, after the steep climb to the ski resort at Alpe d'Huez. Lemond initiated the reconciliation, wrapping an arm around Hinault's shoulder and suggesting that he should take the honour of crossing the finish line first. The Badger, as Hinault was nicknamed, wasn't about to refuse and the pair crossed the line holding hands in a shaky display of unity, with the Frenchman's front wheel just a few inches ahead.

At a press conference the next day, Hinault's desperate ambition got the better of him once more. He turned on the American, insisting feistily that the Tour wasn't over. Despite the Frenchman's boast, Lemond, his nerves frayed by Hinault's mind games, survived to become the first English-speaking winner of the Tour. To this day relations between the two are frosty at best, with each accusing the other of selective amnesia.

The tense drama of the 1986 Tour, in which cycling's old

world, personified by Hinault, squared up to the shock of the new, embodied by Lemond, was to have a profound influence on the development of the sport. The intense publicity that Lemond's battle with the French legend received around the world opened minds. In Colorado, the teenage Bobby Julich was glued to TV coverage of Lemond's success while far away, in the gloomy confines of eastern Europe, twelve-year-old Jan Ullrich was having his own dreams similarly fired by fuzzy television images wafting through the Iron Curtain from West Germany.

Twelve years on and with Tour victory hanging in the balance, Ullrich, clad in the race leader's *maillot jaune*, led the all-powerful and multinational Telekom team along the valley to the foot of the Croix de Fer; the climb where he and Julich, although worlds apart, had seen their own adolescent dreams take shape.

We drove through the dank valley of the Romanche river, overshadowed by towering, forested cliffs, to the foot of the Croix de Fer. There, as the *route du Tour* swung left off the main road to head up into the hills, we pulled over beyond the road-block and, after diving into a nearby bar for a quick *café au lait*, joined the expectant crowds waiting to see the Tour pass by.

In the drizzle, there was a palpable tension. We all knew, as did the man himself, that this must be Pantani's hour; the earlier attacks in the Pyrénées might have shaken Ullrich's confidence, but they had failed to dislodge him. If the Italian, or for that matter Bobby J, wanted to win the Tour, then here and now, at the foot of these giant and forbidding mountain passes, was their moment.

Cars sped past, some familiar from the press convoy; others splattered with the logos of TV and radio companies seen for the first time since the crammed confines of Dublin Castle, some three weeks earlier. Finally the first vehicles in the police escort came into view, and then after a long pause, the first commissaire cars. A ripple of cheering spread down the roadside as the first break of the day, containing Ullrich's team-mates Erik Zabel and Rolf Aldag, the Italian Oscar Pozzi and, almost inevitably, Jacky Durand sped past. A minute or so later the main field swept by. I glimpsed Ullrich, riding on the outside of the group, seemingly in the wrong position and too far from the front as he began the long haul up to the Croix de Fer.

From the desolate high pastures of the Croix de Fer they faced the long and often bumpy thirty kilometre descent to the Maurienne valley, a thin strip of flat meadowland between the giant peaks, blighted by frequent ugly factories. The Arc river ran alongside the road as the route took them to the foot of the next obstacle, a mammoth forty-six kilometre haul over two notorious adjoining passes, the Col du Télégraphe and the giant Col du Galibier. The Galibier's final switchbacks top out at 2,645 metres above sea level, making it the highest point on the route of the 1998 Tour.

Zabel, Durand, Aldag and Pozzi had been quickly swept up on the first steep ramps of the Croix de Fer as the favourites moved forward and set a punishing tempo which relegated a large group of riders to the back of the field. Up at the front, about forty riders rode towards the summit, leaving well over a hundred professionals hanging on for survival. Appropriately enough, Massi, clad in the King of the Mountains jersey, was first over the top; he was followed by Laurent Jalabert, who with Daniel Baal's assurances in mind seemed to have forgotten the traumas of Tarascon-sur-Ariège. Pantani, despite an inconsequential tumble on the climb, sat calmly in the front group, biding his time. By the

205

time they got to the foot of the Télégraphe and the climb out of Saint-Michel-de-Maurienne, a break of six riders had gone ahead, climbing up into the low, swirling cloud hanging over the mountains. Max Sciandri, usually not at his best in the high passes, was one of them; but they held out little hope of staying clear over the top of the mountain. A little-known rider called Christophe Rinero, one of Bobby Julich's French team-mates, was also there, as Cofidis again showed their surprising strength in depth.

In the dim, cold conditions, the colours of their bright jerseys dulled by the filthy spray thrown up from the road, the main group rode on, climbing inexorably towards the Télégraphe. Slowly but surely the break of six fell back with only Rinero, joined now by Massi and Spain's Marcos Serrano, showing signs of persisting. Jalabert, his lank black hair drooping over his brow, cracked soon afterwards and was dropped by Ullrich and the other favourites, despite the exhortations of his team manager, Manolo Saiz. One by one, as the stage wore on, the cluster of potential rivals at the race leader's side was diminishing. Even so, Telekom were riding in a jittery fashion with Riis, Ullrich and the experienced Udo Bolts all flitting to and fro, unsure whether to dictate events or to save their strength for Pantani's anticipated assault.

There was a brief five kilometre drop from the ridge of the Télégraphe into the hanging valley at the foot of the Galibier to the ski resort of Valloire, grim and neglected in the grey summer rain. From there, Serrano, Massi and Rinero led the way up the Galibier, their efforts diminished by the monumental landscape as the sweeping screes frowned down on the steep road. Behind them Riis, Leblanc, Escartin and Ullrich moved to the front, testing their companions once more. Every little change in pace saw more riders lose contact, as Ullrich anxiously continued to defend his lead. But he hadn't got rid of his main rivals – Julich and Pantani. They hovered menacingly on his shoulder, crowding the young German and his remaining team-mates Bolts and Riis as Leblanc attacked yet again. Ullrich responded in an effort to assert himself over his rivals, but only succeeded in putting his two Telekom aides in serious trouble. The signs of uncertainty in the champion were growing and, as the road ramped up and up once more, Pantani could smell blood.

By now two riders, Italian Fabrizio Guidi and José Luis Arrieta, a Spaniard from the Banesto team, had abandoned, suffering from hypothermia. On this foul, desolate day the Galibier wanted more from the Tour *peloton* than climbing prowess and stamina; it searched their souls for something beyond endurance, questioning their will to carry on. Ullrich's stamina, doubted all spring by the media, was holding; but with Riis and Bolts falling behind and the steepest gradients of the Galibier still to come, he was alone and at his full physical extent – with Pantani, Julich, Boogerd, Escartin and Leblanc for company.

And then, in a moment, it was over.

Without any team-mates to protect him, Ullrich had been forced to exhaust himself chasing a succession of sharp accelerations from Leblanc and Escartin. The door had at last been prised ajar; Pantani seized the moment and bolted through it.

The next morning, the papers said that the 1998 Tour was decided on the stage's final climb to Les Deux Alpes: certainly, the champion died a thousand deaths on that short ascent; but the fatal wounds were inflicted in a split second, with an assassin's practised skill, just four kilometres from the top of the Galibier. Pantani's turn of speed into the fog and drizzle was so decisive that for a moment nobody knew quite where he'd gone. 'Elephantino' had ridden into hyperspace, leaving us all wondering at events, trying to get to grips with his stupefying acceleration. The TV motorbikes sped off in optimistic pursuit, focusing on lone riders as they searched for the little Italian in the thick murk that had descended on the mountain.

One by one, Pantani caught up with and passed Massi, Serrano and Rinero, the trio who'd been ahead since the foot of the Galibier, leaving them stunned by his pace. Even though they tried, none of them could hope to stay with him and by the summit, he'd already taken almost three minutes back from Ullrich. The champion knew that things were bad, but without Riis or Bolts to prompt him, Ullrich seemed stricken with uncertainty. And Julich, who could have stolen an opportunity and tried to join his team-mate Rinero, still riding ahead of him, seemed equally dumbfounded by the finality of Pantani's move.

Once over the summit, Pantani had vanished into the mist and cloud, apparently untroubled by the conditions; yet the biting cold was causing problems for many riders.

'The cold was killing me,' said Jalabert afterwards. 'I knew the stage would be tough, but I didn't realise how tough. I couldn't recover and my muscles wouldn't respond. My teeth were chattering in the descents and I felt like my circulation had stopped,' he continued. 'If I hadn't been so high on the overall classification, I'd have given up, because I got so cold that I wasn't thinking straight. I was alone and things were getting dangerous.'

The situation was equally threatening for those struggling at the back of the race, riding more than twenty minutes behind the flying Italian. Magnus Backstedt, so nonchalant after surviving the demands of the Pyrénées, was one of those dropped by the high pace and found himself fighting to stay in the last group on the road, riding far behind Pantani. Towards the top of the Galibier, as he climbed the last four kilometres to the summit, Backstedt had thought that it was over for him.

'I couldn't turn my legs around,' he said later. 'I started thinking that I might have to get off, but I was still determined to get to the finish, even if I wasn't sure whether I could make it inside the time limit.'

For the taller, heavier riders, the major mountain stages – especially those which fall towards the end of the race – are purgatory. They know that if they finish outside the calculated time limit, which in the Tour is based on a complicated percentage calculation of the stage winner's average speed, then they will be disqualified – even if they ride the whole route and finish the stage. But as he struggled on, past the Galibier's forbidding snowfields and its eerie rocky spires, Backstedt was saved by the team-mate whose interests he had defended earlier in the race, on the flat stages heading south through the west of France.

'Stuart O'Grady came alongside me,' Magnus explained, 'and saw that I was in trouble. He gave me a push and started to encourage me. That helped me to get a little speed up and I tried to maintain that for as long as possible.'

Even though the Australian was himself struggling to stay in the race, he did his best to motivate the big Swede. 'He was yelling, "Come on! We're going to Paris – the Eiffel Tower's just over the top!" I was in the *grupetto*, but I was struggling – really struggling – to hang on.'

On the long run to the foot of the first climb, the Croix de Fer, Backstedt had been steeling himself for the test that the first Alpine stage would set him. Those who know that they will struggle through the mountain passes – the sprinters and the team helpers – band together in the long ascents, combining their pacemaking strength and experience to form the 'bus', or as it's known by Italian professionals, the *grupetto*. Backstedt's wily Italian team-mate Eros Poli has an intimidating reputation as the 'bus driver', the rider who decides when, with the climbers and team leaders far ahead, the *grupetto* must pool its resources and start working together to ensure survival.

'We were about five kilometres up the Croix de Fer when it started to hurt a bit, so we called the big *grupetto*,' said Backstedt. 'Eros and me are normally the guys who say "OK, that's it – *grupetto* time." Usually I'm riding at the other side of the *peloton* and he looks across to me with that look in his eyes, a look that says, "Is it *grupetto* time or not?" So after we've decided, we start riding a good tempo, steady but easy. Eros picks the pace because he's got all the time limits worked out in his head. He knows exactly how many minutes we can afford to lose on each climb to stay within a safe margin and he knows that we can take some time back on the flat roads between each climb.'

Reinstatements after finishing outside the time limit are rare, although there have been a few examples. Britain's Paul Sherwen, now a television commentator, is one of those riders. His courage after an horrendous fall moved the race organisation so deeply that his failure to finish within the time limit was ignored.

With the rain falling and the temperature dropping, not to mention Pantani and Ullrich fighting hammer and tongs, Poli and Backstedt knew that this would be a tough and long day.

'It's not so easy with a climber like Pantani attacking,' admitted Magnus, 'but in a stage like that, Eros spends the whole time calculating how fast Pantani can ride up the hill. He makes sure he gets regular information from the second team car and he always allows a little extra, so that we have spare time just in case anything goes wrong.'

Backstedt had been riding so slowly on his way up the Galibier that he had started to feel the bitter blasts of cold air swirling around the summit even before beginning the long descent towards the valley.

'When I finally got to the top of the Galibier, I didn't stop to put on a cape or anything. I just carried on because I was too worried about losing touch with the others, so I descended in arm-warmers and a short-sleeve jersey. It was only four degrees at the top, but I knew if I lost thirty metres on the *grupetto* that I'd never catch them again and that it would be the end of the Tour for me. Even on the way down from the Galibier, I was struggling to hang on. I was freezing,' he smiled wryly, 'and my legs were gone.'

It was wet, misty and cold as Backstedt began the fast drop towards the gorge of the river Durance, yet he joined the balletic line of riders, fearlessly diving through the slick bends.

'Descending is no problem for me,' he said. 'I like descending, whatever the weather. I think it helps that I was an Alpine skier before I was a cyclist, because I can read the corners and find the best line without too much of a problem. You always feel like you're losing your grip a little and you might have a couple of skids, but that's what you get used to when you're racing at speed.'

There are no protective guard rails, trees or low walls to prevent a rider from tumbling into space on the descent from the Galibier, but Backstedt, O'Grady and Poli, desperate to avoid elimination from the Tour, touched speeds of almost ninety kilometres per hour as they hurtled down from the top of the mountain.

Ahead of them all, Marco Pantani was on the threshold of

greatness. The Tour has many famous tales, stories of riders surviving terrible hardship and legends of mythical solo attacks. *Il Pirata*'s solo break to Les Deux Alpes fitted the bill and would be a perfect addition to that fabled archive – providing he survived the final kilometres of the stage. Riders did try to chase him, throwing caution to the wind on the drop from the Galibier and descending at high speed, before realising that without thermal clothing, hypothermia and exhaustion were just minutes away.

'I was completely frozen, locked up,' said Luc Leblanc. 'I was so cold on the descent that I couldn't even see clearly. It was as if I was cross-eyed – when I saw the others go past me at eighty kilometres per hour, I didn't know where I was any more.'

By the time he reached the valley, Ullrich was in a similarly desperate state as Riis and Bolts fought to race back to him. Alone, and with Pantani now almost five minutes ahead of him, he suffered the final blow – a puncture at the foot of the last climb, the nine-kilometre drag up to the ski resort at Les Deux Alpes. The champion stood shivering and bedraggled at the roadside while Telekom's staff frantically fitted a new wheel to his bike, but their efforts made little difference. When he got going again, Ullrich was a spent force. Joined by Bolts and Riis, he was barely able to turn the pedals. The TV motorbikes closed in on him voyeuristically, focusing on his dark, puffy eyes and grimacing expression. Was he crying or were his eyes just watering from the cold wind?

Pantani was closing on the finish line as Ullrich struggled past the four-kilometres-to-go mark. The gulf between the two was so marked that it was almost impossible to remember that only a year earlier, the German had been the Tour's unstoppable winner, tipped as the champion for the Millennium. Now he could only pedal leadenly towards the finish,

The crowds flock to the mountains to watch the stage finish at Plateau de Beille.

Magnus Backstedt takes time to rest and recover in his hotel room as the Tour heads south towards the Pyrenees.

Eros Poli and team-mate Backstedt pacing the *gruppetto* to the summit finish at Plateau de Beille.

TVM's Lars Michaelsen packs his bags after being eliminated from the race.

Biding his time: Marco Pantani in the build-up to the mountain stages.

Pantani makes his point at the rider protest in Tarascon.

Onlookers restrain Manolo Saiz as tempers start to flare at Tarascon.

Casino's Rodolfo Massi leads his team away from the riders' strike as Max Sciandri, wearing 129, looks on.

obby J talking up his chances
or the folks back home.

Jill and Marty Jemison snatch a rare moment
together before the stage start in Albertville.

élo Club: Gérard Holtz welcomes Rodolfo Massi to another edition of the
ost-stage chat show.

Udo Bolts, Telekom's experienced team captain, puts his point of view to the German media.

TVM's Serguei Outschakov asks Pantani for his support at the chaotic start in Albertville.

Caught in the middle: Bjarne Riis struggles to make his voice heard.

Paris welcomes a weary *peloton* to the cobbles of the Champs-Elysées.

Marco Pantani, eventual winner of the 1998 Tour de France, in full flight in the Pyrenees.

egged on by Riis and Bolts, who watched helplessly as lesser riders, dropped far behind on the way up the Télégraphe and the Galibier, made up lost ground and rode away from them. After hesitating when Pantani had shown the way, Julich, Boogerd and Escartin had finally attacked Ullrich, ruthlessly making the most of his dramatic collapse. Pantani, now almost nine minutes ahead of the outgoing champion, galloped up to Les Deux Alpes, to the stage victory and the overall race lead. It had been a devastating and epic afternoon of racing.

As Jan Ullrich disappeared into his room at La Farandole in the heart of Les Deux Alpes' ugly collection of squat ski hotels, the Telekom team's staff set about resuscitating and reviving their fallen star. He was back in the bubble, in the womb of the team that had first unleashed him on the Tour in the summer of 1996. Riis was willing to talk, however, and launched into a tirade against the uncharitable fans who had booed Ullrich as he crossed the finish line.

'They were yelling insults,' the Dane complained. 'He didn't deserve that – why can't they respect him as the good rider that he is?'

But he acknowledged that Ullrich's inexperience had let him down. 'We should have had a man at the top of the Galibier with a thermal jacket for him,' said Riis, 'because he lost so much energy on the descent. He suffered from his lack of experience today – he tends to panic a little when I'm not around.'

Quizzed by the German media as soon as he got out of Telekom's number one team car, Ullrich's team manager Walter Godefroot was philosophical.

'In principle,' he shrugged resignedly, 'the Tour is lost. We have to be realistic. He's not going to get six minutes back on

Pantani in Saturday's time trial.'

Out on the road, plenty of riders were still fighting for survival. 'By the time we reached the last climb,' recalled Magnus Backstedt later, 'I'd started to feel better again. But then it was Stuart's turn to struggle. When I saw him dropping off a bit, I went back to help him. I couldn't push him because I didn't have the strength to, but I rode alongside, talking to him, and we managed to make it back up to the *grupetto* and stayed with them all the way to the finish.'

Backstedt knew that he'd been lucky to survive what he called the hardest day of his career. 'I was so happy to get to the finish,' he said, 'just to get there within the time limit. I was really tired as well, but I felt this massive sense of relief.'

But the day's brutal demands took their toll. 'When I got back to the hotel, I just lay down on the bed in all my wet gear – helmet, shoes, everything – and fell asleep. Eros woke me up about ten minutes later and told me to get out of my gear and get into the tub, so I did and then went back to bed again. I can't remember exactly,' Magnus said, 'but I think I must have slept through the whole of that evening.'

Stage winner: Marco Pantani, Italy (Mercatone Uno)

Overall race leader: Marco Pantani, Italy (Mercatone Uno)

Points classification leader: Erik Zabel, Germany (Deutsche Telekom)

Team classification leader: Cofidis

Mountains classification leader: Rodolfo Massi, Italy (Casino)

Day 20

Stage 16

Tuesday 28 July
Vizille–Albertville, 204 km

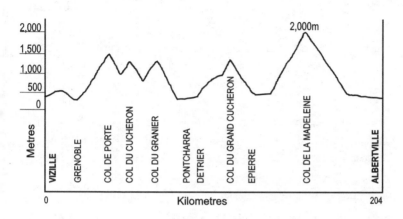

'He's young and he recovers well,' Telekom manager Walter Godefroot had said pointedly of Jan Ullrich after his young protégé's terrible defeat on the slopes of the Col de Galibier. While the defending champion hadn't been totally written off, his collapse at Les Deux Alpes had been so utterly complete that most of the race convoy now expected him to slip further down the classification. At the *village départ*, in the shadow of Vizille's seventeenth-century château, one ex-professional even suggested that the twenty-four-year-old might struggle to finish the race. But while doubt centred on the fallen German star, there was universal praise for Pantani's epic victory.

'Pantani was incredible,' said Bobby Julich. 'I knew he was dangerous, but I didn't know he was capable of what he did – it made the rest of us look silly. But the race isn't over and now the pressure is on his team to take control.'

As more team cars pulled into the start area, the fans spilled in, surrounding tired riders and seeking out autographs. After the stresses of the previous day, some of them flashed filthy looks at the impatient, pushy kids as they jostled them and shoved magazines under their nose. A grizzled and weary-looking Udo Bolts, ignored by those hunting Riis or Ullrich, stopped and shook hands as behind him the crowds pressed around the Telekom team's mobile home. He'd spent much of the previous evening talking to the shattered Ullrich, pulling him back on his feet.

'When you're his age, it's tough,' mused Udo. 'But worse things happen in your personal life than anything that happens when you're racing. We're all tired, though. I just hope it's not too hard in the first climb today.'

Over at US Postal's cars, Marty Jemison was still recovering from the previous day's efforts. 'I'm pretty tired,' he admitted, 'but I don't think today will be so bad. Yesterday was hellish and it was dangerous, too.'

Finally, wearing his personalised bandana and the Tour's *maillot jaune*, Marco Pantani stepped out of Mercatone Uno's giant camper van to a rapturous reception. Flanked by his team-mates and grinning sheepishly, he made it through the packed crowds and headed up to the start line on a tide of cheers and whistles.

The last real mountain stage of the Tour took in four lesser climbs – the Porte, Cucheron, Granier and Grand Cucheron – before the long and steep ascent of the 2,000-metre-high Col de la Madeleine. The vertiginous descent from the Madeleine towards Albertville was just as tiring as the climb, and required agility and concentration over its twenty-five kilometres.

Udo Bolts was to be disappointed. His hopes of a quiet start to the stage were forgotten as early as the second kilometre, when Italian breakaway specialist Fabio Roscioli tried his luck. In pursuit came Stéphane Heulot of the La Française des Jeux team, Telekom's lanky Rolf Aldag and Andrei Teteriouk from Kazakhstan, riding with the Lotto team. The first climb, the Col de Porte, put paid to Roscioli who slipped back towards the chasing field, but the remaining trio were still ahead of the field as they dropped from the Grand Cucheron and rode through the feed zone at Epierre, just ten kilometres from the foot of the Madeleine.

At the bottom of the Madeleine, as the road climbs up from the drab village of La Chambre, a series of steep switchbacks reach up the mountainside. Heulot, far more of a climber than either of his companions, moved ahead, tapping out a steady rhythm as he made his way up the mountain. Behind him, Telekom and Mercatone Uno were vying for control of the *peloton*. Riis and Ullrich rode close to the front with Pantani alongside, as the speed picked up on the fast approach to the Madeleine. As the leaders hit the Madeleine's eight per cent gradient, the large front group exploded as several riders were reduced almost to walking pace. A group of twenty-two including most of the favourites set a quick pace, rounding the bends and powering up the steep ramps as the valley receded from view. Telekom had planned to set a high tempo in the hope that later, near the top of the long climb, a recovered Ullrich might be able to attack and regain the ground lost to Julich at Les Deux Alpes, twenty-four hours earlier.

But ten kilometres from the summit, as the Cofidis team moved to the front, the defending champion seized the initiative when his rivals and his team-mates were least expecting it. Later, a story circulated that Ullrich had changed his plan after hearing a struggling Bobby J ask his team-mates to drop the pace a little. Whatever the reason, his sudden attack caught the race by surprise. Even Pantani looked momentarily shocked to see the rider he had so wholly dominated the previous day now go on the offensive. But the Italian recovered quickly enough, sprinting up to Ullrich's back wheel as behind them, Julich and the others grimaced with the effort.

Later, Ullrich said that he attacked to 'thank his team', yet his bold move had the aura of a champion repairing his wounded pride, a rebuff to those who would have written him off. With the leader's jersey on his back, Pantani was happy to follow in Ullrich's slipstream, although he did assist with the pacemaking from time to time. Mostly, though, their attack was dominated by the German's ferocious power. The move worked well for them both as they sought to distance the weakening Julich. Just to make sure of victory, Pantani wanted more time on the American prior to the final time trial, while Ullrich was just as keen to ensure that he was in contention for second place.

They soon caught and passed Aldag and Teteriouk, although the Telekom rider did make a huge effort to set the pace for his team leader. In the event though, Aldag was able only to ride alongside Ullrich for a few hundred metres, his mouth gaping in exhaustion, before he was dropped by the fast-moving pair. Just short of the summit, as the full impact of Ullrich's re-awakening began to hit home, they passed the tiring Heulot.

'I'd hoped to stay with them, so that I could try and win the stage,' said Heulot, 'but I didn't want to put myself in the red. When they came up to me, it was like two motorbikes going past.'

Pantani let Ullrich pass first over the summit of the Madeleine, but with only a two-minute lead on Julich and the American's time-trialling abilities in mind, he plunged full tilt into the Madeleine's narrow and technically demanding descent. Behind them, Bobby J was weighing up his options.

'I used my head,' he said afterwards. 'I couldn't follow at the front, so I looked around to see who was there. I was with a team-mate and the other major favourites, so I figured that I wasn't in such bad company. After that, I gritted my teeth and concentrated on limiting my losses.'

The drop from the summit of the Madeleine served Ullrich well. By the time he and Pantani had reached the valley of the Isère some 1,500 metres below the col's high green pastures, they were too far ahead to be caught, even allowing for the fact that they would inevitably concede time to a chasing group on the flat final approach to Albertville. In fact, with Julich now distanced, there was even time to talk.

It is one of the archaic traditions of professional cycling that deals are arranged on the road, often at the climax of great races. No real attempt is made to hide the transactions, as riders barter over the arrangements, swapping stage victories for promises of support or solidarity. Ullrich, having instigated the decisive move and reassured that Julich no longer posed a real threat either to him or to Pantani's race leadership, wanted to strike a deal. Quite openly, they rode alongside each other, presumably discussing the pros and cons of the German's suggestion that he take the stage win, while Pantani, with two stage successes already under his belt, contented himself with tightening his grip on the yellow jersey.

They were still chatting as they rode into the suburbs of Albertville, although the sudden proximity of the finish line made them both realise that they had to make it look good for the cameras. So, as they entered the final few hundred metres, Pantani began a theatrical sprint, doing his best to persuade those watching that he really was trying very hard indeed. But to the Italian's consternation, Ullrich, hovering sluggishly off his right shoulder, seemed to be having trouble working up much of a head of steam and could barely manage to draw level with the Pirate, let alone pass him. In exasperation and with the finish line just metres away, Pantani slowed for a split second – just enough for Ullrich to drift ahead of him as they crossed the line, and for him to keep their gentleman's agreement.

A little under two minutes later, Julich, despite suffering from cramp, wearily led a group of nine riders including Rinero, Riis, Boogerd, Escartin and surprisingly Axel Merckx, son of the great Eddy, across the line. The American seemed to have done enough to ensure a top three finish.

'That's the Ullrich I know,' said Bobby J admiringly of his German rival. 'It's impressive after what happened to him yesterday. I suffered a lot on the Madeleine but I was determined to hang on. All I could think about was the people with American flags. That kept me going, along with the e-mails and the positive vibes that people have been sending. Pantani and Ullrich are greater riders than me, but if I can get on to the Paris podium alongside them, well, that will make a nice photo.'

In victory as in defeat, Ullrich remained as enigmatic as ever. 'I'd planned to attack on the Madeleine to help forget the Galibier,' he told the German media later in the evening, having snubbed the scheduled stage winner's press conference. 'I wasn't trying to take the yellow jersey from Pantani because he's clearly the strongest, but just to make up lost time and to make sure of second place on the podium.'

The skies were overcast as we headed out of Albertville on the *autoroute* towards the Hôtel Welcome in Moûtiers. After the best part of two scandal-free days of gripping mountain racing, we had started to think that perhaps the 1998 Tour de France would miraculously redeem itself. We checked in, taking our keys from the surly Barbara Windsor lookalike manning the front desk; but just as I began to think of dinner, of a bottle of wine and of a rare early night, the phone rang.

It was another rumour, but one that was this time well founded. The Reims judiciary had authorised a further search of the TVM team's hotel and of all their bags and vehicles. As we sat down to eat, the French authorities were getting ready to pounce on the Tour convoy once more.

Stage winner: Jan Ullrich, Germany (Deutsche Telekom)
Overall race leader: Marco Pantani, Italy (Mercatone Uno)
Points classification leader: Erik Zabel, Germany (Deutsche Telekom)
Team classification leader: Cofidis
Mountains classification leader: Rodolfo Massi, Italy (Casino)

Leading overall placings after stage sixteen:

1. Marco Pantani, Italy (Mercatone Uno), 3,051.6 kilometres in 77 hrs, 38 mins 24 secs
2. Bobby Julich, USA (Cofidis) at 5 mins 42 secs
3. Jan Ullrich, Germany (Deutsche Telekom) at 5 mins 56 secs
4. Fernando Escartin, Spain (Kelme) at 6 mins 3 secs
5. Christophe Rinero, France (Cofidis) at 8 mins 1 sec
6. Michael Boogerd, Holland (Rabobank) at 8 mins 5 secs
7. Rodolfo Massi, Italy (Casino) at 12 mins 15 secs
8. Jean-Cyril Robin, France (US Postal) at 12 mins 34 secs
9. Leonardo Piepoli, Italy (Saeco) at 12 mins 45 secs
10. Roland Meier, Switzerland (Cofidis) at 13 mins 19 secs

Other placings:

14. Bjarne Riis, Denmark (Deutsche Telekom) at 14 mins 45 secs
16. Axel Merckx, Belgium (Polti) at 16 mins 15 secs
21. Laurent Jalabert, France (ONCE) at 24 mins 21 secs
29. Luc Leblanc, France (Polti) at 33 mins 55 secs
60. Marty Jemison, USA (US Postal) at 1 hr, 26 mins 9 secs
80. Max Sciandri, GB (FDJ) at 1 hr, 45 mins 52 secs
93. Stuart O'Grady, Australia (GAN) at 1 hr, 58 mins 17 secs
109. Jacky Durand, France (Casino) at 2 hrs, 11 mins 17 secs
116. Magnus Backstedt, Sweden (GAN) at 2 hrs, 16 mins 1 sec
128. Jeroen Blijlevens, Holland (TVM) at 2 hrs, 32 mins 35 secs

Day 21   Stage 17

Wednesday 29 July
Albertville–Aix-les-Bains, 149 km

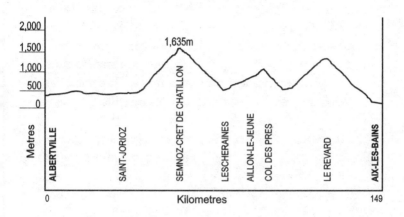

The French say that professional cycling is a sport for the head and the legs; that even when your strength fails and your legs turn to jelly, you can still succeed if you keep your cool, bluff your opponent and use your tactical nous to save the day.

Wednesday 29 July was the 85th Tour's darkest day; a day that started in clear Alpine sunshine and ended in bitter, angry tears as the world's best riders finally lost their heads and totally forgot about using their legs. The frail hope, emerging from two days of great racing, that the 1998 Tour might somehow resurrect itself and preserve its dignity was snuffed out as chaos and defeatism engulfed the convoy. From the moment the caravan rolled uncertainly away from Albertville at the start of the Tour's seventeenth stage, race director Jean-Marie Leblanc was little more than a stricken spectator as the lack of solidarity between the riders was finally exposed for all to see.

When the inevitable protest against the police raids on the TVM team finally came, it was incoherent, shambolic and damaging, throwing into stark relief the *peloton*'s inability to grasp the gravity of the situation. Riders tore their race numbers off and threw them to the ground, arguing among themselves, cursing the French authorities and the Tour organisation and turning their backs on the great race. They rode at a snail's pace and left furious spectators standing snarling at the roadside, until, late in the afternoon, as the sharp Alpine shadows lengthened, it seemed they had finally broken the Tour's old and ailing heart.

At the end of the day, the summer night settling over Lac Bourget, I sat alone with a drink on the hotel terrace and stared into the dark, starry sky, dazed by disillusion, wondering how it had come to this.

Anxious for news of the TVM police raids, I'd climbed out of bed early that morning and pushed open the shutters in the Hôtel Welcome to a view of rooftops and sleepy, scruffy cats lounging in the first pools of morning sunlight. Beyond the Moûtiers skyline, the Tarentaise Alps climbed towards the icy towers of the Parc National de la Vanoise and the Italian border. Steep wooded slopes gave way to higher open pastures and beyond that, misty glaciated peaks. It was a very French perspective – shabby on one level, but so very grand and inspiring on another.

I phoned down to 'Babs' for coffee, flicked on the TV and set about shaving, keeping an eye through the bathroom door on France 2's breakfast news report. The overnight news was dominated by more doping scandals. There was shaky footage of a besieged hotel at night; this time, the TVM team's Hôtel Million in the centre of Albertville. Stunned men in tracksuits and polo shirts stood around in the entrance of the hotel, blinking in the glare of arc lights as policemen came and went, lugging holdalls and sagging bin bags. I sat sipping coffee on the end of the bed and realised that, as far as the French judiciary were concerned, police raids had now become professional cycling's only effective dope controls. While the UCI looked on bemusedly, the cosy drug controls of the past had been swept aside by this startling new approach: raid them, search them and bang them up.

After the stage finish the day before, the police had come looking for TVM, taking Blijlevens, De Jongh, Ivanov, Voskamp, Knaven and Outschakov to Albertville hospital for medical tests. Soon afterwards, with more camera crews and journalists arriving at the hotel by the minute, *directeur sportif* Hendrik Redant and *soigneur* Jan Moors had been taken into custody. They finally let the riders go after midnight. Later on, they released Redant – at five in the morning – but Moors was kept in custody, awaiting further investigation.

The TVM raid demolished the fragile stability established by Pantani and Ullrich's forty-eight hours of heavyweight sparring in the Alps. We were back where we'd started. Voskamp, Outschakov and the others had fled the hospital in panic and unwittingly provided one of the most haunting images of the whole affair. Faced with a barrage of cameras, they pulled their jackets over their faces and stretched out their hands to try and cover the intrusive lens. The raids, together with those on the ONCE, BigMat and Casino teams proved, as if proof were needed, that it wasn't just Festina who were under suspicion – the whole of professional cycling was under the microscope. The rot had irrefutably set in.

Blijlevens told the TV reporters that he'd only finally got to bed at two in the morning. 'I had to get up again at nine,' he complained. 'It's not possible to recover under those sort of conditions.'

The Dutch sprinter's tale was soon to have massive repercussions for the whole Tour convoy. It reached some riders as they dutifully trooped out of their hotels and headed towards the stage start for another day on the Tour's front line.

I finished off my coffee and, as I began packing my bag, picked up the remote and flicked over to M6, the sanitised French channel offering a diet of Johnny Halliday pop videos and shopping telly. Natalie Imbruglia's doe-eyed gamine features filled the screen.

'*I'm all out of faith*,' she sang mournfully, with a strange, timely poignancy. '*You're a little late – I'm already torn . . .*'

Down at the *village départ*, in the shadow of Albertville's Winter Olympic stadium, the usual troupe of VIPs strolled from buffet to buffet, setting their shades nonchalantly on their foreheads as if after two days of gripping racing, free from rider protests or strikes, the Tour had somehow resumed normal service. They seemed oblivious to the tense, conspiratorial huddles of journalists and riders swapping notes on the TVM raids.

'The police were acting like Nazis,' echoed one emotive quote from the TVM camp, no doubt inspired by the fact that Albertville hospital had taken hair samples from the team's riders. It rebounded through the village from rider to journalist and back again. In one corner, the bouffant Sergei Outschakov, still apparently with all his blond curls, found himself besieged by the Italian hacks; while across the village, the mild-mannered Jeroen Blijlevens was at the centre of a mass of Dutch media as he recalled the previous night's events.

'When I got back to the hotel, a man pushed a police identity card under my nose and told me to follow him,' said Blijlevens. 'We went up to the bedrooms – after that it was

226

like some American movie. They pulled Bart Voskamp out of the shower straight away and then started searching the place. They went through the cupboards, the bags and stripped the beds down. One of the officers was bilingual and read our personal letters. They didn't let us take a shower or get a massage – just took us straight to the police station and then the hospital.

'When we got there,' continued the Dutchman, 'there was nothing arranged, so we had to wait a while for the tests. We had nothing to say – only to do what we were told. They took blood and urine, measured our heart rate and took samples of our hair. By the time we got out of the hospital, it was after midnight.'

As in the rest-day raid in Pamiers, the police investigators were from Reims, squaring the circle of intrigue that had begun almost four months earlier when the TVM vehicle had been stopped by customs officers near Reims back in March. The powder keg trail was about to lead to the start line in Albertville, bathed in warm bright sunshine on a beautiful summer's day.

I walked between the team cars, exchanging *ça vas* and handshakes and searching for the right moment to approach those in the thick of the controversy. Leaning on the hood of an ONCE team car, the burly Manolo Saiz was holding forth emotionally in a barely intelligible soup of French and Spanish. Since that explosive run-in with the Tour's direction at Tarascon-sur-Ariège, the Spanish team's *directeur* had been a man on the edge. What he had to say only confirmed the fear that the Tour was close to collapse, that a mass walk-out by the top teams was just a hair's breadth away.

'ONCE came to France to race,' he protested, 'but we'll change everything after what's happened during this Tour de

France. We will change our programme,' he said again, 'because the French are going to finish off the sport of cycling. If it continues like this, then it's over – it's the end for cycling. We're a family heading for a divorce, because the Tour has no respect for the riders any more – in fact, nobody respects anybody else any more.'

Then with tired, red eyes and his fists clenched with emotion, Saiz asked, 'Where is the president of the UCI? The biggest crisis in the history of cycling and where is the president of our governing body?'

Back in the village, riders from Telekom and GAN were gathering at the Maison du Café stand. As the ripples of anxiety and uncertainty spread through the convoy, few of them were willing to talk. Magnus Backstedt, uncharacteristically tight-lipped, looked stunned as I relayed Blijlevens' account of the police raid at the TVM hotel. Alongside the Swede, an eavesdropping Udo Bolts shook his head in disbelief.

'I don't think I'll ride this race again,' the German said wearily. 'Next year, I might just do the Giro and the *Vuelta* – I don't really like the Tour de France any more.'

But the constant threat of police intervention wasn't the only thing bugging a world-weary Bolts.

'There's been too much abuse of Jan during this Tour,' he said, referring to the French fans' treatment of his young team leader. 'If it's only one or two fans then that's OK, you expect that; but when it's so many people, it's hard to bear, especially for a young guy like him.'

As the riders headed off for the start line, we walked away from the village back to the car for the short drive along the *autoroute* to the finish at Aix-les-Bains. But we held back, watching from the *presse arrière* parking area as we waited for the riders and team cars to move off. Peering through the cars and motorbikes and the crowd of riders and officials under the start banner, we could tell that something was delaying the start. There was a long pause, a few shouts and jeers and a palpable moment of uncertainty. Finally, the procession began to move slowly away, to relieved applause and cheers from the fans leaning against the barriers.

What we didn't know, at least until we arrived at the *permanence* in Aix-les-Bains, was that the stage had nearly failed to start altogether. As Pantani stood on the start line, TVM's Outschakov had sidled alongside and begun muttering darkly in the little Italian's prominent left ear. The Ukrainian had given Pantani further details of the raid on his team's hotel, of their long night in Albertville's police station and of the hair and blood samples taken from them in hospital. Maybe he'd repeated that now-famous line, accusing the police of behaving 'like Nazis'. Whatever, he wanted a show of support from the *peloton* – some form of protest at their treatment by the French police.

His words obviously made an impression, both on Pantani and the increasingly harassed and tense Jean-Marie Leblanc, who was soon out of his race director's car, manhandling photographers away from the start line and imploring Pantani and Outschakov to get on with it. But Pantani had already acknowledged the Dutch team's need for some form of protest, even if there were those on the start line, such as Telekom's Erik Zabel, who looked to be losing their patience with raids and protests and the '98 Tour's relentless game of stop-start. Finally, as a consoled Outschakov made his way defiantly back to his team-mates to relay Pantani's apparent solidarity, the riders eased away from the line and headed out towards the green climbs of the Chaine des Aravis.

By then, we were well on our way to the press room. We joined the sparse stream of traffic heading east through the

Alps on the A43 *autoroute* and sat chatting over the rights and wrongs of the police investigation. Arriving in the genteel town of Aix-les-Bains we swung away from the Promenade du Lac into the car-park at the press room, rolled to a halt under a tree, and stepped into the stifling heat. I began sifting through the wads of press releases, newspaper cuttings and results in my bag. I fiddled with the stacks of magazines and newspapers spilling across the boot but gave up in exasperation when it became clear that the next Alpine hairpin would soon throw my archives into chaos once more. I slammed the boot shut and then sat on the grass for ten minutes soaking up the midday sun. If I'd known what was happening at Saint-Jorioz, after only thirty-two kilometres of the race route, then I might have forgone the sunbathing and hurried towards the shadows of the press hall with a little more urgency.

After a while, I got to my feet, strolled across the nearby football pitch, pushed my shades on to the top of my head and walked into the darkness of the *salle de presse*. As the cool air hit me, I stopped in my tracks, stunned by the images filling the bank of TV screens at the far end of the long shabby hall. Chaos had descended on the Tour once more. As I stared open-mouthed at the screens, it wasn't easy to make out what had happened. At first, I thought that there had been some almighty crash or that the race had been halted by fans or protesters. But as I got nearer to the monitors, I was able to take in the sad sight of the riders milling around in the middle of the road, arguing among themselves – it was enough to break poor Jean-Marie's heart.

All of the riders had stopped. They stood in groups in the road or on the verge, some sitting disinterestedly under the shade of nearby trees. As in Tarascon, factions had formed, dividing the riders by nationalities rather than team allegiances. From the circling helicopter pictures, it looked like a shambles. Jan Ullrich sat glumly on the tarmac, bike laid on the road by his side, staring morosely at some distant horizon, surrounded by bemused fans. Nearby, Pantani was at the centre of an animated Italian-speaking huddle, while Laurent Jalabert, apparently wholly supported by team manager-cum-shop-steward Saiz, had already climbed into his team car in disgust.

What were they doing? Was this the best they could come up with? Dithering and dawdling, teetering on their racing shoes, wagging fingers at each other? Didn't they know that the world was watching? This time, Jalabert was almost – but not quite – speechless with rage. He sat alongside the burly Saiz, affecting nonchalance as he nibbled on a choc-ice.

'I've had enough,' he shrugged as microphones were thrust through the open car window. 'I'm fed up to the back teeth with it.'

As the chaos around him continued, Jalabert, clad in the French champion's jersey, turned his back on the Tour, apparently with Saiz's blessing. It should have been a shock, an outrage, a disaster for the Tour. Instead, it was oddly inevitable that this diffident character, so weary of the French nation's demands upon him, should prompt a walk-out of all the Spanish teams.

With panic setting in, Jean-Marie Leblanc was soon on Radio Tour, pleading for common sense.

'The riders are traumatised and I understand their feelings,' he said. 'I'm seeking guarantees from the authorities that any further investigations are carried out in a manner appropriate to the dignity of athletes of the highest level.'

It was hardly enough to calm their brittle nerves, but with the fans baying for blood and the race director making an emotional plea for them to continue, the Tour field dragged itself off the canvas once more.

'If we're carrying on, then it's only for the fans,' said the enraged Luc Leblanc, as he swung back into the saddle.

Somehow, under the impetus of the Mercatone Uno and Telekom teams and, in particular, of Bjarne Riis, with the words of Leblanc ringing in their ears, the riders restarted – but without Jalabert and his ONCE team-mates. The convoy may have got moving once more, but we all knew that it wasn't over. What would they do next?

They soon answered that question, tearing off their race numbers as they pedalled at a snail's pace towards the first climb, the Cret de Châtillon, a wooded peak known to locals as Le Semnoz. Were they so lacking in self-awareness that, after everything else that had happened, they had no idea how terrible this looked to those watching? Some of them were even laughing as they rode along. Led by Pantani and the Spaniards, they continued to peel off their race numbers, effectively ensuring the neutralisation of the stage. The gesture was met with abuse and cries of 'shame' from the furious crowds at the roadside.

The Tour's cultural manual says that the summit of Le Semnoz offers remarkable views. On this sunny Wednesday afternoon, it took on a particularly dramatic perspective. A few metres ahead of the riders, Riis, prompted by the Telekom team, took it upon himself to ride up alongside Jean-Marie's car and act as the riders' spokesman, their *porteparole*. It may have been a well-intentioned and conciliatory gesture, but for some of those riders watching the Dane chatting with Leblanc, clinging to the roof of the red Fiat and free-wheeling alongside, it was tantamount to fraternising with the enemy. Half-way up the climb, after barely fifty kilometres of the stage, with Riis still tactfully explaining their grievances to Leblanc, the riders ground to a halt yet again.

Another groan of disbelief rolled around the press room, as the 1998 Tour, for the second time in half an hour, stared into the abyss of sporting extinction.

As the crowd again spilled on to the road, there were some who simply didn't want to know any more. Magnus Backstedt, Eros Poli, Erik Zabel and, curiously, Jalabert's kid brother and erstwhile breakaway companion in Tarascon, Nicolas, found a shady tree and sat awaiting the outcome of the latest bout of foot-stamping petulance. The rest of the riders, unsure of themselves, hovered uneasily, one foot on the pedals, the other on the tarmac, waiting for a lead.

Riis meanwhile had made his way back to the centre of the main group of riders and was beginning to explain his conversation with the race director. Those listening were unimpressed by his impromptu speech.

'He said a load of stuff about how we couldn't carry on like this but had to finish the stage for the public,' said one rider the next day. 'Riis said that the UCI would meet with the riders that night to decide whether the Tour should continue, but some of them were saying that most of that was bullshit.'

But Riis was interrupted when Luc Leblanc blew yet another fuse and forced his way to the front of the throng to confront Telekom's team captain, although Leblanc claimed later that all he had said to him was that no rider could speak on behalf of everybody else.

Overhead, the all-seeing TV helicopter trained its cameras on the chaos and beamed images of the stricken Tour live around the world. Pine trees swayed in the down-draught from the rotor blades as the chopper hovered. On the ground below, Leblanc wagged his finger threateningly at the tall Dane. In the days of Anquetil, Merckx and Hinault, there was some semblance of solidarity and professional dignity. Back then, rider protests – however misplaced – had some kind of authority, an almost military precision and unity. But this oh-so-nineties protest was shambolic. Rather than dignify their profession with a coherent display of outrage, the *peloton* came across as a bunch of spoilt brats arguing over their toys on Christmas morning.

For those looking on in horror, this was one of sport's darkest moments. It was akin to Mike Tyson biting Evander Holyfield's ear, that aborted Grand National, Michael Schumacher shunting Jacques Villeneuve and David Beckham's ill-tempered swipe at Diego Simeone. Bobby Julich held his head in his hands and stared at the ground while the fans around him, many still demonstrating their support for Virenque and his departed Festina team, began to jostle the riders as the jeering and abuse reached a crescendo.

Meanwhile, José Miguel Echavarri, manager of Olano's Banesto team, was talking on his mobile to his sponsor back in Spain. Half an hour later, the team that sponsored Miguel Indurain, perhaps the greatest Tour rider in history, would also have quit the 1998 race. And things were about to get worse.

Something got the riders moving again but at the top of the climb, the crowd had been hanging around for long enough. Furious at the long wait for the passage of the race and stung by the exclusion of their beloved Virenque, they ignored the overwhelmed *gendarmes* and stood across the crown of the road. By the time the *peloton* reached the summit of Le Semnoz, the road was blocked by fans. Some spat insults and swore graphically at the shocked riders and the following cars; others dropped their shorts and mooned at the race director's car as it struggled through the mêlée. From here on in, the remaining ninety kilometres to Aix-les-Bains were little more than a humiliating procession with a dwindling cast of characters, most of whom didn't even know their lines. Leblanc came on the radio again, insistent that the authorities had guaranteed to respect the 'dignity and humanity' of the riders. Soon afterwards, the news broke that the ONCE team, who'd sped back to Chambéry following their walk-out, had been greeted on their arrival at the Château de Candie hotel by police investigators from Lille.

The press room took on a frenzied atmosphere as photographers working on the race phoned in their eyewitness accounts of the disputes between riders and the crowd to their men on the ground. Uncertainly, we began writing, wondering whether the usual daily report would turn out to be an obituary. '*The 1998 Tour de France stood on the brink of collapse,*' I began.

Meanwhile, the grim procession of riders, now two hours behind schedule and meandering pointlessly through a sporting no man's land, was still taking up live TV air time. French TV presenters didn't know what to make of it. On the one hand, everything was set up for *le spectacle* – the magnificent Alpine scenes, the sunny skies, the crowds lining the route. On the other was the nightmarish reality.

Beneath the TV screens, a hastily arranged press conference dais was being put together. A sheet bearing an Aix-les-Bains logo was wrapped around the table, and chairs and microphones were quickly put in place. Across the room, the information screens hesitantly relayed more bad news. All of the Banesto team had climbed off at the feed zone in Lescheraines, and the three remaining members of the Riso Scotti team had also called it a day. With Olano long gone and none of their other riders in overall contention, Banesto's solidarity with Jalabert's deserting ONCE team was inevitable.

Yet abandoning the race in its hour of need betrayed the

Tour's old ethic of the simple honour of finishing in Paris. It was a cynical and faithless act on the day when the Tour most needed a show of loyalty and support. Sponsors who owed much of their international success to the reputation of the great old race, who'd build huge wealth on the link between themselves and the Tour de France, turned their back on the race.

The sun was dropping behind the hills by the time the riders finally appeared in the streets of Aix-les-Bains. Incredibly, the crowds had stayed at the finish and, swelled by those on their way home from work, had even grown in number, pressing voyeuristically against the barriers. Were they there to support the TVM team, to express solidarity with Outschakov, Blijlevens and Luc Leblanc? Or had they come to gawp at these desensitised athletes – professionals so out of touch with the real world that they still failed to grasp the awful truth of their plight?

Shortly before half-past seven, more than two hours behind the original finish time, they rode into the final kilometre with the TVM team fanning out across the road at the head of the bunch, much as the Motorola team had done in 1995 following the death of their Italian team-mate, Fabio Casartelli. But that July day in the Pyrénées had been heavy with sadness and loss, not anger and bitterness. In the last rays of golden sunlight, Outschakov, Voskamp and the others finally crossed the line with hands raised, as if they'd achieved a great and memorable victory.

After everything else that had happened, that sad finish would have been enough for one day, but there were more shocks still to come. Soon after the finish, Riis was dragged on to the set of *Vélo Club* and quizzed by a flustered Gérard Holtz.

'I was trying to save the Tour and to save cycling as a sport,' the tall Dane said firmly. 'Nobody asked me to act as spokesman but Jean-Marie Leblanc gave me his word that he would ask the authorities to show respect. I told him that if things carried on as they had done, then the Tour was over – that the riders would go home,' Riis explained. 'He said that the treatment given to the TVM team wouldn't be repeated. All the riders want to go to Paris. Cycling's our life – we suffer, year in and year out, but the police don't understand that. We've the right to act as we did,' he concluded. 'If the police go to the hotels tonight, then tomorrow we go home.'

But even as he spoke, personnel from the ONCE, La Française des Jeux and Casino teams were watching helplessly as the police searched team bags, vehicles and hotel rooms; while the two remaining Spanish teams, Kelme and Vitalicio Seguros, were under intense pressure from their departed peers to drop out of the race.

At the finish, Jacky 'Dudu' Durand, the joker in the pack, had dropped his usual laughing-boy image.

'The fans were treating us like rapists, like criminals,' he protested indignantly to French journalists. As he headed back to his hotel in Chambéry, the police were waiting for him and his Casino team-mates.

In the *salle de presse*, the press conference dais still stood, surrounded by vacant chairs. The clock ticked on and the heat of the day died away, yet there was still no sign of any officials from the Tour direction. By nine in the evening the rumours were flying thick and fast. Kelme and Vitalicio *had* pulled out of the race and perhaps BigMat and Casino too. I scanned the results to check on how many riders would still be left in the race following such a dramatic cull.

My mobile rang. BBC News 24 wanted to do a live 'Tour crisis' piece in their ten o'clock bulletin. The paper called and said that they wanted to make the strike a lead story on the back – and the front – page. Slowly but surely, the Tour was heading for media meltdown. Still there was no sign of Killy or Leblanc. Eventually a crew appeared and began unplugging speakers and dismantling the dais, carefully unpinning the sagging Aix-les-Bains logo as they did so.

I looked through the open doors at the far end of the hall and saw that darkness had fallen. The Spaniards, with no riders left to follow, came round and said their farewells before beginning the long drive home. We sat, speculating on the real possibility of the Tour ending here and now, four days from Paris. Writing our near-obituaries and with no words of comfort or defiance emanating from the race organisation, we were left to draw our own conclusions. The race was spinning out of control, deep into a twilight zone.

I put the phone down after sending my last story, stretched and then strolled back to my laptop, stopping off to check any further revelations as I passed colleagues along the way. It was gone eleven, but Steve still had stories to file and the press room was still lively. As I began clearing up, staff from the Tour press office slumped wearily into nearby chairs. We chatted for a few moments and I asked them if there was a political agenda to the Tour's humiliation. None of them really knew for sure, but they suggested that the Tour's parent company, the Amary Group, had critics within the French establishment. It was too late in the day and we were all too far gone to take the conversation any further, but the implication was clear.

Steve was finally ready, so, after the best part of ten hours in the *salle de presse*, we stepped through the open doors and out into the warm night air. We were both fried, wrung-out, exhausted. It took us an hour to find the Hôtel Dauphinois, an hour wasted on the empty ring roads and roundabouts of Aix-les-Bains. We joined the group of familiar faces on the terrace and ordered what we could at midnight – omelette, chips and salad.

The tortured shadows of the past, of Tour legends Coppi, Merckx and Hinault, seemed to haunt us as we sat drinking. A BBC man had latched on to us, name-dropping furiously. He was looking for that bit extra for his 'story'. As I sleepily downed another beer, he was beginning to wind me up. But by this time, I'd had it with the spin and the scandal; I'd grown weary of the fraud and deceit. The race was holed below the waterline and was steadily sinking into the depths.

I ordered another beer, finished the one I was drinking, scowled at Beeb-man and began to slip down with it.

No results were issued for stage seventeen, following a rider protest. The overall positions following stage sixteen there-fore remained unchanged.

PART FIVE

Day 22   Stage 18

Thursday 30 July
Aix-les-Bains–Neuchâtel, 215 km

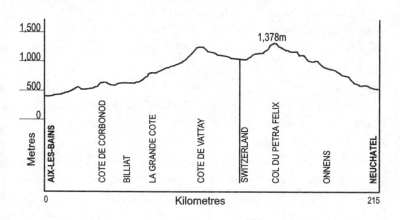

The next morning, I hurried out of the faded and musty room in the Hôtel Dauphinois, away from the smell of disinfectant and cheap cigarettes, the dark uneven corridors and rusting wrought-iron balconies, eager to get out into the fresh sunlight and clean air. Down in the courtyard, Stephen and I chatted across the breakfast table, wondering aloud if we'd be home before the weekend. Even with a few hours' sleep under our belts, we were still stunned, incredulous that we were somehow expected to feel that nothing had changed – that business was supposed to continue as usual. But of course, after stage seventeen of the 1998 Tour de France, everything had changed – for good.

Ten years earlier, I'd bought into the Tour dream, seduced by the toiling brown figures battling heroically against the backdrop of snowy mountain passes in the Alps and Pyrénées. There'd been a slow realisation back then that doping was part of the sport, but I hadn't realised the extent of abuse that went on. The truth had shocked me.

It wasn't just Bobby Julich's dream that was being betrayed – it was my teenage dream and that of every kid who'd looked at riders and had seen only sacrifice and selfless-ness. The more I'd listened to certain star riders bleating over the injustice of it all, the cruelty of the police and the lynch-mob mentality of the media, the more irritated by their arguments I became. They were turning into undignified parodies of themselves, vain drama queens, wagging their fingers and behaving as if they were beyond society's normal ethical expectations.

I found it hard to see them as hard done by. They'd filled garages with sports cars and quad bikes, built massive rambling dream homes overlooking Lake Geneva or Lake Como, put their kids down for private schools, stashed millions made from sponsorship endorsements in high-interest accounts – often on the back of victories born from canny use of a syringe and the advice of a sports doctor. Too many of them were frauds; they'd cheated the public and they'd cheated themselves. Too many of them, even though they'd been caught with their hands in the till, didn't have the guts to own up to it. Instead, the French police were doing what the sport itself couldn't – or wouldn't – do. The great rain had finally come and was washing the streets clean.

In the warm morning sunlight, I strolled over the road and picked up all the French newspapers, each of which led with banner headlines pointing to the moral and ethical death of the Tour. One had a cover shot of a particularly *sauvage* and gnarly *derrière* bared shamelessly at the roadside, protruding from the crowd and mooning at the hapless Jean-Marie

Leblanc's car as it drove mournfully towards the previous day's finish. I rolled the pages of newsprint under my arm and walked up the Avenue de Tresserve to the Telekom team buses, where a typical Tour mix of autograph hunters – adolescent boys and girls and old men and women – crowded around the entrance of the Hôtel Agora.

Earlier on, unseen by the crowds, Bjarne Riis – only a few hours earlier the self-styled saviour of the Tour – had been outside the hotel, race number in hand, assuring journalists that, yes, he would be starting the stage. Numbers clipped neatly to the frames, the sleek Pinarello bikes leaned against the team van as the mechanics sat nearby, keeping themselves to themselves. Through the crowd loomed Matthias Schuman's tall figure. We exchanged a handshake over children's heads.

'So what do you think about all this?' I asked. 'Is the team definitely starting today?'

'Yes, yes, we're starting,' he answered in precise English. 'The Tour has to go on and Telekom want us to go on, but what's happened here is not good,' he shrugged.

'But isn't the sponsor getting nervous because of all of this?'

'Not really, because Telekom has no worries. They can come to the hotel if they want and search everything, but they won't find anything because we're clean,' he insisted. 'Telekom is clean.'

Down at the start village overlooking the Lac du Bourget, the crowds seemed smaller than usual, less enthusiastic and more subdued. As the sun blazed down, there was a palpable sense of unease in the air. Out on the lake, windsurfers and water-skiers shimmered across the water in the shadow of the steep sides of the Mont du Chat. It was an idyllic setting for what threatened to become a wake.

As I walked into the *village départ*, nobody knew whether the riders would start or not. With the Spaniards long gone and Massi out of the picture, rumours spread that Casino would stage a loud and public protest and then leave. Riis' tentative threat of the previous evening – 'we're all going home' – echoed resoundingly in my mind.

There was a sudden flurry of activity as cameramen and *gendarmes* jostled for position at the entrance to the village. Out of the scrum, dressed in team-issue casuals, emerged the red-faced, frowning Luc Leblanc, who marched into the village and sat at the nearest table. A burly human pyramid of journalists teetering over him, Leblanc began speaking quietly. With elbows and lenses battering my head, I strained to hear his quiet voice; but in fact, we all knew what he was going to say. Like Laurent Jalabert before him, Leblanc was soon denouncing the impossible working conditions, claiming solidarity with Jalabert and saving a few choice words for the absent Hein Verbruggen.

'I'm quitting the Tour with my head held high,' he said. 'This is without doubt the most important decision of my career. What's happened here is a bad thing but in the long term, it will lead to better things. It's unforgivable that the UCI president is on holiday in India. This is one of the most serious crises in the history of cycling – at least he could have been here at our side. We must find a new president.'

Yet his words had little real impact. After days of sudden scandal and high-speed revelations, the atmosphere seemed leaden and dead, the air thick with an awful sense of inevitability. The frenetic pace had finally dropped and we were walking through treacle, going through the motions, engulfed by an overpowering sense of defeat and pointlessness. Without riders like Olano, Leblanc, Zulle, Virenque, Jalabert, Dufaux, Escartin and, yes, even Massi, the King of the

Mountains arrested the night before – without any of them, the classification had an absurd look to it. They'd gone but we were all still here, watching the race hang on for grim death. As I headed out of the village towards the team cars, I realised why there was so much free and uncluttered parking space around the start village – it was because there were only fourteen teams left in the race. Most of the big air-con team buses had gone, leaving just some of the smaller team vans. And there were fewer riders pedalling back and forth, killing time before the start and fewer team cars to gravitate towards – just plenty of still, dead air.

Meanwhile, big Magnus Backstedt, grinning readily in spite of everything, pedalled into view and slapped me on the shoulder. I was pleased to see his tall frame and wide strong features. I asked him how he was feeling. He knew straight away that I wasn't talking about his legs.

'I had a bad night. Yesterday was a crazy day – my head's messed up because of all this,' he said bluntly. 'It's been getting to me, all this shit. I've been calling my mum at home for about thirty or forty minutes every night, just to talk and to try to bring out the positive things. But yesterday was too much to experience in my first Tour,' he admitted. 'I felt like I didn't need that. It made me want to go home, because when we stopped yesterday, I just didn't want any part of what was happening. I didn't want to do it any more.'

While Riis and Leblanc had squared up to each other under the gaze of the world's media and Bobby J had bowed his head in anguish, Magnus, confused and disillusioned, had walked away in disgust.

'I took my bike off the road and laid it in a ditch, walked up into the woods and sat at the foot of a tree, thinking, "Shit, this is not true – this can't be happening." I was just sitting on my own, looking at it all going on. I didn't want to get

247

involved with it because it was just stupid. The image was terrible and I didn't want to have anything to do with it.'

When the bunch finally climbed back on and reluctantly moved off, Magnus was one of those on the fringe of the battle, struggling to come to terms with the situation.

'I didn't know what was happening – I don't think anybody did. Suddenly, I looked around and there weren't any Spanish riders there any more. At first I thought it was because they were riding in a group behind,' he explained, 'or because they knew that the stage was neutralised and that there weren't any times being taken. But I wasn't thinking about them. By then, I was concentrating on the race the next day – wondering *if* it was going to happen. At that point, we still didn't know. I had to fight my own head the whole time, to try and get rid of the negative thoughts. I wanted to keep motivated and focused – I didn't want to fill my head with thoughts about what was the right or wrong thing to do, or start thinking about quitting. That would have felt like giving up on the sport and I didn't want to do that. The team wanted us to continue and Roger said, "Please, for me – stay in the race and carry on doing the best you can."

'Now I just want to get to Paris,' he said after a long pause, before adding, almost as an afterthought, 'and try to win a stage, if I can.'

'But do you know if everybody is starting today?' I asked him.

'I don't know, because some guys are pretty upset,' he said, before heading off in search of a coffee. 'I'll find out from the others.'

In the no man's land between the diminishing number of team cars and the eerily low-key village, Bobby J was holding court to a handful of journos and TV crews. The throng swelled as, warming to his theme, he began a defiant monologue.

'They're killing my dream,' he was saying emotively, as I took my place in the huddle of journalists. 'I don't understand why they want to kill off their race, just because of some judge miles away, looking for fifteen minutes of fame. The Tour must go on – we have to go on. This is my dream,' he said yet again, 'and they're trying to kill it . . .'

The soundbites fell from his tongue, and then, as if stage-managed, a group of American fans appeared waving the star-spangled banner. It was too much. I walked off, wondering if a drooling American film crew, avidly filming the whole scene, had handed over the flag to wave in shot.

A hundred metres away, a wearied Udo Bolts had just emerged from the Telekom bus, almost ignored as he battled through the fans pushing towards the door in search of Ullrich. For a few brief moments, I had him to myself. As usual, Udo was friendly although subdued, but in no mood to throw in the towel.

'If we stop riding, then the police will win,' he stated calmly. 'That will give the French sports minister what she wants. But,' he added pointedly as Bobby J, having finally broken away from the American press corps, arrived by his side, 'we're not criminals – we have rights. We're racing today and we have to carry on to Paris. But being booed like we were yesterday is hard to take,' said Udo quietly. 'It's bad for your soul.'

In spite of his impassioned plea for the race to be left alone, Bobby J didn't seem quite so sure of himself after all. With all of us eavesdropping, he asked Bolts what was happening.

'We race,' said the German unwaveringly. 'Definitely – we go.'

But Bolts was speaking for Telekom, not for the other teams who had been dragged into the fog of allegations and betrayals. There was still uncertainty over what Casino would do in the aftermath of Massi's arrest and anyway, how many riders still had the heart to continue after the previous long day's ride through a corridor of abuse and insults?

Over at the Casino mini-bus, the French sponsor's morose riders were putting the final reluctant touches to their daily ritual of race preparation.

'We're starting today because we have to,' said Stéphane Barthe, Casino's former French national champion.

A brief visit from Tour director Leblanc just a few minutes before the bell rang out across the village to call the riders to the start line had failed to lift the French team's spirits.

'As far as I'm concerned, the Tour is already over,' said the absent Massi's Italian team-mate, Alberto Elli gloomily. 'But all the same, we're going to Paris. The bosses have told us that we have to carry on, but don't count on me for any animated racing.'

Even so, Bolts and the other 102 riders made their way through the barriers, past the quiet crowd and pedalled calmly to the start line. As they came together for the first time since the Spanish walk-out, since Massi's arrest, since Jalabert and Leblanc's emotional exits, we waited for them to decide the fate of the 1998 Tour. I stood alongside the fleet of team cars, their engines running, waiting in line as they did on so many other more humdrum mornings to speed after their sponsor's jerseys once the flag had dropped. There was a long pause. For a moment, we all held our breath; but then, rolling over the heads of the crowd came a muffled cheer and the long line of Fiats slowly moved off in pursuit of the Tour's beleaguered *peloton*.

After they'd finally gone, we walked back to the car and drove slowly through the crowds towards the *autoroute*, again trying to make sense of it all. Would it have been better for the Tour, better for cycling – better for all sport – if the shambolic 1998 Tour had stopped there and then, with a shrug of weary resignation at the lakeside in Aix-les-Bains? Who wanted the race back on the road? The riders? The fans? The media? Nike, Fiat and Crédit Lyonnais? The game was up, the whistle had been blown, yet we were still carrying on, even if most of us – riders included – were now desperate for the race to be put out of its misery. So why were we continuing? Because contracts with stage towns had been struck months earlier, rights had been sold to TV companies on the other side of the world, the big-money sponsors – the Tour's *partenaires* – expected, probably even demanded it.

I felt for Jean-Marie Leblanc, our red-eyed ringmaster. A decent and courteous man, a former professional and accomplished journalist, he knew more than anybody else how shamed the race had become. You just had to look into his eyes to see the strain and heartbreak. As usual, Leblanc's was the first voice to crackle over Radio Tour a few minutes after the start. But instead of the usual roll-call of corporate guests crowded into the fleet of silver Lancias, he spoke clearly and passionately of the catastrophe that had been so narrowly averted.

'This Tour,' he began carefully, 'has been at the same time a magnificent race and one poisoned by scandal. The Tour is so popular and has such meaning that it has found itself in the eye of a storm. Now that storm has blown itself out.'

We drove on in silence, listening intently to his carefully chosen words.

'We want to thank, from the heart, those who have shown solidarity; particularly the 103 riders starting the race this morning and their spokesman, Bjarne Riis, for his concern for the riders' conditions and for the future of the sport. Together, we're going to finish this Tour de France, just like the 84 Tours before it. This morning we're happy to know that we're going to make it to Paris. Even with a slightly bitter taste in the mouth,' concluded Leblanc, 'this is for us a great triumph.'

But not every rider saw it the same way. Carrying on after everything that had happened quickly became too much for Casino's Barthe. The French rider climbed off soon after the *départ réel*, having lost the heart to continue. TVM's stressed and wearied Jeroen Blijlevens joined the Frenchman after losing touch with the bunch in the first hills of the day, and abandoned almost as soon as the race crossed into Switzerland.

'I started this morning to honour the race and in honour of Cees Priem and Andrei Mikhailov,' Blijlevens explained later. 'But when I saw them all racing as usual, I felt it showed a lack of respect. So I decided to abandon – symbolically – just after the frontier. Now I can forget about France.'

In the car, as we headed north towards the border crossing into Switzerland just south of Geneva, there was time to scan the French papers. All of them led with the previous day's farce. The headlines made it clear that the tide of French public opinion had hardened against the Tour and the riders. In *France-Soir*, Bernard Gravet, director of the French judiciary, sneered at the riders' protests.

'The riders have been maltreated? Dream on!' he told the French tabloid. 'I'm appalled by the attitude shown by certain areas of the Tour direction, who want to distract attention from the real problem. They have to understand that the authorities have declared war on doping,' asserted Gravet. But the riders couldn't or wouldn't see the big picture; all they saw was a concerted personal attack on their own careers.

The radio signal faded away in the valleys between the *autoroute* and the race as we drove past the genteel lakeside town of Annecy and homed in on the Swiss border at the southern tip of Lac Leman. There'd been rumours that the convoy would be forced into buying a year's motorway tax just for the privilege of spending a couple of hours on the Swiss *autoroutes*. Sure enough, as we lined up at border control, a beaming policewoman leaned in through the passenger window and heartlessly relieved me of the best part of 200 francs, in spite of my spluttering protests.

Further on, as we rejoined the race route, a garage with VISA signs plastered across its windows charged commission for paying with credit card for a tank full of gas. 'Visa only accepted for repair work,' snapped the man behind the counter mechanically, through his bushy backwoodsman beard. 'No good for petrol,' he said strictly.

We drove on, joining the race route as it skirted the foot of the Jura mountains, through scenes of ordered but soulless pastoral vistas. The villages were neat, picturesque and smart with no sign of litter or, in fact, of any human activity. Switzerland may be a beautiful country but it can leave the heart cold.

The race radio crackled back to life as we neared Neuchâtel. There was a breakaway of four riders who'd slipped clear of the main field after forty-eight kilometres. GAN's long-distance breakaway star, Cédric Vasseur, was trying his luck once more in the company of two other Frenchmen, Cofidis rider Laurent Desbiens and Christophe Mengin of La Française des Jeux. Italian Massimo Donati of the Cipolliniless Saeco team had tagged along too. These weren't four clueless kamikazes. Vasseur had a proven pedigree as long-term *maillot jaune*, while both Desbiens and Mengin had also picked up stage wins in 1997. But it was a strange move, one born out of a need to put the record straight; to show that there was more to the '98 Tour's final days than police raids, team walk-outs and rider protests.

The quartet, who at one point had led by six minutes and forty-five seconds, faded fast as Telekom, led by the *porte-parole* himself, Bjarne Riis, and Mapei, working for a third Tom Steels success, chased hard on the run-in to the Lac de Neuchâtel, aided by some fast downhill stretches and a lively following breeze. In reality, there were two, maybe three men capable of winning the stage. Steels was the obvious favourite, while the moody Zabel, who'd suffered some tough luck earlier in the race, was hoping to make the best of his team's hard work. Rabobank's Robbie McEwen, who despite a series of high placings had never looked likely to beat either Steels or Zabel to the line, had hung on through the mountain stages and was desperate to pick up some success before the race ended in three days' time.

But McEwen, whose feisty attitude fits the 'plucky Aussie' cliché to a tee, was about to have another unlucky day. Six kilometres from the line in Neuchâtel's Avenue du Premier Mars, Mapei and Telekom led the shattered field past the breakaway and Steels moved into pole position. After that, it was a formality for the big Belgian rider, who was again simply too quick and too powerful for the increasingly frustrated Zabel. Afterwards, Steels was happy enough, even if he did admit to missing Cipollini, the long-gone Lion King.

'It's not because I always want to beat him,' mused Steels, 'but a win against Cipollini has a bit more worth. It's a real shame that he's gone home.'

McEwen notched up another high placing, despite a brush with some of the unmemorable memorabilia thrown into the crowd by the *caravane publicitaire*. As he wound up his sprint, the Australian was slapped in the face by a spectator leaning over the crowd barriers and waving one of the PMU giant hands.

'I moved up on the right to overtake Zabel but I got smacked full in the face with one of those bloody green things,' he said afterwards. 'Bit of a shock, really.'

I didn't want to stay in Switzerland that night. I wanted the anonymity of a Novotel or a Mercure, an Ibis or a Sofitel; but most of all, I wanted somewhere away from the race, with a well-stocked mini-bar. Besides, we'd been pre-booked into the far side of the lake, even deeper into the staid Swiss countryside and a good hour's drive from the next day's start in La Chaux-de-Fonds. So, as the evening sky darkened over the lake and a steady rain began to fall, I climbed back into the car and headed up into the dark hills of northern Jura. Pontarlier, about fifty kilometres east into France, looked the best possibility for a room. I'd had a soft spot for the place since watching Bernard Hinault power through its streets during the 1985 Tour. I obviously wasn't the only one who wanted to head back to France; as I headed along the winding mountain road, the tail-lights of a convoy of slow-moving Tour vehicles loomed through the rain in front of me.

It was after ten by the time I found Pontarlier's out-of-town estate of Campaniles, Sofitels and Fimotels, all fully booked. But on the other side of the ring road, beckoning through the dark, was a McDonald's. It was late, I was tired and what the hell, I was hungry.

Standing bleary-eyed in the queue was a group of German

journalists, a dishevelled Danish TV crew and one very well-known but anxious looking *directeur sportif*, together with a rep from the *caravane publicitaire*. Even though I'd spoken to this particular *directeur* many times, he looked straight through me, unrecognisingly. But then team bosses being as they are, there was nothing unusual in that. Yet it was odd that he should be there with this other man, especially as this particular *directeur* should have been tucking his boys up in bed, back at the team hotel.

I munched my way disinterestedly through my filet-o-fish, but instinct made me home in on their conspiratorial huddle a few tables away. As I watched, slowly, through the fog of exhaustion and disillusion, the penny dropped. The race convoy would cross back into France the next day, and might just possibly fall foul of customs officers at the border crossing at Le Locle. EPO needs to be kept in fridges but if this *directeur* had any sense, all he had left in his team fridge was a pungent chunk of *chèvre* and a couple of half-eaten energy bars.

So what?

Well, the vehicles in the *caravane* are sometimes staffed by old pros, many of whom still have good contacts with those at the wheel of team cars. And those vans, having safely crossed back into France that evening, were parked up across the road outside the hotel complex. Were the fridges only stocked with water and soft drinks or did they contain something altogether more energising?

Stunned by the realisation, I stood up and followed the pair out into the damp night, wondering if my imagination was finally running away with me. In the rain, through bleary and bloodshot eyes, through the darkness on the edge of town, I tried to piece the puzzle together.

You are free to pass your own judgment, free to think

what you like about this fuzzy late-night encounter. But I know what conclusion my befuddled and stupefied mind came to, as I wearily climbed once more behind the steering wheel and headed on towards Besançon.

Stage winner: Tom Steels, Belgium (Mapei–Bricobi)

Overall race leader: Marco Pantani, Italy (Mercatone Uno)

Points classification leader: Erik Zabel, Germany (Deutsche Telekom)

Team classification leader: Cofidis

Mountains classification leader: Christophe Rinero, France (Cofidis)

Day 23   Stage 19

Friday 31 July
La Chaux-de-Fonds–Autun, 242 km

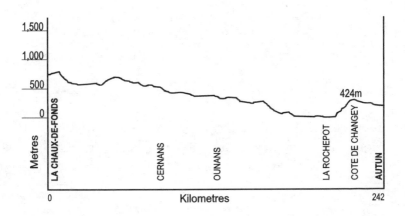

I overslept the next morning but the sun came creeping through the blinds at the Besançon Mercure hotel much earlier than I wanted. Lifting my head gingerly from the pillow, I eyed the array of empty beer and miniature wine bottles lined up on the dressing table. I'd drunk quickly and determinedly until one in the morning, relishing my distance from Planet Tour's claustrophobic, cracked world. Brimming with red wine, I'd flirted with the idea of following Stéphane Barthe's tearful example of making an early return to the real world, wondering woozily and sentimentally how many hours it would take to drive up to Calais and a boat home.

Yet the previous night's disturbing experience under the golden arches on the outskirts of Pontarlier was weighing on my mind. I still needed to know more, to be sure that what I'd seen was real. At least I didn't have to rely on whispered rumours in the press room or suffer convoluted denials to understand what I'd seen: peering through the rain in an empty car-park, I'd had my own brush with the Tour's dark heart.

I took a hot shower and ordered up some coffee to kick-start the day. After the harrowing start at Aix-les-Bains, I'd resolved to skip the *village départ* that morning and, with deadlines pressing, head straight to the press room in Autun.

The final week always tests the convoy's endurance but the '98 Tour's second-longest stage on the day before the final time trial didn't promise any sensations, except perhaps an unremarkable lone breakaway by those with nothing to lose, a frantic pursuit towards the finish and another bunch sprint. But things didn't quite run to plan. As I cruised west along the A36 'Comtoise' *autoroute*, Magnus Backstedt had set about making a name for himself. That, added to the news that the TVM team had quit the race the night before rather than return to French soil, gave me plenty of food for thought. Maybe I should have stayed in Switzerland after all . . .

It had finally got too much for TVM's remaining riders, Bart Voskamp, Steven de Jongh, Sergei Ivanov, Servais Knaven and Sergei Outschakov. Blijlevens' disillusioned withdrawal the day before as the Tour headed into Switzerland had proved to be the straw that broke the camel's back.

'All of TVM's riders have decided not to start the nineteenth stage of the Tour de France,' explained Jean-Marie Leblanc. 'It was a decision taken by the riders and only by the riders.'

Leblanc had been called at 8.30 that morning, by TVM's remaining manager, Guido van Calster. 'Leblanc said that he respected their decision,' van Calster explained, 'and that he regretted that it had come to this.'

★ ★ ★

The press tent, a huge marquee set at a jaunty pitch on the shore of Lac Vallon on the edge of Autun, was quiet when I arrived at lunch-time. A few metres away, another marquee dedicated to the local beef and dairy products was far busier, packed with VIP guests, press car drivers, retired professionals, TV commentators and even the odd hack. After elbowing, barging and then finally shoving my way to the groaning tables laden with meat and cheeses, I loaded up for the afternoon. At the far end of the tent, I watched the Tour's weary foot soldiers queue with growing impatience for a free bottle of local red, courtesy of Autun's *comité local*.

I moved outside, soaking up the sun and watching the throng mill around the tents, waiting for another journalist to emerge so that I could share the burden of knowledge of the Pontarlier incident.

I hid behind my shades in the hot sun, feeling hungover and unsteady, reeling from the shocking revelations that had overloaded my senses during the previous three weeks. Two days from Paris and, like many of those working on the race, I was wrung out and disillusioned, ready to believe just about anyone and anything.

Meanwhile Magnus, to his credit, was clinging to his dream of a stage win and had seen a promising opportunity. With almost half the field gone and too many riders running on empty, the big Swede had recovered from his harrowing time in the Alps and was eyeing up the possibilities.

'I don't know why, but I felt geed up this morning and wanted to get into a break,' he said after the stage. 'I hadn't been in a good long break since the Tour started and I felt like I really needed to get into one. And it turned out to be just that – 220 kilometres out front,' he admitted. 'I told Stuart

O'Grady, "I'm going off in the break," and he came with it too. It took a while to get going, but after about twenty kilometres, I put the hammer down as hard as I could for five kilometres. When I looked around there were about a dozen guys with me and we started working together.'

Backstedt worked hard, dragging a group of twelve riders, including team-mate O'Grady, clear of the main field as the race headed back into the French heartlands of the Saône-et-Loire region. Among the GAN pair's breakaway partners were two of Casino's French riders, inevitably including Jacky 'Dudu' Durand, and two US Postal hopefuls, Frankie Andreu and Pascal Deramé. Casino, with Massi still being questioned and team manager Lavenu protesting his rider's innocence, needed a break more than any of us realised at the time; while US Postal had ghosted through the Tour, there or thereabouts on most days, but with a list of missed opportunities haunting them.

During the first week, the unassuming George Hincapie had come within two seconds of the yellow jersey on that long Bastille Day break from Roscoff to Lorient. Meanwhile, Tyler Hamilton, whose main claim to fame prior to the Tour was as winner of the Mount Washington hill climb in the States, had yo-yoed through the race, giving Ullrich a run for his money during the stage seven time trial in Corrèze, but then tumbling down the classification on the approach to the Pyrénées. Later, in the Provençal hills, Marty Jemison had flown the flag on the tough and baking stage into Carpentras following all the right wheels, only to find himself agonisingly outsprinted by Italian Daniele Nardello. The very next day, the American team had Peter Meinert-Nielsen in the attack of six riders that moved clear on the road to Grenoble. But the Dane fluffed his finishing straight move and could only watch as O'Grady sealed another

GAN success. Now four days later, with the Alps receding into the distance and the Tour defiantly bludgeoning its way to Paris, Derame had a chance to make up for the team's earlier disappointments.

As the day wore on, I glanced at the TV screens in the press room. The break of thirteen riders, with no contenders for any of the classifications in the move, was now more than seventeen minutes clear of the disinterested *peloton*. In fact, it was so far ahead of the field that the next time most of them would see their team-mates would be at the dinner table that night. Even then, late in the long, hot afternoon, as the twenty-eight-year-old Deramé attacked to split the breakaway in two as it crested the fourth-category climb of the Côte de Changey, few of us watching believed that the Frenchman could win. Neither, as it turned out, did Marcus Backstedt.

'I knew six kilometres from the finish that I was gonna do it,' Backstedt said later. 'I knew from the way the others were riding. Deramé was basically riding for me. I know he didn't mean to be, but everything he did was perfect for me. I'm sure that he didn't even know that he was doing it himself.'

With the lead group reduced to just four riders – Backstedt, Deramé, Rabobank's Maarten Den Bakker and Saeco's Eddy Mazzoleni – and only sixteen twisting kilometres left to race, Magnus bided his time. Deramé, meanwhile, knowing that he had virtually no hope of outsprinting any of his three remaining companions, was getting nervous. With only a stage win in the lowly Tour of Poitou-Charentes to his name since turning professional, the US Postal rider began tentatively attacking on the lumpy run-in to Autun. Three kilometres from the uphill finishing straight, Deramé looked to have broken decisively clear; but with the others reacting quickly, he was unable to open enough of a gap.

'I got away from them,' explained Deramé later, 'but I was tired. I couldn't go again to move further clear and that cost me the stage.'

But Backstedt, facing a dream opportunity to become Sweden's first Tour stage winner, was staying cool and allowed Den Bakker and Mazzoleni to haul him back up to the desperate US Postal professional.

'I tried everything,' a defeated Deramé told the huddle of French journalists who swarmed around him beyond the finish line, 'because it's not every day that a guy like me gets the chance to win a stage in the Tour.'

Derame's fumbling tactics were unable to cope with the surprisingly canny Swede and when the Frenchman led the quartet into the final kilometre, Backstedt was still sitting calmly at the rear of the group, waiting to unleash his sprint.

At the same time, back home in Sweden, Magnus's parents were watching live TV coverage.

'I think my dad almost had a heart attack, because he'd never seen me act like that,' Backstedt recalled later. 'My parents had never seen me be so calm, so they were sitting there screaming at the television, thinking that I'd left it too late for the sprint.'

Yet when Den Bakker, not such a bad sprinter in his own right, sped past the flagging Deramé with Mazzoleni in his slipstream, Backstedt's graceful power took him smoothly ahead of the trio. The big blond crossed the line with out-stretched arms and an exultant howl of delight.

'I didn't know whether to laugh or cry,' he smiled later that evening. 'Instead I just screamed for joy. It's been my dream since I was twelve or thirteen years old, just to ride the Tour de France. But then to win a stage made everything feel like a movie. It was almost too much for me . . . I was so surprised that I actually did it,' Magnus admitted, 'so surprised that I stayed so cool. I let the other guys do all the work and then just waited until the last 150 metres. I've never played it like that in my whole life before. I've never ever waited for the other guys to do the work for me because I've never had the mental strength to ride like that before.'

GAN had started the Tour with the troubled Frédéric Moncassin as their top sprinter; now, two weeks later, they could call on O'Grady or Backstedt for opportunistic stage wins, leaving Moncassin increasingly sidelined as the team's protected fast finisher.

'I started the year trying to lead out Fred and staying with him for the sprints,' recalled Backstedt, 'making sure he got in a good position for the finale.'

That much had been achieved but the Toulousian sprinter, after his long run of painful near misses, had failed to notch up a single truly significant win for the best part of two seasons. By the late spring, Moncassin's crisis in confidence was about to work in Backstedt's favour.

'One day at a race before the Tour,' Magnus explained, 'Fred said, "I'm not feeling so good – why don't you do the sprint today and I'll lead you out?" I was shocked because I'd never had a lead out before and, since I was a junior, everybody's always told me that I'm not fast enough. Having Fred say that to me – a guy who's been my idol from years back – came as a surprise. Anyway, he did a good job that day and I got second in the sprint, so since then things have changed. I've got more confident in myself when I'm sprinting and the team has got more confidence in me.'

Moncassin, his morale broken yet again by another run of near misses in the Tour's first week, had abandoned the Tour together with sixteen other riders during the apocalyptic tenth stage to Luchon. Once thought of as a rival to Cipollini, Moncassin's talent seemed on the wane while GAN's English-speaking youngsters, O'Grady and Backstedt, were very much on the rise. So the twenty-nine-year-old Frenchman from the Haute Garonne wasn't at the dinner table in Montceau-les-Mines to see his Swedish protégé celebrate with a bottle of champagne.

'When I got back to the hotel that night,' said Backstedt after the Tour ended, 'the phone didn't stop. I had a hell of a lot of calls, from Sweden, Norway, Denmark, France – in fact, from all over the world. It was fun but it was tiring as well, because I wanted to sit down at the dinner table with the team and drink champagne, to celebrate with the guys who'd helped me to win. Afterwards, I couldn't get to sleep. In fact, it took me until 1.30 in the morning before I dropped off. I was still hyped up. It took me until the next morning to understand how much it meant and that I'd really done it.'

But while Backstedt basked in his success, a mournful Deramé, complete with hair dyed in the colours of the French *tricolore*, had some explaining to do in his native national papers.

'I've got nothing more than getting to the Champs-Elysées in mind,' he told *L'Equipe*. 'That will mean the Tour's ended and that everybody – riders, mechanics, physios – can get the rest we're waiting for. We're keen for this race to end.'

But the Tour's waves of scandal were far from over. As Magnus and his team-mates sat down to toast his success in the Grill Hotel and the sun dropped behind the tall woods lining Lac Vallon, the near-deserted press room came alive again as the latest doping bombshell dropped.

Hundreds of miles away in Lille, Bobby J's 'fifteen minutes of fame' man, Judge Patrick Keil, was again shaping the outcome of the 1998 Tour de France. The news broke at 8.30 – just at the time when most weary hacks were thinking of dinner and a glass or two of local Bourgogne.

Casino's Rodolfo Massi, the Tour's detained 'King of the Mountains', one of the most established Italian professionals in the bunch, had been charged with drug trafficking. Massi, along with ONCE's team doctor, Nicolas Terrados who was also charged, had been released on bail. The thirty-two-year-old, winner of the Pyrenean stage to Luchon where he'd held off Marco Pantani's furious pursuit, was charged with importing, distributing and transferring what the French authorities referred to as 'poisonous substances'.

Earlier in the evening, Bjarne Riis had marched heatedly into a hastily arranged press conference, refuting a story that had emanated from the Spanish and Swiss media quoting his alleged description of Massi as a 'drug dealer'. Up in Lille, Massi was about to be charged by Patrick Keil, even as Riis was struggling to keep his Nordic cool while denying that he would ever cast any doubts about Massi's character. But it was too late. Events had overtaken his denials and Massi had been charged. Judge Keil clearly wasn't listening to big Bjarne's words.

'The police are doing their job,' Riis mused in his rambling and unscripted statement, 'and they have to do that job in order to clean up the sport. Everybody must pull together to end this crisis. But cycling isn't finished,' he insisted. 'I don't agree that this has been a dreadful Tour. That's the wrong attitude to take. To move on, you have to compromise – otherwise everything breaks down. If everybody had quit the Tour, where would we be? Do you think cycling would be better off today?'

I took another deep breath and set about rewriting my story. Magnus's joyful victory, one that I'd been thrilled by and wanted to do justice to, was soon relegated to only the briefest mention. Yet again, doping scandals took over the back page headlines.

Massi had been seventh overall and unassailably leading the King of the Mountains competition when the police had arrested him in Chambéry. He'd been around a long time, turning professional in 1987 and riding with some of the smaller Italian sponsors, like Jolly Club and the Vatican-approved pro-lifers Amore e Vita, prior to joining Casino in 1997. While he had always held his own as a limited but moderately successful rider, with stage wins in races like the Tour of Italy and Sicilian Week, 1998 had already been his most successful season by far. In his second professional year, while with the Alba Cucine team, he'd been badly injured in a crash during the first week of the Tour of Italy. Massi had collided with an ancient Roman arch in Santa Maria Capua Vetere, north of Naples. The impact was such that it shattered his femur and his collar-bone, leaving him with one leg shorter than the other following surgery and forcing him out of racing for more than a year. In 1993, Massi crashed once more, again breaking his collar-bone and forcing him to take further time out from the sport. He came back to racing in 1994, and finally, after seven years in the pro ranks, took his first win at the Italian stage race Sicilian Week.

'I've always been dogged by bad luck,' he'd told the press, following his spectacular win on the stage from Pau to Luchon.

In twelve seasons, the dapper, stocky climber from Ancona had ridden for no fewer than eight sponsors. But it was with the all-conquering Casino, unstoppable in the early months of 1998, that he'd found his best form.

Now, with the Italian facing court proceedings, Casino were plunged deeper into the mire. Massi's success in Luchon had been the team's forty-fifth victory of the year, but it was soon forgotten as the Tour convoy's rumour mill went into overdrive. The French and Italian press alleged that corticoids had been found in his room, along with a substantial amount of cash; that his supposedly frequent trips to Mexico weren't to enjoy the benefits of altitude training, but for more sinister purposes. Anonymous riders still racing in the Tour were said to be queuing up to reveal what and how much they'd bought from Massi in recent years.

It was a hard fall for a long-suffering rider who, only a few days earlier, following his solo ride through the Pyrénées, had been hailed as a star. Ironically, his arrest came as he enjoyed his greatest success, an unexpected victory in the Tour's prestigious King of the Mountains competition.

But the Italian's own disgrace was nothing to the further damage done to the Tour's credibility. Massi's success in the Pyrénées had been swallowed unquestioningly by the Tour machine, with the Italian triumphantly stepping on to the podium every evening to pick up his latest polka-dot climber's jersey. He had been shaking hands, waving to the crowds and basking in the full glare of the Tour's publicity juggernaut. If there were any vestiges of hope left for cycling's self-regulation, then the Massi affair finally, irrevocably killed them off. The police had taken over, leaving the Société du Tour de France powerless. Ignorance had left the riders in moral and ethical free fall, unable to break free of the professional scene's culture of denial, now so ruthlessly exposed by the French authorities.

As the race faced up to its final weekend, Killy and Leblanc were sure to achieve their goal of taking the ailing

Tour to Paris. But it was no longer even a wounded beast. All that remained of the festival spirit of the 1998 Tour was a glassy-eyed impostor, clinging doggedly to a life-support machine.

Stage winner: Magnus Backstedt, Sweden (GAN)

Overall race leader: Marco Pantani, Italy (Mercatone Uno)

Points classification leader: Erik Zabel, Germany (Deutsche Telekom)

Team classification leader: Cofidis

Mountain classification leader: Christophe Rinero, France (Cofidis)

Day 24   Stage 20

Saturday 1 August
Montceau-les-Mines–Le Creusot 52 km:
individual time trial

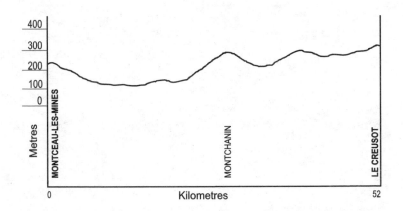

Steady rain drummed against the windows of the Hôtel Athanor in Beaune, greeting the first day of August and the last weekend of the 85th Tour de France with grey and mournful skies.

Now, even Pantani was said to be privately admitting that the stress of leading the 1998 Tour had left him longing for Paris. The stage twenty time trial, effectively a showdown between the Italian and Ullrich, was his final obstacle to victory.

For the Tour's big-hitters, it was a day of consolidation; Ullrich sought to preserve his champion's honour with a stage win and second place overall, while Pantani needed to limit his losses in order to secure his grip on victory. Bobby J, meanwhile, who had shown signs of fallibility in the final week of the race, was desperate to preserve his place on the Champs-Elysées podium of top three finishers. And even though little Marco led Ullrich by the best part of six minutes, there was always the possibility of crashes and punctures, particularly on a heavy, wet day such as this.

We expected Ullrich to reclaim perhaps three minutes, but if Pantani was unlucky enough to crash or have a puncture, then Telekom's young leader would suddenly have everything to play for. But we were all willing the Pirate on, united behind him, desperate for some positivism to emerge from the dread that had stigmatised the whole race. His success would restore balance to the overwhelming pessimism that had gripped the weary convoy. Against the unrelenting backdrop of syringes and police vans, of arrests and raids, of desperate, outflanked grey men, Pantani shone, his brilliance lifting the race when no other rider was capable of it. His ride at Les Deux Alpes and his attacks a month earlier in the Giro d'Italia transcended the fog of scandal which had since descended on the sport.

Pantani's almost inevitable triumph would be a long-awaited success emulating that of the deified Italian Fausto Coppi, winner of the Giro and the Tour in 1952. Coppi's story, outwardly one of success and glory, was also filled with poignancy and sadness. At the height of his powers, Coppi was condemned by the conservative Italy of the 1950s for an extra-marital affair with a woman who became characterised by a sanctimonious media as the mysterious 'White Lady'. The subsequent scandal left Fausto bitter and isolated. His beloved brother Serse, also a professional, was killed after a heavy fall while racing in Italy in the Tour of Piedmont, the year after Fausto's Giro–Tour double. Serse's death devastated the 'campionissimo', as Coppi was universally known. It took his family and close friends several months to dissuade him from abandoning the sport altogether. Yet Coppi's stamina in the high mountains hid a frail constitution. It finally caught up with him in January 1960, when he died suddenly after a bout of malaria was wrongly diagnosed as flu. He was only forty years old.

Since then, Italy had enjoyed the Tour de France wins of Gastone Nencini in the year of Coppi's death, and Felice Gimondi, our man in the Dublin Sports Café, in 1965. There had been others of course, such as Claudio Chiappucci and Gianni Bugno who had knocked on the door in the early 1990s, but neither rider had been able to overcome the dominant Indurain. Chiappucci valiantly led the 1990 Tour for the best part of a week, only to be caught in the finishing straight by an unflappable Greg Lemond. He then squared up to Indurain and in 1992 took a memorable and emotional stage victory at Sestrières ski station, site of one of Coppi's finest hours, after an epic lone attack through the high Alpine passes. But the self-styled 'il diablo', something of a self-publicist, was never able to overcome his weaknesses in time trials, despite his inspirational breakaways in the mountains.

In Bugno's case, it was lack of self-belief that proved to be his stumbling block. Elegant, thoughtful and with dark, brooding good looks, the gravel-voiced Bugno was one of the most charismatic riders in the bunch. He won the Giro d'Italia in 1990 with a powerful combination of time trialling and climbing, creating intense speculation that, at last, Italian cycling had a worthy successor to Gimondi. The *tifosi*'s anticipation was heightened further when he won the World Championships in 1991 and 1992 and finished in the Tour's top three in both those years. But in the seasons that followed, his nerves and moodiness got the better of him. Bugno hummed Mozart to get over his fear of descending, but despite that apparent inner calm, he was still unable to overcome his hesitancy and self-doubt. Slowly but surely, the Italian fans, who had greeted his arrival as a Tour contender with such high expectations, turned on him as the near misses added up. His public standing began to parallel that of Roberto Baggio, the Italian footballing Buddhist, vilified for his penalty miss in the 1994 World Cup final.

Once, during the 1994 Giro, when Bugno was having a particularly torrid time at the hands of the Italian media, I arrived at his team hotel for a pre-arranged interview. But Gianni wasn't there. I waited long into the evening, until, at about ten-thirty, he turned up, with one side of his face badly swollen. Bugno stared at me blankly and then, with a sudden flicker of recognition, broke into profuse apologies for keeping me waiting. He had been to an emergency dentist, he explained, for treatment of an abscess. Could we do the interview in the morning after breakfast? So the next morning we sat awkwardly in the hotel restaurant; sadly, the easy charm of the previous night had frozen over. Bugno was evasive, secretive and uncertain, his nervy manner betraying the stress of unfulfilled expectations imposed on an Italian superstar. He clutched his mobile phone and, seemingly with the weight of the world on his shoulders, twitched and shrugged his way through a series of curt, non-committal answers.

Bugno's star seemed to be falling that summer, but Pantani was becoming the new hope of Italian cycling, after taking two spectacular wins in the Giro's toughest mountain stages. Pantani had emerged from the *peloton*'s anonymous ranks during that year's Giro, finishing second to Evgeni Berzin in the Italian race and then, on the back of a growing buzz of excitement, placing third to Miguel Indurain in the Tour de France. But he had humiliated the great Indurain in that year's Giro, much as he devastated Ullrich during the 1998 Tour, leaving the Spaniard exhausted in the Dolomite mountains as Pantani took back-to-back stage victories.

Even so, few believed that the balding Italian would ever pose a serious long-term threat to the mid-1990s domination of all-rounders such as Indurain, Berzin, Olano and, latterly, Ullrich. His weaknesses in the time trial were deemed to prove that Pantani, for all his thrilling climbing skills, would never win one of the major national Tours. Those who believed that he could follow in the footsteps of similarly mercurial climbers such as Charly Gaul, Federico Bahamontes and Lucien van Impe were dismissed as hopeless romantics. But that theory overlooked his telling result in the 1994 Giro's second time trial, a hill climb, rising up from the Ligurian coast to the scented woods of the Passo del Bocco. Pantani finished third in that stage, under a minute and a half behind Indurain and only one minute and thirty-seven seconds behind stage winner Berzin.

Perhaps during that hot Mediterranean afternoon, Pantani found the touchstone of future success and realised that he was far more of an all-rounder than he'd been given credit for. Now four years later, he was set to confound the cynics and thrill the romantics in the grey drizzle hovering over Montceau-les-Mines. To safeguard final victory, Pantani had to survive Ullrich's inevitable assault over the fifty-two kilometre course; but even allowing for his near six-minute lead, he knew that a puncture or a crash could be his downfall.

'I haven't forgotten that the time trial is Ullrich's speciality,' *Il Pirata* insisted before the stage. 'You can always have problems. I'll be on my toes until the finish in Paris.'

Despite Pantani's caution, Ullrich acknowledged that final victory was now beyond him. 'I dreamed of the *maillot jaune* for a long time before the Tour,' he said, 'and when I got it, I thought I could hold on to it; but in the space of one day, I lost everything. I have to be realistic. Making up six minutes on Pantani is mission impossible. But I can make sure of a place on the podium and a third stage win – that's something to be proud of.'

Ullrich's failure to defend his title wasn't reflected by viewing figures on German television.

'More than five million people, with peaks of more than seven million, have watched the race each day,' announced German TV company ARD's PR company. 'In a phone poll we held, 87 per cent of spectators wanted the Tour to go on and 77 per cent supported the riders in their protests against the police action.'

Even so, there was little doubt that the powerful Telekom team had expected to win the race for the third year running.

'I've learnt my lesson,' said Ullrich contritely. 'I won't make the same mistakes again. Not after this Tour or during the winter break. And next year I'll be back – to win.'

In the Telekom leader's firing line was the jubilant Bobby J, who was doing little to dispel the impression that he was thrilled merely to be keeping company with such illustrious talents. Julich was clinging on to second place overall, with a mere fourteen second advantage over Ullrich following the German's devastating breakaway over the Col de la Madeleine.

'This time trial's going to be a great duel, but I don't feel any pressure,' enthused Bobby J. 'I know it will be tough against Ullrich, but this second place is important to me and I don't want to lose it. I've been dreaming of the Tour podium for thirteen years.'

Bobby's *directeur*, Bernard Quilfen, had been impressed by the American's confidence. 'He told me that he wants to do the ride of his life to hold on to second place,' said Quilfen.

With three Cofidis riders fighting for a finish in the Tour's top ten and two inside the top four placings, Quilfen had every reason to be proud of his team.

'Before the Tour began, we'd never have imagined that we would have been in this situation, but today,' he said on Saturday morning, 'we're close to a real achievement.'

Consolidation day didn't begin well for Ullrich, but he soon made up for it. Somehow, in another lapse of concentration that said as much about Telekom's management team as for the outgoing champion himself, he almost missed his start time, arriving flustered at the start ramp only half a minute or so before he was due to race. In spite of that stress and the lack of his aerodynamic racing helmet – Pantani, on the other hand, revealed that he'd simply shaved his cranium that bit closer the previous evening – Ullrich set off determinedly, brimming with aggressive attitude. He led through all the checkpoints, catching Christophe Rinero of Cofidis, who had started three minutes ahead of him, after only thirty kilometres. As Ullrich entered the finishing straight, his brown face strained into a rictus of effort, he closed down on the unnerved Michael Boogerd of Holland, who had started six minutes before him. Now there was no doubt that the German star would win the stage.

But Pantani was not about to fold in the face of Ullrich's determination. He sped off, the race leader's jersey on his back, as he had done earlier in the summer in the final time trial of the Giro d'Italia. Back in June, his advantage over the second-placed rider Pavel Tonkov of Russia had been under a minute and a half; but with the *tifosi* passionately imploring him to hang on to the race leader's pink jersey, Pantani had actually increased his lead over the former army officer. A repeat performance was out of the question against the far more accomplished Ullrich; nevertheless, the Pirate held second place throughout the stage and lost only two minutes and thirty-five seconds to the 1997 champion.

'After five kilometres I knew he was riding well,' said Pantani's *directeur*, Guiseppe Martinelli. 'So I told him not to take any risks. I think it was the best time trial he's ever ridden – better even than the one in the Giro. This was longer and harder.'

Pantani's success, the first by an Italian in thirty-three long seasons during which French, Belgian, Spanish and even American riders had dominated the Tour de France, was finally assured.

In fact it was Julich, despite second place on the stage, who suffered most at Ullrich's hands, losing the runner's-up spot by sixty-one seconds and settling for third overall. But Bobby J, forever upbeat, wasn't really that bothered. He rolled through the finish line to be met by the usual scrum of media and officials, hugged his father, and then, floating on a cloud of euphoria, launched into another celebratory speech.

'I wanted to ride this time trial as hard as I could,' he admitted. 'I thought maybe I was going too fast, but when I saw my name written on the road, I couldn't slow down. Too many people wanted me to ride for me to do that. But I'm happy – it's a big honour for me to share the Paris podium with Marco Pantani and Jan Ullrich. Now, no matter what else happens to me in life, I can say that I finished third in the Tour de France. Today, I believe that I can follow Greg Lemond and one day win the Tour. That's my dream – and I'm dreaming about next year already.'

Shortly after six o'clock, Pantani, together with his personal *soigneur* and Mercatone Uno *directeur* Guiseppe Martinelli, strolled into the *salle de presse* for one final question and answer session. Barring his path with outstretched arms was a beaming Gimondi. The two Tour winners embraced and a ripple of applause spread around the room, greeting the new champion as he settled down in front of a mass of cameras and microphones.

'Whoever wins this Tour will inevitably be the "King of the Dopes",' Laurent Jalabert had said bitterly, as he exited the Tour in reaction to what he saw as the media's lynch-mob mentality. But Jalabert, not for the first time, had got it wrong. Pantani had risen above the doom and gloom, lifting the Tour with his stylish performance. His unaffected panache had warmed cold and jaded hearts. Now he sat before us, in a rare moment of quiet, away from the crowds; occasionally, in a slightly regal manner, referring to himself in the third person.

Marco, what did you think when you realised for sure that you would win the Tour?

'That I'd won on a route that wasn't really suited to a climber. But even so, this has been the most difficult Tour I've ridden. As well as the concentration needed for the race, there's been so much tension about the scandals.'

Is this a different feeling to winning the Giro d'Italia?

'I suffered a lot under pressure at the Giro, because it was my big objective of the year. I came to the Tour more relaxed and I rode more intelligently. The stage over the Galibier is my best memory, even though I was frozen on the descent. But what I did that day had a special flavour; everything came together: my courage, my endurance and my strength. I felt incredibly determined.'

Before the race started, you said you came to the Tour with no ambition of winning and that you had poor form; you said it again in the Pyrénées. Were you playing games?

'Absolutely not! But in a big race as long as this, you go through a lot of moods – some days are better than others. I'm maybe more honest than some of the others, because when I said those things, that was how I was thinking, even if deep down I still had thoughts of winning.'

Were you worried that you might lose everything if the Tour was abandoned because of the scandal surrounding the race?

'I think everybody was frightened that we might have to stop, but we were too close to Paris. My team had made a lot of sacrifices; we'd all fought hard for my yellow jersey and stopping the race would simply have fed further doubts. It's hard to know the truth in all of this, but those who've made errors should have to pay.'

People have had the impression that some of the riders didn't care about what was happening as long as they themselves weren't under suspicion. How did you get through it all?

'It's true that at the start with the Festina affair, we weren't that bothered. I thought it was just down to one *soigneur* and that the scene itself, as a whole, wasn't touched by it. Then events overtook us. It's clear that it doesn't do any good to go on strike, that justice has its job to do.'

This Tour de France has been like no other. Do you think that the scandal has had the effect of making it a cleaner race?

'Everyone has had difficult moments. There's no other sport that makes the demands that cycling does, where you race for three weeks without a break. But the power of the law scares everyone, so maybe the investigations have made this Tour a cleaner race.'

Are you aware that by achieving the Giro–Tour double you've become a legend?

'I'm not any less or any more aware of that. You know, if Pantani hadn't come along, nobody would have noticed. They would have said that Ullrich was the strongest. But maybe I've won because this year we've seen a different Pantani, more mature and better prepared.'

What does it mean to you to become the first Italian to win the Tour since Felice Gimondi, thirty-three years ago?

'It's a huge joy and thrill. Luciano Pezzi [the Mercatone Uno team's technical director who died a month earlier and had guided Gimondi's challenge in the 1965 Tour] dreamed of seeing me win the Tour one day. He passed on all his experience to us. Without being pretentious, I wanted to do something for him, because he would have been so happy to see me win.'

Stage winner: Jan Ullrich, Germany (Deutsche Telekom)
Overall race leader: Marco Pantani, Italy (Mercatone Uno)
Points classification leader: Erik Zabel, Germany (Deutsche Telekom)
Teams classification leader: Cofidis
Mountains classification leader: Christophe Rinero, France (Cofidis)

Day 25   Stage 21

Sunday 2 August
Melun–Paris-Champs-Elysées, 147.5 km

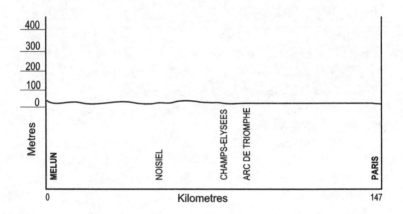

This time, there were no black cats crossing his path and causing him to crash; no rogue drivers speeding towards the *peloton* on the race route, shattering his bones: Marco Pantani – the 'divine Marco' as the French were calling him – rode into Paris, survived a momentary scare with a puncture and then stood, waving to the crowds, on the top step of the 1998 Tour de France podium. Overnight, he'd dyed his goatee blond to match the hair colour sported by the rest of his team. Through the drizzle falling on the cobbles of the Champs-Elysées, he and his team-mates were unmistakable: the golden Mercatone Uno *squadra* shone through the drab afternoon.

    The sun finally came out after the rain as Pantani, Ullrich and Julich stepped up on to the podium together. Ullrich smiled, content with his recovery from the catastrophe that was Les Deux Alpes and seemed genuinely to be enjoying

282

Pantani's moment; while Julich was delirious with joy, his head thrown back in exultation. Now he would have his photo of the three of them together.

There should have been more of a party atmosphere in the final start village of the 1998 Tour de France, yet the only real celebrations centred on Pantani and his Mercatone Uno team-mates. Elsewhere there was a palpable sense of relief that at last the race, this unholy Tour, was almost over.

Magnus Backstedt, who'd begun the Tour in anonymity, emerged from the GAN wagon, again surrounded by autograph-hunting kids and those who just wanted to shake his hand and slap him on the back. This time he didn't mind the attention. 'I've been floating,' he grinned. 'Since I won the stage, I've been floating.'

Marty Jemison had finished another Tour. He'd done his work in the shadows working hard for the team, looking after George Hincapie in the first week of the race and then doing his best to restore Tyler Hamilton after his near-collapse at Pau. Only once had Marty ridden for himself and not for the team, on the day he came close to a stage win in Carpentras.

'Everybody's relieved that this one is over,' he replied as I offered congratulations. 'I was really tired a few days back, but I feel better now.'

Jemison and the rest of his team were scheduled to host a party for one hundred people in Paris that evening, but, he admitted, he wasn't that enthusiastic about the idea. 'It's for a load of sponsors who want to party in Paris,' he shrugged, 'but they don't understand how tired we are.'

From Paris, Marty and Jill were heading back to Spain for a week's rest prior to his next race, the San Sebastian Classic the following weekend. 'I'll be on the beach with Jill by Tuesday,' he said, with a tired smile.

The crowd pressing around Pantani's team bus cheered, whistled and screamed as the divine Marco emerged to sign on for the stage start. Now, like so many other Tour winners before him, he was adopted as an honorary Frenchman; crucially, one who had rescued the reputation of the nation's greatest event. It was fifty-six days since Pantani had ridden through the rain into Milan clad in the final pink leader's jersey of Giro d'Italia leadership. Since then he'd made the transformation from erratic mountain climber to the fearsome champion of European professional cycling. His inspirational performances had brought comparisons with many of the great names from the past, such as Colombian climber Luis Herrera, Spaniards Luis Ocana and José-María Fuente, both Eddy Merckx's great rivals; and with Belgian Lucien van Impe, the last of the out-and-out climbers who won the Tour in 1976.

Yet Pantani, supposedly nothing more than a pure climber, had not won a particularly mountainous Tour and his ride in the final time trial defused the argument that he was a frail rider against the clock. In fact, he'd won the fastest-ever edition of the Tour, run off at an average speed of 39.9 kilometres per hour and he'd beaten Jan Ullrich, probably the best time triallist in the world. Forty-seven years after Fausto Coppi won the Giro–Tour double and thirty-three years after Felice Gimondi celebrated Italian success in Paris, Pantani became the sixth Italian to win the Tour. His predecessor, the ever-elegant Gimondi, had been among the first to congratulate him.

'Marco is like Fuente,' said Gimondi, as he watched the 1998 Tour play out its final moments of racing. 'He can attack where he wants, when he wants. That allows him to attack on the steepest slopes where nobody can follow. But he's an intelligent rider. He chooses his moment and knows how to measure his efforts. He knew that it was on the Galibier that he could win the Tour, and he did it – thanks as much to his head as to his legs.'

Somehow, against the mountain range of obstacles it had encountered *en route*, the eighty-fifth Tour de France made it through the storm to Paris. It said a lot for the strength and determination of the race organisation, for Jean-Marie Leblanc's staying power, that he had guided his ship into harbour when most had expected it to sink.

The final promenade stage usually allows plenty of time for play, as the riders goof around and pose for the photographers. This time, though, there were fewer of the traffic-cone-on-head or tall-rider-swaps-bikes-with-short-rider jokes going on. Although Italian champion Andrea Tafi shared a glass of champagne with the divine Marco while riding along-side the race winner, it was a muted finish to the great race – nobody wanted to seem blasé about what had gone before. And the doping scandals had taken their toll in other ways. The Tour's showpiece finish attracted fewer VIPs than before as those in the government made their excuses, pointing uncertainly to prior engagements. Once more, Jean-Marie seemed a lonely figure, preoccupied by what the future might hold, as the stage drew to a climax.

After the slow, conversational ride into Paris, the circuits up and down the Champs-Elysées are traditionally taken at breakneck speed as the riders jubilantly fight to squeeze out every last drop of energy. Pascal Chanteur of Casino, himself a Parisian, was first on to the wide boulevard, haring clear of the bunch on the first of twelve laps up and down the cobbles and past the Tuileries. But apart from Pantani's unscheduled wheel change, it was all for show. A bunch sprint finale to the Tour's most prestigious finish line was inevitable and there was one rider who was determined to win it. Telekom's Erik Zabel, despite winning the points competition for the third successive year, was unhappy at his lack of stage wins. Since his Tour début in 1995 he'd won no less than seven stages; but this year, with Mapei's Tom Steels dominating him, he'd been unable to add to his tally. Yet try as he might, he was again unable to overcome the burly Belgian champion. After the flurry of futile breakaways were over, it all came down to the final few hundred metres. Zabel, Stuart O'Grady and Hincapie all tried, but Steels was too quick and powerful for them. It was his fourth stage win of the race.

Behind him, not quite lost in the *peloton*'s flashing colours, Marco Pantani beamed and momentarily raised his arms in triumph as Jean-Marie Leblanc, the dark shadows etched under his eyes, looked on.

Stage winner: Tom Steels, Belgium (Mapei)

Overall race winner: Marco Pantani, Italy (Mercatone Uno)

Points classification winner: Erik Zabel, Germany (Telekom)

Team classification winner: Cofidis

Mountains classification winner: Christophe Rinero, France (Cofidis)

1998 Tour de France Final Overall Standings
  1. Marco Pantani, Italy (Mercatone Uno), 3,458.2 kilometres in 92 hrs, 49 mins 46 secs
  2. Jan Ullrich, Germany (Deutsche Telekom) at 3 mins 21 secs
  3. Bobby Julich, USA (Cofidis) at 4 mins 8 secs
  4. Christophe Rinero, France (Cofidis) at 9 mins 16 secs
  5. Michael Boogerd, Holland (Rabobank) at 11 mins 26 secs
  6. Jean-Cyril Robin, France (US Postal) at 14 mins 57 secs
  7. Roland Meier, Switzerland (Cofidis) at 15 mins 13 secs
  8. Daniele Nardello, Italy (Mapei–Bricobi) at 16 mins 7 secs
  9. Guiseppe di Grande, Italy (Mapei–Bricobi) at 17 mins 35 secs
 10. Axel Merckx, Belgium (Polti) at 17 mins 39 secs
 11. Bjarne Riis, Denmark (Deutsche Telekom) at 19 mins 10 secs
 12. Dariusz Baranowski, Poland (US Postal) at 19 mins 58 secs
 13. Stéphane Heulot, France (La Française des Jeux) at 20 mins 57 secs
 14. Leonardo Piepoli, Italy (Saeco) at 22 mins 45 secs
 15. Bo Hamburger, Denmark (Casino) at 26 mins 39 secs
 16. Kurt van de Wouwer, Belgium (Lotto) at 27 mins 20 secs
 17. Kevin Livingston, America (Cofidis) at 34 mins 3 secs
 18. Jorg Jaksche, Germany (Polti) at 35 mins 41 secs
 19. Peter Farazijn, Belgium (Lotto) at 36 mins 10 secs
 20. Andrei Teteriouk, Kazakhstan (Lotto) at 37 mins 3 secs

21. Udo Bolts, Germany (Deutsche Telekom) at 37 mins 25 secs
22. Laurent Madouas, France (Lotto) at 39 mins 54 secs
23. Geert Verheyen, Belgium (Lotto) at 41 mins 23 secs
24. Cédric Vasseur, France (GAN) at 42 mins 14 secs
25. Evgeni Berzin, Russia (La Française des Jeux) at 42 mins 51 secs
26. Thierry Bourgignon, France (BigMat Auber) at 43 mins 53 secs
27. Georg Totschnig, Austria (Deutsche Telekom) at 50 mins 13 secs
28. Benoit Salmon, France (Casino) at 51 mins 18 secs
29. Alberto Elli, Italy (Casino) at 1 hr 13 secs
30. Philippe Bordenave, France (BigMat Auber) at 1 hr, 5 mins 55 secs
31. Christophe Agnolutto, France (Casino) at 1 hr, 11 mins 3 secs
32. Oscar Pozzi, Italy (Asics) at 1 hr, 14 mins 54 secs
33. Maarten Den Bakker, Holland (Rabobank) at 1 hr, 16 mins 21 secs
34. Patrick Jonker, Holland (Rabobank) at 1 hr, 16 mins 49 secs
35. Pascal Chanteur, France (Casino) at 1 hr, 19 mins 32 secs
36. Massimiliano Lelli, Italy (Cofidis) at 1 hr, 20 mins 15 secs
37. Massimo Podenzana, Italy (Mercatone Uno) at 1 hr, 20 mins 47 secs
38. Vjatcheslav Ekimov, Russia (US Postal) at 1 hr, 22 mins 40 secs
39. Denis Leproux, France (BigMat Auber) at 1 hr, 25 mins 5 secs

40. Beat Zberg, Switzerland (Rabobank) at 1 hr, 26 mins 8 secs
41. Lylian Lebreton, France (BigMat Auber) at 1 hr, 28 mins 19 secs
42. Andrea Tafi, Italy (Mapei–Bricobi) at 1 hr 29 mins 22 secs
43. Rolf Aldag, Germany (Deutsche Telekom) at 1 hr, 29 mins 27 secs
44. Koos Moerenhout, Holland (Rabobank) at 1 hr, 29 mins 37 secs
45. Peter Meinert-Nielsen, Denmark (US Postal) at 1 hr, 29 mins 52 secs
46. Riccardo Forconi, Italy (Mercatone Uno) at 1 hr, 30 mins 33 secs
47. Fabio Sacchi, Italy (Polti) at 1 hr, 31 mins 53 secs
48. Marty Jemison, USA (US Postal) at 1 hr, 34 mins 27 secs
49. Nicolas Jalabert, France (Cofidis) at 1 hr, 38 mins 45 secs
50. Massimo Donati, Italy (Saeco) at 1 hr, 38 mins 59 secs
51. Tyler Hamilton, USA (US Postal) at 1 hr, 39 mins 53 secs
52. Simone Borgheresi, Italy (Mercatone Uno) at 1 hr, 40 mins 4 secs
53. George Hincapie, USA (US Postal) at 1 hr, 40 mins 39 secs
54. Stuart O'Grady, Australia (GAN) at 1 hr, 46 mins 4 secs
55. Filippo Simeoni, Italy (Asics) at 1 hr, 47 mins 19 secs
56. Jens Heppner, Germany (Deutsche Telekom) at 1 hr, 50 mins 43 secs
57. François Simon, France (GAN) at 1 hr, 52 mins 41 secs

58. Frankie Andreu, USA (US Postal) at 1 hr, 53 mins 44 secs

59. Thierry Gouvenou, France (BigMat Auber) at 1 hr, 55 mins 20 secs

60. Roberto Conti, Italy (Mercatone Uno) at 1 hr, 55 mins 33 secs

61. Laurent Desbiens, France (Cofidis) at 1 hr, 56 mins 28 secs

62. Erik Zabel, Germany (Deutsche Telekom) at 1 hr, 56 mins 57 secs

63. Leon van Bon, Holland (Rabobank) at 1 hr, 57 mins 30 secs

64. Paul van Hyfte, Belgium (Lotto) at 1 hr, 58 mins 2 secs

65. Jacky Durand, France (Casino) at 1 hr, 59 mins 42 secs

66. Christophe Mengin, France (La Française des Jeux) at 2 hrs 35 secs

67. Frédéric Guesdon, France (La Française des Jeux) at 2 hrs, 5 mins 8 secs

68. Wilfried Peeters, Belgium (Mapei–Bricobi) at 2 hrs, 6 mins 16 secs

69. Rik Verbrugghe, Belgium (Lotto) at 2 hrs, 6 mins 17 secs

70. Magnus Backstedt, Sweden (GAN) at 2 hrs, 8 mins 30 secs

71. Eddy Mazzoleni, Italy (Saeco) at 2 hrs, 10 mins 19 secs

72. Fabiano Fontanelli, Italy (Mercatone Uno) at 2 hrs, 11 mins 37 secs

73. Stefano Zanini, Italy (Mapei–Bricobi) at 2 hrs, 12 mins 11 secs

74. Alain Turicchia, Italy (Asics) at 2 hrs, 14 mins 12 secs

75. Mirco Crepaldi, Italy (Polti) at 2 hrs, 15 mins 5 secs
76. Diego Ferrari, Italy (Asics) at 2 hrs, 15 mins 46 secs
77. Xavier Jan, France (La Française des Jeux) at 2 hrs, 15 mins 51 secs
78. Pascal Lino, France (BigMat Auber) at 2 hrs, 16 mins 13 secs
79. Fabio Roscioli, Italy (Asics) at 2 hrs, 17 mins 53 secs
80. Christian Henn, Germany (Deutsche Telekom) at 2 hrs, 19 mins 52 secs
81. Viatcheslav Djavanian, Russia (BigMat Auber) at 2 hrs, 21 mins 31 secs
82. Rossano Brasi, Italy (Polti) at 2 hrs, 22 mins 10 secs
83. Jens Voigt, Germany (GAN) at 2 hrs, 25 mins 14 secs
84. Pascal Derame, France (US Postal) at 2 hrs, 26 mins 25 secs
85. Tom Steels, Belgium (Mapei–Bricobi) at 2 hrs, 26 mins 30 secs
86. Eros Poli, Italy (GAN) at 2 hrs, 31 mins 56 secs
87. Alexei Sivakov, Russia (BigMat Auber) at 2 hrs, 33 mins 19 secs
88. Aart Vierhouten, Holland (Rabobank) at 2 hrs, 35 mins 6 secs
89. Robbie McEwen, Australia (Rabobank) at 2 hrs, 36 mins 32 secs
90. Paolo Fornaciari, Italy (Saeco) at 2 hrs, 37 mins 50 secs
91. Massimiliano Mori, Italy (Saeco) at 2 hrs, 38 mins 12 secs
92. Bart Leysen, Belgium (Mapei–Bricobi) at 2 hrs, 39 mins 43 secs
93. Francesco Frattini, Italy (Deutsche Telekom) at 2 hrs, 43 mins 16 secs

94. Franck Bouyer, France (La Française des Jeux) at 2 hrs, 43 mins 45 secs
95. Mario Traversoni, Italy (Mercatone Uno) at 2 hrs, 44 mins 42 secs
96. Damien Nazon, France (La Française des Jeux) at 3 hrs, 12 mins 15 secs

Epilogue

I awoke with a start as the train burst out of the darkness of the tunnel and into the bright autumn sunlight. It was a crisp November morning and I was on the Eurostar, on my way to Paris for the presentation of the 1999 Tour de France route.

Despite the brave and inspiring words spoken in Paris that cold morning by a chastened Jean-Claude Killy and Jean-Marie Leblanc, there are no tidy, happy endings to this story. Maybe others think there can be; but no, for many, this everyday story of fudge and corruption ends with doubt still permeating their minds. So much has been said since July of 1998, yet I am unsure what has been achieved. As the 1999 season began, the French police had already picked up where they left off, searching vehicles from the Mapei team on their way back to Italy via the South of France.

After the 1998 Tour de France ended, the scandal really began. There were endless police interviews, uneasy meetings between riders and promoters; yet a wisp of hope hung in the air, giving rise to the belief that change was possible. But as the weeks passed and Willy Voet, Richard Virenque, Jean-Marie Leblanc, Manolo Saiz, Hein Verbruggen and Laurent Jalabert, among others, had their say, the plot, if it had ever been evident, was lost.

Saiz, still smarting from the confrontational scenes at Tarascon-sur-Ariège, spent most of the autumn berating the Tour organisation and the French media. 'We have stuck a finger up the Tour's arse,' he had said, soon after quitting the race in disgust back in July. His brutal language returned when confronted with Alex Zulle's supposed admission, dur-

293

ing the July police interrogations, of EPO use at ONCE.

'Anyone who gets a finger stuck up their arse in a police station at five in the morning will say anything,' commented Manolo, who was soon afterwards elected president of the professional team managers' association.

The Festina team made their return to top-level racing in the San Sebastian Classic in August, the first post-Tour World Cup race. The event, one of the ten most prestigious one-day races in the world, is promoted and run under the jurisdiction of the UCI. Shortly after winning the race, Italian Francesco Casagrande of the Cofidis team tested positive and was banned until the following season. In contrast with French race organisers, the Spanish, outraged by the treatment of their own trade teams by the French during the Tour, welcomed the Festina 'martyrs' with open arms, no questions asked. Three weeks after San Sebastian the team, led by Virenque and Zulle, rode the Tour of Spain. Although the race was won by Abraham Olano, Festina came close to putting the apparently reformed Alex Zulle in a top three placing. Soon after the Vuelta ended, the Swiss cycling federation announced sanctions on the trio of Festina riders under their jurisdiction – Zulle, Laurent Dufaux and Armin Meier. While the Swiss proposed eight-month bans, which would have effectively ruled the threesome out of competition until 1 June 1999, the UCI overruled them and reduced the punishment to seven-month bans. That curious decision allowed them to come back to racing on 1 May – leaving them with just enough time to prepare for the 3 July start of the 1999 Tour de France.

The French federation meanwhile, stymied by a lack of admissible evidence, was forced to adjourn its own enquiry, leaving Virenque's trial by media to continue unchecked. His former masseur and confidant, Willy Voet, became his chief accuser as he claimed in a series of press interviews that Hervé and Virenque were among the team's most enthusiastic dopers. As the autumn wore on, both Hervé and Virenque continued to deny knowingly using doping products and rejected Voet's claims.

In interview after interview Voet scoffed at the UCI's blood-test health checks, pointed to by Verbruggen as the best available safeguard against EPO use.

'They're a joke,' Voet told the press, before explaining that the UCI's doctors could be fooled by riders being quickly rehydrated with water and sodium prior to a blood test. 'Twenty minutes later,' claimed Voet, 'the haematocrit level has dropped by about three points.'

In a press conference at the World Championships in Holland, Verbruggen came under fire over the UCI's leniency with the Swiss trio. He was asked if Zulle, who according to further revelations in his leaked police testimony had admitted to using EPO over a four-year period, including his time with Saiz's ONCE team, would be stripped of victories dating back to that period. But Verbruggen quickly moved on to emphasise the legal complexities of any further action.

Neil Stephens, devastated by the whole affair, got out while he could and, after a controversial selection for the Australian Commonwealth Games team, abruptly retired from the sport. At thirty-four, he was known to be thinking of quitting anyway – the Festina affair just helped to make up his mind.

'Stevo' had consistently maintained his innocence, claiming that he had never knowingly doped himself, as had Pascal Hervé and most notably Richard Virenque, both of whom claimed that they had been unaware of the administration of banned products within the Festina team. Hervé opted for a self-imposed ban, in what he described as solidarity with his sanctioned Festina team-mates, that would bring him back to racing prior to the 1999 Tour de France.

ONCE team doctor Terrados and the Tour's erstwhile King of the Mountains, Rodolfo Massi, both charged by the French courts, also consistently denied all charges. The Italian climber, who left the Casino team over the winter and headed back to Italy and the Liquigas squad, instructed his lawyer to request that the charges against him be dropped, but in mid-February 1999, a court in Douai in northern France rejected his appeal and the case against him seemed set to go ahead.

Hervé, his reputation affected by persistent media rumours linking him to doping excesses, which he has also consistently denied, took a pay cut and opted to stay with Festina. He remained loyal to his friend Richard Virenque, even as the controversy surrounding him threatened to ostracise Virenque from the sport.

By November, when the following year's Tour de France launch came around, the continuing aftershocks had left the sport in disarray. The UCI still fought shy of decisive action, while the riders and teams insisted that they were mere victims in a political battle centred on the French Ministry for Sport. Yet reports emanating from the French police were said to reveal that all of the TVM riders taken away by police in the Albertville night raids had tested positive for drugs. The cocktail was said to include steroids, growth hormones, EPO, amphetamines and cannabis. Meanwhile the team doctor, Andrei Mikhailov, was still in custody, having confessed to providing the batch of EPO which had been discovered at Reims in the spring.

So when the lights dimmed in the Palais des Congrès in Paris, just a stone's throw from the Champs-Elysées, the sport badly needed resuscitation and leadership. The French government expected nothing less from the nation's flagship sporting event, yet the Société du Tour de France knew that they had only a limited influence. Stern-faced, Jean-Claude Killy strode on stage and in a cathartic moment told the assembled audience of riders, team managers, sponsors, promoters and journalists that 'we all touched rock bottom' the previous July.

'We thought doping was the problem of one team,' said Killy, 'but we quickly understood that it was the problem of the sport as a whole. Everybody knew it but nobody admitted it. The Tour lives on but it will never again be a symbol of doping, but instead a symbol of the fight against doping.'

Later, race director Leblanc promised that in future the Tour organisation would closely vet teams. 'We reserve the right to withdraw a team's invitation,' he said. 'We'll start the Tour with sixteen or fourteen teams if we have to.'

On the same day, Virenque reached the end of the road with Festina. His constant denials of doping had made him an isolated figure. Few inside the sport had faith in him any more, even though a poll in *L'Equipe* revealed that he'd retained much of his popularity among French sports fans. But Festina announced that the French climber had refused to take the pay cut they had wanted to impose on him and that their negotiations were at an end. Stung by his long-term employer's sacking, Virenque desperately scoured the market for a sponsor. Although there was some interest, most notably in Italy, the upshot of Judge Keil's inquiry, suggesting that he had used EPO, soon left him shunned by the sport and without any potential employers.

'All the tests prove scientifically that I am not doped,' Virenque insisted ebulliently after his December meeting with Judge Keil. 'I'm relieved. I'm sure this is the end of a nightmare.'

But his situation only further alienated those who would have signed him up. It took an emotional televised plea from his brother Lionel and former team-mate Pascal Hervé to rescue his endangered career. Presented by his two allies as the sole Frenchman currently capable of winning the Tour, his phone started ringing again. There was talk of teams in Spain or perhaps Portugal; finally, in January 1999, he signed a lucrative deal in Paris with the Italian team Polti. Still proclaiming his innocence and six months after being expelled from the 1998 Tour de France, Richard Virenque, leader of the infamous Festina team had been saved and could look forward to returning to the race in 1999.

Now, almost a year later, what do I think?

I think that professional cycling has received a long overdue wake-up call; that cycling's institutions and the UCI, shown to be out of step with the outside world, need to radically alter their perspective; and I think that the sport – ideally, perhaps all sports – should be run by wholly independent bodies, with no vested interests in TV franchises, timing systems, clothing deals or global marketing.

And maybe some of the riders need a few sharp reminders of their obligations, not to themselves or to their team, but to the millions who keep the faith and line the roadsides each season. Being a professional sportsman may be tough, but it's also a blessing and a privilege. Maybe they need to remember how it all looked from the outside, to remember their own teenage dreams, long before the old men in tracksuits and the sports agents gathered around and dangled financial incentives. They need to remember when they stood excitedly alongside the *route du Tour* and reached for the free hats tossed out from the passing *caravane publicitaire*; they need to remember when they had posters on their walls and when

298

they stared into the eyes of the Tour's riders and saw only devotion and sacrifice, heroism and suffering.

Maybe in the end the characters in the 1998 Tour's sorry scandal just don't get it. Maybe they just don't realise that bloodied syringes in bin bags do not form part of any sports fan's dreams. Maybe they don't see that professional cycling – that *all* top-level international sport – doesn't belong to them, because it transcends individuals. An event as grandiose and dramatic as the Tour is about all our lives, because we all invest in it and give it meaning. We love the riders and treat them as heroes for their ability to make the impossible seem possible. We believe in them, in their devotion, their integrity and their dignity – or at least, we once did.

As I drove north from Paris, towards Calais and the boat home, one image stayed with me. It was a few days after Festina had been thrown off the Tour. Alone in the car, I drove along the stage route as the race turned away from the Mediterranean, inland towards the low hills of the plateau de Vaucluse. I was at least three hours ahead of the race convoy, heading to the press room. There was no rush. I cruised past families at the roadside, picnicking in the hills towards Carpentras. They smiled and waved, still keen to support the Tour and the 140-odd riders left in the race.

Then I saw him, as I slowed for a tight right-hand hairpin. He was standing alone under a shady tree, wide-eyed and expectant, smiling and waving, waiting for his dreams to be fulfilled. He looked about six years old, with thick, milk-bottle glasses and uneven teeth and the kind of open, innocent and eager face that only children of that age can have. I slowed to a virtual halt on the bend and our eyes met. I took in his oversized Festina jersey and cycling cap, the Coca-Cola flag in his hand – and the excitement in his eyes.

I wanted to stop and talk to him, to try to explain; to tell him that men are weak and greedy, that they grow old and faithless and forget their dreams.

I wanted to tell him that I was sorry – that we were all sorry for the lies and the silence, for the cynicism and the loss of innocence. I wanted us both to believe again.

Glossary

arrivée – finish
caravane publicitaire – publicity caravan
classement – classification
col – mountain pass
contre la montre – individual time trial from A to B
côte – hill climb
coureur – rider
départ – start
directeur sportif – cycling team manager
échappée – breakaway ahead of main field
échelon – formation of riders taking shelter against a cross wind
équipe – team
équipier – team-mate
étape – stage
maillot jaune – race leader's yellow jersey
partenaire – sponsor
peloton – main field of riders
permanence – race HQ
ravitaillement – rider feed zone
salle de presse – press room
soigneur – principally a masseur, but also confidant and aide
   to a professional rider
village départ – temporary start village

List of Riders

85th Tour de France
11 July – 2 August 1998

21 teams
189 riders
Abbreviations
ab. = abandon
st. 10 = stage 10
d.n.s. = did not start
* = team withdrew from race
** = disqualified by race jury
elim. = eliminated by time limit
dis. = disqualified

TEAM DEUTSCHE TELEKOM
Directeurs sportifs: Walter Godefroot, Rudy Pevenage

1	Jan Ullrich GER	6	Jens Heppner GER
2	Rolf Aldag GER	7	Bjarne Riis DEN
3	Udo Bolts GER	8	Georg Totschnig AUT
4	Francesco Frattini ITA	9	Erik Zabel GER
5	Christian Henn GER		

FESTINA Watches **
Directeurs sportifs: Bruno Roussel, Michel Gros

11	Richard Virenque FRA	16	Christophe Moreau FRA
12	Laurent Brochard FRA	17	Didier Rous FRA
13	Laurent Dufaux SWITZ	18	Neil Stephens AUS
14	Pascal Hervé FRA	19	Alex Zulle SWITZ
15	Armin Meier SWITZ		

NOTE: FESTINA TEAM EXPELLED FROM RACE, 17 JULY

MERCATONE UNO – BIANCHI

Directeurs sportifs: Giuseppe Martinelli, Alessandro Giannelli

21 Marco Pantani ITA

~~**22** Sergio Barbero ITA ab. st. 15~~

23 Simone Borgheresi ITA

24 Roberto Conti ITA

25 Fabiano Fontanelli ITA

26 Riccardo Forconi ITA

~~**27** Dimitri Konyshev RUS ab. st. 10~~

28 Massimo Podenzana ITA

29 Mario Traversoni ITA

MAPEI–BRICOBI

Directeurs sportifs: Patrick Lefevere, Fabrizio Fabbri

~~**31** Franco Ballerini ITA ab. st. 16~~

32 Giuseppe di Grande ITA

33 Bart Leysen BEL

34 Daniele Nardello ITA

35 Wilfried Peeters BEL

36 Tom Steels BEL

~~**37** Jan Svorada CZE ab. st. 16~~

38 Andrea Tafi ITA

39 Stefano Zanini ITA

ONCE – DEUTSCHE BANK *

Directeurs sportifs: Manolo Saiz, Sebastian Pozo

~~**41** Laurent Jalabert FRA ab. st. 17~~

~~**42** Johan Bruyneel BEL ab. st. 10~~

~~**43** Rafael Diaz Justo SPA ab. st. 17~~

~~**44** H. Diaz Zabala SPA ab. st. 17~~

~~**45** Marcelino Garcia SPA ab. st. 17~~

~~**46** Javier Mauleon SPA ab. st. 17~~

~~**47** Melchor Mauri SPA ab. st. 17~~

~~**48** L. Perez Rodriguez SPA ab. st. 17~~

~~**49** Roberto Sierra SPA ab. st. 17~~

RABOBANK

Directeurs sportifs: Théo de Rooy, A. van Houwelingen

51 Michael Boogerd HOL

~~**52** Erik Dekker HOL d.n.s. st. 2~~

53 Maarten Den Bakker HOL

54 Patrick Jonker HOL

55 Robbie McEwen AUS

56 Koos Moerenhout HOL

57 Leon van Bon HOL

58 Aart Vierhouten HOL

59 Beat Zberg SWITZ

CASINO

Directeurs sportifs: Vincent Lavenu, Laurent Biondi

61	Bo Hamburger DEN	66	Alberto Elli ITA
62	Christophe Agnolutto FRA	67	Jan Kirsipuu EST ab. st. 10
63	Stéphane Barthe FRA ab. st. 18	68	Rodolfo Massi ITA d.n.s. st. 18
64	Pascal Chanteur FRA	69	Benoit Salmon FRA
65	Jacky Durand FRA		

BANESTO *

Directeurs sportifs: Eusebio Unzue, Jose-Luis Jaimerena

71	Abraham Olano SPA ab. st. 11	76	José María Jimenez SPA ab. st. 16
72	Marino Alonso SPA ab. st. 17	77	Miguel Angel Pena SPA ab. st. 17
73	José Luis Arrieta SPA ab. st. 15	78	Orlando Rodrigues POR ab. st. 17
74	Manuel Beltran SPA ab. st. 17	79	César Solaun SPA ab. st. 17
75	V. Garcia-Acosta SPA ab. st. 17		

GAN

Directeurs sportifs: Roger Legeay, Serge Beucherie

81	Chris Boardman GB ab. st. 2	86	Eddy Seigneur FRA elim. st. 15
82	Magnus Backstedt SWE	87	François Simon FRA
83	Frédéric Moncassin FRA ab. st. 10	88	Cédric Vasseur FRA
84	Stuart O'Grady AUS	89	Jens Voigt GER
85	Eros Poli ITA		

LOTTO – MOBISTAR

Directeurs sportifs: J.-L. Vandenbroucke, Jos Braeckevelt

91	Laurent Madouas FRA	96	Kurt van de Wouwer BEL
92	Peter Farazijn BEL	97	Paul van Hyfte BEL
93	Joona Laukka FIN d.n.s. st. 13	98	Rik Verbrugghe BEL
94	Andrei Tchmil BEL d.n.s. st. 16	99	Geert Verheyen BEL
95	Andrei Teteriouk KAZ		

TVM – FARM FRITES *

Directeurs sportifs: Cees Priem, Hendrik Redant

101 Laurent Roux FRA ab. st. 10
102 Jeroen Blijlevens HOL ab. st. 18
103 Steven de Jongh HOL d.n.s. st. 19
104 Serguei Ivanov RUS d.n.s. st. 19
105 Servais Knaven HOL d.n.s. st. 19

106 Lars Michaelsen DEN d.n.s. st. 11
107 Serguei Outschakov UKR d.n.s. st. 19
108 Peter van Petegem BEL ab. st. 15
109 Bart Voskamp HOL d.n.s. st. 19

SAECO – CANNONDALE

Directeurs sportifs: Antonio Salutini, Bruno Vicino

111 Mario Cipollini ITA ab. st. 9
112 Giuseppe Calcaterra ITA ab. st. 16
113 Massimo Donati ITA
114 Gian Matteo Fagnini ITA ab. st. 10
115 Paolo Fornaciari ITA

116 Eddy Mazzoleni ITA
117 Massimiliano Mori ITA
118 Leonardo Piepoli ITA
119 Mario Scirea ITA ab. st. 10

LA FRANÇAISE DES JEUX

Directeurs sportifs: Marc Madiot, Yvon Madiot

121 Evgeni Berzin RUS
122 Franck Bouyer FRA
123 Frédéric Guesdon FRA
124 Stéphane Heulot FRA
125 Xavier Jan FRA

126 Emmanuel Magnien FRA ab. st. 10
127 Christophe Mengin FRA
128 Damien Nazon FRA
129 Maximilian Sciandri GB d.n.s. st. 17

COFIDIS. LE CREDIT PAR TELEPHONE

Directeurs sportifs: Bernard Quilfen, Alain Deloeuil

131 F. Casagrande ITA ab. st. 10
132 Laurent Desbiens FRA
133 Philippe Gaumont FRA ab. st. 10
134 Nicolas Jalabert FRA
135 Bobby Julich USA

136 Massimiliano Lelli ITA
137 Kevin Livingston USA
138 Roland Meier SWITZ
139 Christophe Rinero FRA

Yellow Fever

TEAM POLTI
Directeurs sportifs: Gianluigi Stanga, Giovanni Fidanza

141 Luc Leblanc FRA d.n.s. st. 18
142 Rossano Brasi ITA
143 Mirco Crepaldi ITA
144 Fabrizio Guidi ITA ab. st. 6
145 Leonardo Guidi ITA ab. st. 15

146 Jorg Jaksche GER
147 Silvio Martinello ITA d.n.s. st. 6
148 Axel Merckx BEL
149 Fabio Sacchi ITA

ASICS – CGA
Directeurs sportifs: Serge Parsani, Mario Chiesa

151 Carlo Marino Bianchi ITA ab. st. 10
152 Alessio Bongioni ITA ab. st. 9
153 Diego Ferrari ITA
154 Oscar Pozzi ITA
155 Fabio Roscioli ITA

156 Samuele Schiavina ITA ab. st. 4
157 Aleksandre Shefer KAZ ab. st. 10
158 Filippo Simeoni ITA
159 Alain Turicchia ITA

VITALICIO SEGUROS – GRUPPO GENERALI *
Directeurs sportifs: Javier Minguez, Jose Luis Lopez-Cerron

161 Santiago Blanco SPA d.n.s. st. 18
162 Francisco Benitez SPA d.n.s. st. 18
163 Hernan Buenahora COL ab. st. 10
164 Angel Casero SPA d.n.s. st. 18
165 Andrea Ferrigato ITA d.n.s. st. 18

166 David Garcia SPA ab. st. 10
167 F. Garcia Rodriguez SPA ab. st. 5
168 Prudencio Indurain SPA d.n.s. st. 18
169 Oliveiro Rincon COL elim. st. 8

KELME – COSTA BLANCA *
Directeurs sportifs: Alvaro Pino, José Ignacio Labarta

171 Fernando Escartin SPA d.n.s. st. 18
172 Francisco Cabello SPA d.n.s. st. 18
173 Carlos Contreras COL ab. st. 10
174 José de los Angeles SPA ab. st. 15
175 José Javier Gomez SPA d.n.s. st. 18

176 Santos Gonzalez SPA d.n.s. st. 18
177 José Rodriguez SPA ab. st. 16
178 Marcos Serrano SPA d.n.s. st. 18
179 José Angel Vidal SPA d.n.s. st. 18

US POSTAL SERVICE
Directeurs sportifs: Mark Gorski, Johnny Weltz

181	Jean-Cyril Robin FRA	186	Tyler Hamilton USA
182	Frankie Andreu USA	187	George Hincapie USA
183	Dariusz Baranowski POL	188	Marty Jemison USA
184	Pascal Deramé FRA	189	Peter Meinert-Nielsen DEN
185	Vjatceslav Ekimov RUS		

RISO SCOTTI – MG MAGLIFICIO
Directeurs sportifs: Emmanuele Bombini, Alberto Volpi

191	Fabio Baldato ITA ab. st. 15	196	Federico de Beni ITA ab. st. 4
192	Vladislav Bobrik RUS ab. st. 11	197	Nicola Minali ITA ab. st. 17
193	Ermanno Brignoli ITA ab. st. 17	198	Roberto Pistore ITA elim. st. 8
194	Roberto Caruso ITA ab. st. 10	199	A. Spezialetti ITA ab. st. 17
195	Stefano Casagranda ITA ab. st. 10		

BIGMAT – AUBER 93
Directeurs sportifs: Stephane Javalet, Pascal Dubois

201	Pascal Lino FRA	206	Thierry Gouvenou FRA
202	Ludovic Auger FRA d.n.s. st. 2	207	Lylian Lebreton FRA
203	Philippe Bordenave FRA	208	Denis Leproux FRA
204	T. Bourguignon FRA	209	Alexei Sivakov RUS
205	Viatcheslav Djavanian RUS		

307